# Roadside History of
# NEVADA

Roadside History of
# NEVADA

Richard Moreno

Mountain Press Publishing Company
Missoula 2000

For Pamela, Hank, and Julia

Third Printing, January 2006

Cover painting "The Mountain behind Jim's House" by Jeff Nicholson.

Photographs not otherwise credited are by the author.

Maps by William L. Nelson.

Library of Congress Cataloging-in-Publication Data

Moreno, Richard.
    Roadside history of Nevada / Richard Moreno.
        p. cm.
    Includes bibliographical references and index.
    ISBN 0-87842-410-5 (alk. paper)
    1. Nevada—Tours. 2. Nevada—History, Local. 3. Historic sites—Ne-
vada—Guidebooks. 4. Automobile travel—Nevada—Guidebooks. I.
Title.

F839.3 .M69 2000
917.9304'34—dc21
                                                                00-042366

PRINTED IN THE U.S.A.

Mountain Press Publishing Company
P.O. Box 2399 • Missoula, MT 59806
Phone (406) 728-1900

# CONTENTS

# Acknowledgments

My sincere thanks to the many individuals who provided me with invaluable historical information about Nevada during preparation of this book. In particular, I would like to thank Nevada state archivist Guy Louis Rocha, who has long instructed me to never assume anything. I would also like to thank the past and present staffs of *Nevada Magazine*, where I'm fortunate to work. For more than six decades they have produced an amazing publication that truly tells the Nevada story.

I am also indebted to the many folks who provided assistance, whether intentional or unintentional, during the writing of this book. They include K. J. Evans and A. D. Hopkins of the *Las Vegas Review-Journal*; Nevada state historic preservation officer Ronald M. James; Phillip I. Earl, curator of history at the Nevada Historical Society; author Shawn Hall; David Moore, editor of *Nevada Magazine*; Deke Castleman, managing editor of Huntington Press; Mike and Barbara Land; Stanley W. Paher, publisher and editor at Nevada Publications; writer David W. Toll; and my friend Rick Dower.

I would also like to thank Dan Greer, a former editor at Mountain Press, for his encouragement, and Gwen McKenna, my current editor at Mountain Press, for her patience.

Lastly, my most heartfelt thanks to the many Nevada historians and writers who helped to show me that there is a lot more to the state than one-armed bandits, cheap buffets, and Elvis impersonators.

# Nevada Chronology

1776   Father Francisco Garcés leads an expedition into the future Nevada. He becomes the first non-Indian to enter the Great Basin.

1827   Returning from a trapping excursion in California, Jedediah Smith and party become the first non-Indians to cross the Great Basin.

1828   On November 9 trapper Peter Skene Ogden discovers the Humboldt River, which he calls Unknown River.

1829   Antonio Armijo leads a trading expedition from Santa Fe to Los Angeles via southern Nevada, establishing the Old Spanish Trail as a viable commercial route.

1833–34   Explorer Joseph R. Walker guides a trapping party into northern Nevada. In October 1833 the group battles with the local Northern Paiute at the Humboldt Sink. This is the first known hostility between whites and Indians in Nevada.

1841   John Bidwell and John Bartleson head the first overland emigrant party from Missouri to California; the group includes the first white woman and child to enter Nevada and brings the first cattle.

1843   John C. Frémont and Kit Carson lead an expedition to explore and map the Great Basin.

1844   In February Frémont and Carson make the first winter crossing of the Sierra Nevada into California via the Carson Pass.

1846–47   A group of eighty-seven emigrants traveling across Nevada to California, led by John Reed and Jacob Donner, become trapped for months in the snowy Sierra Nevada. More than half perish.

1851   John Reese, a Mormon, opens a trading post in the Carson Valley and names it Mormon Station. Later renamed Genoa, it is Nevada's first permanent community.

On September 9 Congress establishes the Utah Territory, of which Nevada is a part. On November 12 at Mormon Station, residents of western Utah set up the first organized, but unofficial, government for a separate Nevada Territory.

Eagle Station, now Carson City, is founded in November.

1852     The Utah territorial government outlines county boundaries, including those of future Nevada.

1855     In June a small group of Mormon missionaries establishes a colony in the Las Vegas Valley. It is the first non-Indian settlement in southern Nevada.

1857     Brothers Hosea and Ethan Grosh discover large silver deposits near Sun Mountain (later called Mount Davidson), but both die before developing the claim. The deposit is thought to have been part of what would later be called the Comstock Lode, one of the richest silver strikes in U.S. history.

1859     Miners Peter O'Riley and Patrick McLaughlin discover the Comstock Lode on the slopes of Sun Mountain. A mining camp grows near the site and is later named Virginia City.

           Captain James H. Simpson surveys the Central Overland Trail, which crosses central Nevada. The route reduces the journey to California by nearly 300 miles.

1860     On May 12 Paiute warriors clash with a citizen militia organized by Major William Ormsby of Carson City at the first battle in the Pyramid Lake War. Later that month, the Indians are defeated at the second Pyramid Lake battle.

           Wells, Fargo Express & Banking Company of San Francisco opens a branch office in Virginia City. It is Nevada's first bank.

1861     Congress establishes the Nevada Territory on March 2; James Nye of New York is designated territorial governor. The first territorial elections are held on August 31, and the first territorial legislature meets from October 1 to November 29.

1862     In July, twenty-six-year-old Samuel Clemens takes a job at the *Territorial Enterprise* in Virginia City and soon begins writing under the pseudonym Mark Twain.

1864     President Abraham Lincoln grants statehood to Nevada on October 31; H. G. Blasdel is elected governor.

1867     In December the Central Pacific Railroad line, the western portion of the first transcontinental railroad, begins construction in Nevada; the state's section of the line is completed in early 1869.

1869     Adolph Sutro begins construction of Sutro Tunnel, designed to dewater Virginia City's underground mines; its four miles are completed in July 1878.

1870     Nevada extends the right to vote to non-white males.

Work starts on the Nevada State Capitol in Carson City; the project is completed in 1871.

| | |
|---|---|
| 1873 | The University of Nevada is established in Elko; the campus is moved to Reno in 1885. |
| 1875 | Fire destroys the core of Virginia City; it is immediately rebuilt, but its rich mines are exhausted within two years. |
| 1895 | The state legislature authorizes Nevada's first public library, to be built in Reno. |
| 1900 | In May rancher Jim Butler uncovers a rich silver deposit at Tonopah, triggering Nevada's second great mining boom. |
| 1902 | William Marsh and Harry Stimler find substantial gold deposits thirty miles south of Tonopah. The mining camp, originally called Grandpa, becomes Goldfield, with an estimated population of nearly 20,000 by 1907. |
| 1905 | Las Vegas is founded as a station for the San Pedro, Los Angeles & Salt Lake City Railroad; the town is incorporated in 1911. |
| | The Nevada legislature approves the design for the first official flag of Nevada. The design is revised on March 22, 1915. The current state flag is approved on March 26, 1929, with slight modifications in 1991. |
| 1910 | In Reno, world heavyweight boxing champion Jack Johnson, the first African American to hold the title, defeats challenger and former champ Jim Jeffries, billed as "the Great White Hope." |
| 1913 | The Lincoln Highway, America's first transcontinental highway, is built across Nevada. |
| 1914 | Women gain the right to vote in Nevada. |
| 1916 | The last stagecoach robbery in the American West is committed near Jarbidge. |
| 1919 | Sadie H. Hurst, a Republican from Reno, is elected to the state assembly, becoming the first woman to serve in the Nevada legislature. |
| 1931 | Gambling is legalized in Nevada; the residency requirement for divorce is reduced to six weeks, spawning a lucrative divorce industry. |
| | Construction begins on massive Hoover Dam in Black Canyon; the project is completed in 1935. |
| 1933 | The Nevada legislature approves "Home Means Nevada," by Mrs. Bertha Raffetto of Reno, as the official state song. |
| 1938 | Democrat Dewey E. Sampson of Reno is elected to the state assembly, becoming the first Native American to serve in the Nevada legislature. |

*Nevada state tree, the piñon pine.* —Courtesy Nevada Commission on Tourism

*Nevada state bird, the mountain bluebird.* —Courtesy Nevada Commission on Tourism

*Nevada state flower, sagebrush.* —Courtesy Nevada Commission on Tourism

*Nevada state animal, the bighorn sheep.* —Courtesy Nevada Commission on Tourism

| 1941 | The Las Vegas Army Airfield (later renamed Nellis Air Force Base) opens north of Las Vegas. |
|---|---|
| | The El Rancho Vegas hotel-casino opens, the first hotel-casino built on what later becomes known as the Las Vegas Strip. |
| 1946 | Benjamin "Bugsy" Siegel, a gangster, opens the Flamingo Hotel-Casino, the first high-rise hotel-casino resort on the Las Vegas Strip. |
| 1951 | Above-ground atomic tests begin on the Nevada Proving Grounds (later known as the Nevada Test Site), sixty miles north of Las Vegas. |
| | Nevada Southern University is established in Las Vegas; it becomes the University of Nevada at Las Vegas in 1969. |
| 1959 | The Nevada legislature creates the Nevada Gaming Commission and the Gaming Control Board to regulate the gambling industry. |
| 1964 | Nevada celebrates its centennial. |
| 1966 | Eccentric billionaire Howard Hughes moves to the Desert Inn Hotel in Las Vegas and begins purchasing hotel-casinos throughout Nevada. By 1970 he owns seven resorts and considerable land holdings in the state. |
| | Republican Woodrow Wilson of Las Vegas is elected to the state assembly, becoming the first African American to serve in the Nevada legislature. |
| 1982 | Patricia Cafferata is sworn in as state treasurer, becoming the first woman elected to statewide office in Nevada. The same year, her mother, Barbara Vucanovich, becomes the first woman elected to represent Nevada in the U.S. Congress. |
| 1986 | Great Basin National Park, seventy miles southeast of Ely, becomes Nevada's first national park. |
| 1987 | Nevada's population exceeds 1 million. |
| 1989 | The Mirage Resort, the state's first mega-resort, opens in Las Vegas, signaling the start of an unprecedented hotel-building boom in southern Nevada. |
| 1996 | In April the Stratosphere Tower and Hotel opens in Las Vegas. At 1,149 feet, it is the tallest structure in Nevada. |

# Nevada Facts

Territory: 1861

Statehood: 1864

Name: Spanish for "snow-capped"

Capital: Carson City

Area: 110,540 square miles

Nicknames: Battle Born State, Silver State, Sagebrush State

Motto: All for Our Country

Bird: Mountain bluebird

Animal: Desert bighorn sheep

Flower: Sagebrush

Trees: Piñon pine and bristlecone pine

Grass: Indian rice grass

Precious Stone: Black fire opal

Fish: Lahontan cutthroat trout

Fossil: Ichthyosaur

Song: "Home Means Nevada to Me"

Climate:
Arid mountains and desert, altitudes from 1,000 to over 13,000 feet. Annual average precipitation is nine inches, including snow. Average temperatures vary from seventy degrees in the south to forty-five degrees in the north.

Highest Point: Boundary Peak, elevation 13,145 feet

Lowest Point: Colorado River south of Laughlin, elevation 470 feet

Population (July 1998): 1,855,790

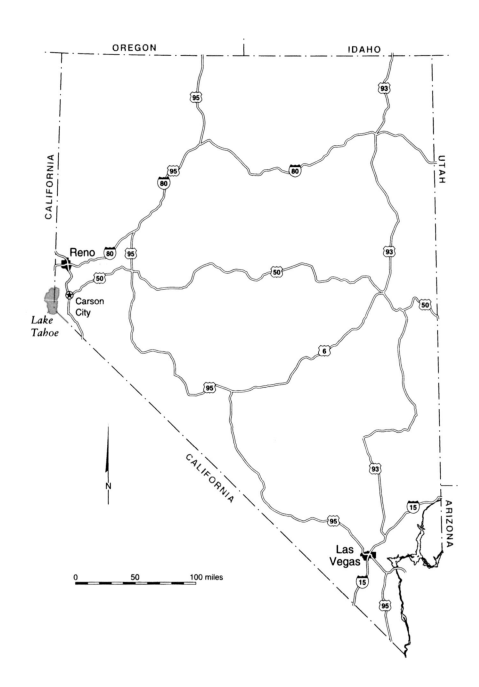

OREGON

IDAHO

CALIFORNIA

UTAH

95

93

95

80

80

80

Reno 80

95

93

50

50

Carson
City

50

*Lake*
*Tahoe*

6

95

CALIFORNIA

93

N

15

ARIZONA

95

Las
Vegas

15

0        50        100 miles

95

# Nevada: An Overview

*Nevada is ten thousand tales of ugliness and beauty, viciousness and virtue.*

—Richard Lillard, *Desert Challenge: An Interpretation of Nevada*

Author Wallace Stegner once noted that to understand the American West you have to get over the color green. No doubt he had Nevada in mind. It is the driest of all states and despite its name, which is Spanish for "snow-capped," is largely a desert. The average annual rainfall is only nine inches, and most of Nevada lies within the boundaries of two designated desert zones, the Great Basin and the Mojave Desert.

But simply calling Nevada a desert does not do the state justice. It is also the most mountainous state, with more than 314 ranges stretched across its 110,000 square miles. Twenty-five of those ranges have summits over 10,000 feet in elevation, and five of those are over 12,000 feet.

From the air, Nevada's true nature becomes obvious: the state is a maze of mountain ranges running mostly north to south, described by one geographer resembling an army of dun-colored caterpillars crawling toward Mexico. These ridges are separated by long, narrow valleys. Together, these mountains and valleys are known as basin and range. Author John McPhee probably described Nevada best when he wrote, "Each range here is like a warship standing on its own, and the Great Basin is an ocean of loose sediment with these mountain ranges standing in it as if they were members of a fleet without precedent, assembled at Guam to assault Japan."

Geologically speaking, the Nevada landscape has survived just about every indignity nature could throw at it during the past 4 billion years. Two billion years ago, about half the land now called Nevada was a shelf underneath the ocean, with beachfront property located somewhere near present-day Reno. Later, additional geological splits, collisions, and fusions drained the water and created a larger land mass with mountains. This was followed by a time of relative calm, when much of Nevada was submerged beneath a shallow ocean. During this time a wide variety of prehistoric birds, dinosaurs, and fish took center stage—including the massive ichthyosaur, a fierce predecessor to the modern whale.

*Pyramid Lake is a remnant of prehistoric Lake Lahontan, which once covered more than 8,665 square miles in Nevada and other western states.*

Modern Nevada finally began to take shape about 17 million years ago during another period of continental tug-of-war that resulted in the formation of most of its mountains and valleys as well as its fault lines. The last major uplift occurred 10 million years ago, when the Sierra Nevada was rammed into existence. These magnificent mountains on the westernmost edge of the Great Basin cast a considerable shadow over the land to the east, changing the region's weather patterns and ultimately creating Nevada's current arid climate.

But prior to this great drying out, Nevada experienced a few more changes. Ice covered portions of the region during the early part of the Pleistocene time, which lasted from about 1.5 million to 10,000 years ago. Melting ice and a wetter climate helped create a gigantic inland body of water known as Lake Lahontan (luh-HAHN-tun), which covered a large portion of northwestern Nevada. At its largest, about 14,500 years ago, the lake covered 8,665 square miles and was about 900 feet deep. It was not, however, a solid body of water. Rather it was a series of long fingers separated by mountains. Today the remnants of Lake Lahontan include a handful of desert lakes, including Pyramid and Walker, in western Nevada.

## The Coming of Man

The earliest evidence of man in Nevada dates to about 12,000 years ago. Scientists hypothesize that between 11,000 and 13,000 years ago, people migrated from Asia to North America over a land bridge across the Bering Strait.

During the end of the last great ice age, these wanderers apparently traveled south into what is now the United States through an opening between two great ice fields. Some ended up in the Great Basin, which at the time still had shallow lakes and marshes where Lake Lahontan had begun to recede. In addition to fish and birds, fossils show the region was home to herds of bison, camels, and horses.

North of Las Vegas, at Tule Springs (now called Floyd Lamb State Park), archaeologists found the oldest known traces of mankind in the state, including nearly a dozen bone tools that have been radiocarbon-dated to between 10,000 and 11,000 years ago. Also found were animal bones with traces of charcoal, another indication of the presence of humans. Excavations at Fishbone Cave have yielded similar artifacts, including fossils proving that early Nevadans had contact with prehistoric camels and horses. These large animals disappeared from Nevada between 5,000 and 10,000 years ago.

Evidence of later, more developed cultures have been found at other sites. In Lovelock Cave, south of Lovelock, scientists have found human mummies, baskets, sandals, duck decoys, feather robes, fish nets, flint knives, scrapers, and other artifacts dating to 2000 B.C. The people who left them, known as the Lovelock Culture, roamed throughout northwestern Nevada. Significant (and older) archaeological discoveries related to the Lovelock Culture have been found at Pyramid Lake, Hidden Cave (near Fallon), and the Leonard Rockshelter (south of Lovelock).

These early Nevadans had a penchant for petroglyphs, or rock carvings, found at more than a hundred locations throughout the state. These mysterious stone scratchings, some dating back to nearly 5000 B.C., have never been definitively deciphered, though many researchers believe they have some relationship to hunting because they occur near springs and other places where hunters could ambush animals. Some of Nevada's better petroglyph sites are in Valley of Fire State Park near Las Vegas, at Grimes Point near Fallon, and in Rainbow Canyon in eastern Nevada. Pictographs, in which images are drawn or painted rather than carved, have also been found at a few places, including Toquima Cave in central Nevada.

Another important link to Nevada's prehistory is the Lost City, a sixteen-mile-long network of pit houses, pueblos, rock shelters, and mines now partly submerged under Lake Mead in southern Nevada. Archaeologists estimate that as many as 20,000 people, known as the Anasazi, may have lived in the Lost City area, also known as Pueblo Grande de Nevada. We know from artifacts found there that these people flourished from about 700 to 1100 A.D., with irrigation systems; crafts such as baskets, jewelry, cloth, and pottery; salt and turquoise mining; and active trade with other peoples. Why the Anasazi abandoned the Lost City is a mystery. An extended drought, the intrusion of hostile tribes, or disease could have been the reason.

*Prehistoric rock carvings, or petroglyphs, such as these found at Grimes Point, are scattered throughout Nevada.*

Almost coinciding with the disappearance of the Anasazi was the appearance of the ancestors of modern tribes. In southern Nevada, this meant the arrival of the Southern Paiute, who also inhabited portions of Utah, Arizona, and California. Western Shoshone settled into northeastern Nevada while Northern Paiute roamed northwestern Nevada, roughly north of Tonopah and west of Winnemucca. The Washo was the smallest of Nevada's tribes, inhabiting the far-western border of the state between Honey Lake, California, and Sonora Pass, and including Lake Tahoe.

Because of limited natural resources, Nevada's tribes were free-roaming hunters, fishers, and gatherers who essentially followed the food. Shelter was a simple hut made from tied bunches of reeds, grass, and tree branches. In winter, dwellings were made a bit more protective, with shallow foundations dug into the ground. The support frame was constructed of poles, tied at the top. This was covered with overlapping bundles of grass, reeds, or bark that kept out rain and snow.

Dining required creativity. While fishing and hunting, mostly for jackrabbits, provided seasonal food, early Nevadans were also proficient at finding wild berries, wild carrots, wild onions, trail potatoes, and white sage, as well as insect larvae. They also collected and stored seeds and nuts, and sometimes crushed them into flour for bread or soup. Among the most important food staples was the pine nut, found in the cones of the piñon tree. Fall was the time for extensive tribal pine-nut gathering. The nuts, which stored well, were crucial to their winter survival.

The emphasis these tribes placed on food is reflected in the names they gave themselves. The Paiute living around Pyramid Lake called themselves the *Cui yui Ticutta,* or Cui-ui Eaters, after a fish found in the lake. The tribe at Walker Lake was known as the *Agai Ticutta,* or Trout Eaters, while those living near Lovelock had the name *Koop Ticutta,* or Ground Squirrel Eaters.

The scarcity of large game in the Great Basin also limited materials for making clothing. While rabbit-skin blankets, particularly among the Washo, and buckskin skirts and loinclothes were fairly common, tribes also fashioned clothing from reeds and sagebrush: the bark was moistened, then pounded into a material that could be used for shoes and skirts. Materials for making elaborate ceremonial costumes, robes, and jewelry were not available to the Great Basin tribes, but both men and women wore necklaces and ear pieces made from bones, feathers, and seashells acquired from California tribes.

One art form Great Basin tribes excelled in was basket making. Using local willow, reeds, and grasses, they crafted beautiful, intricate baskets. Like everything produced by these cultures, the baskets served a practical purpose in carrying nuts and seeds, holding water, and other functions. The Washo are considered the greatest of the basket makers among Nevada tribes, particularly Dat-so-la-lee, a Washo woman who wove hundreds of magnificent baskets in the late nineteenth and early twentieth centuries. Today her work, highly prized by collectors and museums, commands tens of thousands of dollars.

## *Early Explorers*

The first whites to enter Nevada were most likely Spanish explorers establishing a route between Santa Fe, New Mexico, and Monterey, California, which eventually became the Old Spanish Trail. In the spring of 1776, Franciscan priest and explorer Father Francisco Garcés and two Indian guides crossed the Colorado River near a spot believed to be the southernmost tip of the future state of Nevada, making Garcés the first non-Indian to enter the Great Basin.

A more significant entry into Nevada was the 1826–27 expedition led by explorer-trapper Jedediah Smith. Leading a party of fifteen men, Smith traveled from Cache Valley, Utah, to Mission San Gabriel near Los Angeles. His mission was ostensibly to open new beaver-trapping areas, and while he did not find much in the way of fur, he succeeded in becoming the first white man to cross Nevada. The group entered Nevada near present-day Bunkerville and followed the Virgin River to its junction with the Colorado River.

*Explorer Jedediah Smith.*
—Courtesy Nevada Historical Society

Returning to Utah from California that spring, Smith and two companions crossed the middle of Nevada, traveling roughly parallel to today's US 6. Smith and his party thus become the first non-Indians to travel the width of the Great Basin. During the journey, Smith also became the first white to encounter the native tribes of central Nevada and to note the unique geographical features of the Great Basin. Smith returned to Nevada one more time, in late 1827, again following the Virgin River route to California.

The next important visit to Nevada was in 1828–29, with a fur-trapping expedition led by Peter Skene Ogden of the Hudson's Bay Company. Ogden and his party crossed into Nevada near Denio in fall 1828. The group continued south, and on November 9 they encountered the Humboldt River, which Ogden originally named Unknown River. The expedition followed the river westward, and along the way they took nearly every beaver they could find—Hudson's Bay's strategy was to trap out the region to drive away potential competitors. The group returned to Nevada the next spring, this time exploring the area north of the Humboldt River along the Owyhee River, then traveling along the Humboldt to its end, the Humboldt Sink. Ogden made a final trip to Nevada in the fall of 1829.

The last major fur-trapping trek into Nevada was the Bonneville-Walker expedition of 1833–34. Led by Benjamin L. E. de Bonneville, the party traveled throughout Utah and Idaho in an unsuccessful search for trapping grounds not yet exploited by other fur companies. Finally Bonneville instructed Captain Joseph Reddeford Walker to head west into Nevada.

Walker's party retraced Ogden's journey down the Humboldt River to the Humboldt Sink, where in October 1833 they encountered a large number of Paiute. Believing that the Indians stealing their traps, Walker's men confronted them. The dispute escalated and the trappers opened fire on the Indians, killing more than thirty. It was the first fatal encounter between whites and natives in Nevada.

The Walker party continued south to the Carson Sink, fifteen miles south of present-day Fallon, then westward into the Sierra Nevada. In California they discovered the Yosemite Valley and the Merced Grove of giant redwoods. After a few months, the party returned to Nevada via the Walker River. They again encountered the Paiute at the Humboldt Sink and became embroiled in another battle, killing several more Indian men at Toulon Lake, near what is now Lovelock. In addition to their discovery of Yosemite Valley, the Walker expedition established the Overland Trail, later used by thousands of emigrants heading to California.

About seven years after the Walker expedition, a group called the Western Emigration Society publicized its intention to move to California's Central Valley. John Bidwell and John Bartleson led a group of emigrants, including Nancy Kelsey and her small daughter—the first Anglo-American woman and child to make the trip across the Great Basin—from Missouri to California. The Bidwell-Bartleson party followed the Humboldt River across the state and crossed the Sierra Nevada at Sonora Pass.

The last significant explorations of the Nevada region were two overland mapping expeditions conducted in 1843–44 and in 1845 by Captain John C. Frémont. These undertakings were sponsored by the United States government during a time when the country had embraced the philosophy of manifest destiny—the belief that it was America's divine right to expand its borders to the Pacific coast, even though much of the land was still under Mexican or British rule.

Frémont entered Nevada's northwest corner in December 1843, going south around the edges of the Black Rock Desert and encountering a large lake. Frémont wrote:

> We encamped on the shore, opposite a very remarkable rock in the lake, which had attracted our attention for many miles. It rose, according to our estimate, 600 feet above the water; and, from the point we viewed it, presented a pretty exact outline of the great pyramid of Cheops. . . . I called it Pyramid Lake.

From there, Frémont's party, led by scout Christopher "Kit" Carson, followed the Truckee River to present-day Wadsworth, then moved south to the Carson Sink. The group veered west and crossed the Sierra Nevada at Carson

*Captain John C. Frémont.*
—Courtesy Nevada Historical Society

Pass. After resting in California, Frémont's expedition returned east by a southern route that crossed Nevada on the Old Spanish Trail, passing through the future site of Las Vegas.

Frémont's detailed report and the exceptional maps prepared by Charles Preuss, the official topographer, were important to understanding the Great Basin. Frémont gave names to a number of landmarks and features—most are still in use—including the Humboldt River, the Carson River, and the Great Basin. He chose this last name because the land appeared to be an interior drainage, like a huge catch basin. In 1845 Frémont returned for further mapping of the Great Basin.

## The Westward Movement

In the beginning, people could not wait to get across Nevada. Word of the Bidwell-Bartleson party's success along with the wide distribution of Frémont's report attracted the attention of many Americans who believed California could offer a brighter future. The Nevada portion of the route, however, was largely seen as an unfortunate obstacle on the journey to the promised land. It contained some of the most difficult stretches of the entire Emigrant Trail, including the brackish Humboldt River and the Forty Mile Desert.

In May 1845, a group of eighty-seven emigrants set out for California from Missouri. Led by Jacob Donner and John Reed, the group chose to follow directions published in an emigrant guidebook by Lansford Hastings, an entrepreneurial explorer who, unfortunately, had not actually traveled the entire route he outlined. Ignoring the suggestions of some people to stay on the main trail, the Donner party decided to follow Hastings's new route. The band wasted valuable weeks searching for a shortcut in the Ruby Mountains. They finally arrived in the Truckee Meadows in late September 1846, then rested for several days before heading into the Sierra Nevada.

Heavy snows arrived almost immediately as the travelers made their way through the mountains. Within weeks the group was completely snowbound at a lake that would later be called Donner Lake, in California. Eventually, a few of the group made it across the mountains and returned with rescuers in February 1847, but not before some members of the party had resorted to cannibalism to survive. Only forty-seven of the original eighty-seven travelers lived through the ordeal. The tragedy was widely publicized, and for a short time, further overland ventures to California virtually ceased.

But while Nevada's trails remained silent during this time, in Utah there was plenty of activity that would later have an impact on the future Silver State. In 1846 a large colony of Mormons, members of the Church of Jesus Christ of Latter-day Saints, settled at the base of Utah's Wasatch Mountains. The Mormons had been persecuted for their beliefs and forced to flee from New York, where their leader, Joseph Smith, had founded the church. First they fled to Ohio, then Missouri, and later, to Illinois.

By the early 1840s, Smith and his followers had a viable community in Nauvoo, Illinois, including work on an impressive cathedral. Conflicts soon arose with the locals, however, who burned the church and murdered Smith in June 1844. In February 1846, Smith's successor, Brigham Young, led the flock west. The group traveled hundreds of miles before reaching the remote valley of the Great Salt Lake, where Young decided to build his "City of the Saints."

Despite the fact that the region was then under Mexican control, Young also claimed most of the Great Basin and southern California for a proposed American state he called Deseret. Within a few years of establishing Salt Lake City, Young had sent missionaries to build settlements in Deseret, including in the Carson and Las Vegas Valleys.

In 1946, as Young and company were making their way to Utah, President James K. Polk, a firm believer in manifest destiny, challenged Mexico for control of the southwestern portion of North America. The Mexican War of 1846–47 resulted in the 1848 Treaty of Guadalupe Hidalgo, whereby Mexico ceded to the United States ownership of the land that would eventually become the states of Arizona, California, Nevada, and Utah, and portions of New Mexico and Colorado.

Meanwhile that summer, gold was discovered in the gravel beds of northern California's American River, about fifty miles east of Sacramento. Despite efforts to keep the strike secret, by summer hundreds of fortune seekers had flocked to the site to pan for the precious metal. By the end of 1848 word had spread across the nation. The California gold rush had begun.

By early 1849, dozens of sailing ships had set out from the East Coast for California. And within a few months, thousands of people from throughout the United States had begun the treacherous overland journey to the gold-fields. The most traveled route was along the North Platte River across Nebraska, then north into Wyoming. From there, the emigrants headed into southern Idaho before dropping into Nevada. In Nevada the trail followed the curves of the Humboldt River and passed through some serious desert country to either the Carson or the Truckee River, then over the Sierra Nevada. It was a long and dangerous journey through an inhospitable land. Sometimes Indians, threatened by the competition for scarce resources such as water and grass, attacked the emigrants. Still, many braved the trip, believing they would find a brighter future.

## *The First Settlers*

With thousands of people traveling across Nevada to California, which was rushed into statehood in 1849, it was only logical that a few entrepreneurs, led by expansion-minded members of the Church of Jesus Christ of Latter-day Saints, would set up trading posts along the route to supply these pilgrims. In 1850 a group of Mormons led by Joseph DeMont and Hampton S. Beatie chose a spot at the base of the eastern Sierra Nevada to set up a post for the summer, hoping to make a bit of money before heading to the California mines themselves. After constructing a crude, temporary log structure without roof or floor, they began trading with the emigrants passing through, and the enterprise proved reasonably profitable. As planned, the traders abandoned the post at the end of the season.

The following spring, another group of Mormons, headed by businessman John Reese, arrived in the same area. Encouraged by DeMont and Beatie's success at the site, Reese intended to establish a permanent colony there on behalf of the Mormon Church and the newly created Utah Territory. At the time, Utah Territory encompassed most of present-day Nevada. Reese's party brought along ten wagons filled with supplies and immediately began planting crops, building a fort, and erecting fences at a spot about fifty yards south of DeMont and Beatie's trading post. Within months, the new post, called Mormon Station, was thriving, and it became Nevada's first permanent community.

The success of Mormon Station did not go unnoticed, and later that year Frank and Joseph Barnard, George Follensbee, Frank and W. L. Hall, and A. J. Rollins opened in nearby Eagle Valley a trading post, Eagle Station, the future site of Carson City. Other trading posts appeared along the Humboldt and Carson Rivers, including those at Ragtown, near Fallon, and Ponderer's Rest, at Dayton.

On September 9, 1851, Congress established Utah Territory, of which present Nevada was a part. That November the settlers at Mormon Station established an unofficial government for western Utah Territory—a squatters' council that included a justice of the peace and a sheriff. The colony's leaders conducted three organizational meetings and developed rules for recording property and settling legal disputes.

Not wishing to be part of Mormon rule, another group of area settlers, mostly miners, petitioned for California to annex the region. The disagreement ended in the Mormons' favor when the Utah territorial government created Carson County, which included western Nevada, in 1854. Territorial governor Brigham Young appointed Orson Hyde, a Mormon church official, to serve as county administrator. Hyde designated Mormon Station as the county seat and renamed it Genoa, in honor of the birthplace of Christopher Columbus. Despite Hyde's best efforts, the county government floundered because of continuing resistance from non-Mormon settlers.

In 1857 President James Buchanan appointed a non-Mormon governor to replace Brigham Young in an attempt to quell increasing Mormon control of the region. When Young and his followers defied the president's directives, Buchanan sent 2,500 federal troops to Utah. In response to the threats posed by the advancing army, Young recalled all his disciples to Salt Lake City. Fortunately, the so-called Utah War was averted before there was any bloodshed.

During the resulting power vacuum in western Utah (now Nevada), the remaining settlers assumed ownership of Mormon ranches and homes. Despite efforts from the Utah territorial government, local citizens, and the federal government to establish order, there was no effective government in the region during the next few years.

## *The Rush to Washoe*

Everything changed in 1859, the year the fabulously rich Comstock Lode was discovered. The first trace of this immense body of gold and silver ore was uncovered in January of that year near the future site of Gold Hill by John Bishop, James "Old Virginny" Finney, Alec Henderson, and Jack Yount. A few months later, in June, Patrick McLaughlin and Peter O'Riley found the main ledge of the vein.

Immediately, McLaughlin and O'Riley's claim was challenged by others prospecting in the area, most notably Henry Comstock, whose name became forever linked with the lode. Comstock and his partner, Immanuel Penrod, claimed that they had worked the area a few months before. Though not certain of the validity of this claim, the two Irishmen agreed to form a partnership with Comstock and Penrod.

Earlier miners may also have stumbled onto portions of the Comstock Lode, including two brothers, Hosea and Ethan Grosh. In the summer of 1857, the two found what they called a "monster ledge" of silver in a canyon below Sun Mountain (later renamed Mount Davidson). Sadly, the pair never benefited from their discovery. Hosea slammed a pick into his foot and died of blood poisoning two weeks later. Ethan died soon afterward from gangrene following severe frostbite.

At first no one realized the potential of the Comstock Lode. But after particularly rich silver and gold ore samples arrived in Nevada City to be assayed, word started to spread through California. By spring of 1860, the "Rush to Washoe" (WAH-show) had begun, attracting thousands. Many would-be miners had missed out on the gold rush of 1849 and saw this as a second chance to achieve great wealth. Along with the prospectors came other prospective capitalists eager to supply fortune seekers with food, clothing, equipment, and, of course, adult beverages and other distractions. Rude communities rose out of the sagebrush and mud, including Gold Hill, Silver City, and—the Queen of the Comstock—Virginia City.

Prospectors began scurrying all over the region hoping to uncover the next Comstock. Aurora's was the first significant discovery in the state following the Comstock rush. Soon there were many more, including gold and silver strikes in Austin, Unionville, and other locales. The majority of mining camps had very brief lives. In some places mining continued sporadically for about fifty years, but by the early twentieth century most of these, too, had become ghost towns.

While it lasted, all the mining activity did much to unbalance the delicate relationship that Nevada's native peoples had with their environment. The Comstock's mines required enormous quantities of timber to shore up the extensive underground tunnels and to make into charcoal for processing the ore. By 1890, the newcomers had cut nearly every tree in the region to meet the demand, including piñon—whose seeds were an important food source for native people—and the magnificent ponderosa pines of the Lake Tahoe Basin. They also took the best land and built houses and fences that blocked the traditional seasonal trails of native tribes and the migration patterns of animals. The resulting tensions led to a few conflicts between Indians and whites, including the brief but bloody Pyramid Lake War of 1860.

## A State Is Born

By the late 1850s, much of Utah Territory was in political chaos. Due in part to the distance of the territorial capital—Salt Lake City was more than 500 miles from booming western Nevada—it was difficult to govern the region effectively. Other groups attempted to fill the void, including short-lived squatters' governments, two of which attempted to secede from Utah Territory, and the federal government. Finally, in March 1861, Congress and outgoing president James Buchanan created three new territories: Colorado, Dakota, and Nevada.

The original Nevada Territory boundaries were smaller than the borders of today's state. The first expansion occurred in July 1862, when Congress shifted the westernmost portion of Utah Territory into Nevada Territory. In 1866, shortly after Nevada achieved statehood, Congress added another piece of Utah Territory, and in 1867, a triangular wedge of Arizona Territory.

James W. Nye of New York, who had helped the Republican ticket win that state in the 1860 election, was rewarded by President Abraham Lincoln with the governorship of Nevada Territory. Orion Clemens of Missouri was appointed territorial secretary. Clemens arrived in Nevada by stagecoach in the company of his younger brother, Samuel, who hoped to serve as his assistant. Samuel would later write for Virginia City's *Territorial Enterprise* under the pen name Mark Twain. Nye and the elder Clemens were entrusted with governing the territory until an election could be held and a territorial legislature convened to adopt laws.

On October 1, 1861, the Nevada territorial legislature, with its nine council members and fifteen House of Representatives delegates—met in Carson City, which Governor Nye had designated as the capital of the territory. The legislature immediately adopted English common law as the basis for its laws and began passing statutes related to taxation, civil and criminal codes, schools, and other matters. Nine counties were created: Churchill, Douglas, Esmeralda, Humboldt, Lake (later renamed Roop), Lyon, Ormsby, Storey, and Washoe. The territorial legislature met in 1861, 1862, and 1864, and held constitutional conventions in 1863 and 1864. A constitution was required to apply for statehood.

In November and December 1863, the convention met for thirty-two days and produced a constitution similar to California's. The document, however, contained a controversial clause that allowed the state to tax mining shafts and tunnels, productive or not. Mining interests wanted taxes restricted to the proceeds of active mines. Because of the tax clause, the proposed constitution was overwhelmingly rejected on January 19, 1864, by a vote of 8,851 to 2,157.

Statehood for Nevada, however, was not dead. With the 1864 national elections looming, President Abraham Lincoln and the Republican party anticipated that newly created western states would support their antislavery amendment, so Congress approved enabling legislation for Nevada citizens to conduct a new constitutional convention. The legislation also authorized conventions for Nebraska and Colorado. Of the three, only Nevada completed the task in time for the November election.

Nevada's second constitutional convention convened in July 1864. The new draft of the constitution—without the strict mining tax—was put to a vote of the territory's residents on September 7, 1864, and was approved 10,371 to 1,284. With time running out on the deadline, the entire text of the ratified constitution was wired to President Lincoln, at a cost of $4,303.27. At the time it was the longest and most expensive telegram ever sent. After reviewing the document, President Lincoln issued a brief proclamation on October 31, 1864, admitting Nevada as the thirty-sixth state.

On November 8, 1864, Nevada participated in its first federal election—Lincoln easily carried the state—and elected Republican Henry G. Blasdel as its first governor. About a month later, the first state legislature met and elected Virginia City attorney William Stewart and former territorial governor James Nye to serve as the state's first two U.S. senators. Prior to 1914, U.S. senators were elected by state legislatures rather than by popular vote.

## *Bridging the West*

As the state of Nevada was hatching, other events were helping to open its frontiers. In addition to the thousands of emigrants crossing the state on the California Trail, in 1851 George Chorpenning established semiregular mail service between Salt Lake City and Sacramento. Called the "Jackass Mail" because letters were carried by pack mules, the service provided carriers with rest stations every twenty to forty miles. The service was not speedy—it took thirty days for a letter to travel the entire distance—but it was the first attempt to link the far west with the rest of the country.

A few years later, in mid-1859, Captain James H. Simpson of the U.S. Army Topographical Corps was assigned the task of establishing a wagon trail between Salt Lake City and Genoa, Nevada, that would be shorter than the Humboldt River route. Simpson led an expedition of sixty-four scientists, guides, and soldiers across the middle of Nevada. In addition to showing the feasibility of travel through that region, the Simpson survey produced the first color views of Nevada, watercolors made from drawings. The new route, the Central Overland Trail, was almost 300 miles shorter than the old one.

In 1860 William H. Russell, William Waddell, and Alexander Majors, three Missouri businessmen who operated a daily stagecoach line between Missouri and Utah, decided to develop an efficient mail service between St. Joseph, Missouri, and Sacramento, California. Hoping to eventually land lucrative government mail contracts, the men founded the Pony Express, which promised ten-day mail delivery by horseback over the 2,000 miles between the two cities.

To accomplish its goal, the company developed a system of stations along the route. It incorporated existing stagecoach stops when possible and erected additional relay stations, or switch stations (where riders changed horses), in between. Eventually, the Pony Express had 190 stations an average of ten to twelve miles apart.

Nevada presented the biggest challenge Pony Express riders faced. In addition to the long ride through remote, virtually unpopulated country, the mail carriers contended with hostile tribes and a harsh, unforgivingly dry climate. Despite the hardships, the Pony Express never lost a rider in Nevada. The Nevada route incorporated most of Chorpenning's old Jackass Mail stations across the region's midsection. From east to west, the trail first entered Nevada at Antelope Springs, near today's Utah border, then crossed through the center and exited at Friday's Station, near Lake Tahoe.

An express rider carried four small pouches, called cantinas, attached to a flat piece of leather, called a mochila, which fit over his saddle. When full, a mochila carried about twenty pounds of mail. The equipment was designed so that the rider could easily pull the mochila from his horse and throw it over the saddle of a fresh mount. Riders were relieved every 75 to 100 miles.

Pony Express service was expensive—$5 per half ounce of mail. Despite that, or because of it, the Pony Express never made money over its eighteen months of operation, nor did its founders receive the anticipated government contracts. Ultimately, its value was in showing that the central route was the fastest and most practical way to cross the United States. This information would later prove extremely useful to the builders of the transcontinental railroad system. The demise of the Pony Express coincided with completion of the transcontinental telegraph line in October 1861. The express was gradually phased out as the telegraph was extended across the West.

In 1861 engineer and surveyor Theodore D. Judah persuaded California financiers Charles Crocker, Mark Hopkins, Leland Stanford, and Collis P. Huntington to back his dream of constructing a railroad across the United States. The group incorporated as the Central Pacific Rail Road Company of California and signed an agreement with the federal government to build it. Construction commenced in Sacramento, California, on January 8, 1863.

Judah proposed building the rail line over and through the Sierra Nevada and crossing the barren stretches of Nevada and Utah, where it would connect with the Union Pacific Railroad, which was extending its line from the opposite direction. Sadly, Judah did not live to see the completion of the project; he contracted Panama fever while traveling to New York and died in November 1863.

Construction of the first 138 miles consumed nearly five years because of difficulties in building through the Sierra Nevada. In addition to financial problems, the railroad's builders were challenged by steep inclines, unusually heavy snowfall over several winters, and the need to tunnel through granite, particularly at Donner Summit. On December 13, 1867, however, the Central Pacific crossed into Nevada. The hardest part was over. The railroad practically raced across the rest of the state, eventually connecting with the Union Pacific at Promontory, Utah, on May 10, 1869. The last 501 miles of track were laid in less than ten months.

The importance of the new transcontinental railroad line was immediately felt in Nevada. Along the route, the towns of Reno, Winnemucca, Lovelock, and Elko cropped up almost overnight. In the same year the Central Pacific line was finished, work began on the Virginia & Truckee Railroad, completed in 1872. It connected Virginia City to the Central Pacific line in Reno. Now Virginia City's gold and silver could be rushed to far-off markets.

## The Mining Slump

Nevada owed its existence to mining, so it was a severe jolt to the state's psyche when in the early 1880s most of its important mines began to slump. Virginia City—the mother of all Nevada mining camps—saw its silver revenues drop precipitously from about $37 million in 1877 to less than $7 million in 1879. Unlike its previous downturns, this time no new discoveries came along to shake the market from its doldrums. Other once-thriving mines—in Austin, Eureka, and Pioche—also became tapped out. And new finds in Tuscarora and Candelaria did not live up to expectations. Statewide, mining revenues fell from $46 million in 1877 to $8.6 million in 1881.

Aggravating the situation was the so-called Crime of '73 (the 1873 federal Mint Act), which demonetized silver and placed the United States on a gold standard. Nevadans did not feel the effects of the bill immediately because silver production remained high through the mid-1870s. But when the silver-mining industry began its slide, many in Nevada blamed their problems on the Mint Act, claiming it deflated the silver market.

Nevada entered a depression that lasted two decades. Concern about Nevada's viability grew so great that there was talk of revoking its statehood. In 1888, U.S. senator William Stewart of Nevada proposed annexing parts of Idaho and Utah Territories with Nevada to create a larger and, theoretically, more economically sound state. The idea was not well received, and President Grover Cleveland vetoed the proposal. But Stewart countered with another

*Senator William M. Stewart (right) is pictured here at his law office near Rhyolite, Nevada, in about 1908.* —Courtesy Nevada Historical Society

plan that summer, this time suggesting that southern Idaho be added to Nevada, with dual capitals in Boise and Carson City. Idahoans, however, were eager for their own statehood, and Stewart's new proposal died in Congress. In 1890 Idaho was admitted as the forty-third state.

With mining on the skids, ranching and farming became increasingly important in Nevada. By the early 1880s, large ranching outfits had developed in Elko, Carson Valley, Smith Valley, Mason Valley, the Truckee Meadows, Winnemucca, and other areas. As the depression continued, agriculture emerged as a potential solution to Nevada's economic woes. An 1889 state study suggested that Nevada had millions of acres of usable but uncultivated land. Popular opinion was that the only thing lacking in order to transform much of the state into a paradise was water. By the 1890s, Nevada's congressional delegation had begun to promote development of a massive system to store and transport water.

In 1902 U.S. representative Francis G. Newlands of Reno helped to create the U.S. Reclamation Service. The enacting legislation included funding for the Newlands Project, a plan to irrigate 450,000 acres in Churchill County with water diverted from the Carson and Truckee Rivers. The project encompassed miles of canals and the construction of two dams. While it succeeded in transforming portions of the desert into productive farmland, it did not live up to expectations, eventually irrigating only about one-fifth the area originally envisioned.

## *Economic Salvation*

Nevada's economic picture improved in the early twentieth century with the discovery of significant gold and silver deposits in south-central Nevada. The first major strike was at Tonopah in May 1900. Legend has it that a part-time miner named Jim Butler accidentally stumbled onto a ledge of nearly pure silver while chasing an errant mule. Two years after Butler's strike, a substantial gold strike was made about twenty-five miles south of Tonopah at Goldfield. Within a short time, the two cities had become centers of business and politics.

Because of the relative remoteness of Tonopah and Goldfield, several railroad lines were constructed to transfer the tons of valuable ore elsewhere for processing. The routes of these lines, which included the Tonopah & Tidewater, the Las Vegas & Tonopah, and the Tonopah & Goldfield, later provided the right-of-way for many of central and southern Nevada's automobile highways, such as US 95. The Tonopah and Goldfield mining strikes lasted only until World War I, yet they succeeded in easing Nevada's depression and stilled the talk of removing its mantle of statehood.

By the 1920s, as the mining economy continued to wax and wane, Nevada had discovered a new route to profitability: divorce. The state's divorce laws

had loosened in the early 1900s, largely in response to California's requirement of a one-year waiting period. In 1906 the state's "quickie" divorce laws
gained a boost when the wife of William Ellis Corey, president of U.S. Steel,
traveled to Reno to seek a divorce. The case attracted national attention because of the scandalous circumstances—William Corey was having an affair
with a young actress—and enhanced Nevada's reputation as a free, open frontier state.

In 1920 actress Mary Pickford, known as "America's Sweetheart" because of
her squeaky-clean movie image, obtained a Nevada divorce. While there was
no scandal involved, her action made it fashionable to go to Nevada to seek
what was referred to as "the cure."

Catering to divorce seekers became a thriving industry. Dude ranches
cropped up, primarily in the Reno area, to provide divorcees-to-be with os-
tensible addresses to fulfill Nevada's lax residency requirements. Historian
Russell Elliott estimates that the state's divorce "trade" generated some $1 mil-
lion to $5 million annually during the 1930s. Other states sought to cut into
Nevada's action by also lowering their divorce residency requirements, but the
Nevada legislature upped the ante. In 1927 Nevada requirements were reduced
to three months, then in 1931 to only six weeks.

That year the legislature also passed a bill legalizing gambling, which would
eventually have an even greater impact on the state than the divorce laws. At
first the gambling legislation did not make much of an impression because
illegal gambling clubs had operated throughout the state for years. But as anyone who has recently driven down the Las Vegas Strip can attest—passing by
the giant glass pyramid, artificial volcano, faux Roman temple, roller coaster,
and massive neon castle—legal gambling was to shape the fate of Nevada.

Until World War II, Nevada's gambling industry maintained a relatively low
profile. Many of the early casino operators feared a backlash from religious
and moral crusaders should there be too much attention focused on their business. However, increased acceptance of gambling as a recreational pastime,
coupled with the efforts of new and more aggressive casino owners such as
William Harrah and Raymond I. "Pappy" Smith, resulted in a postwar gambling boom.

Las Vegas in particular began to develop in the 1940s as a tourism destination, catering to visitors from rapidly growing southern California. In downtown Las Vegas, known as "Glitter Gulch," more than half a dozen small casinos were clustered along Fremont Street. In 1942 two resorts, the El Rancho
Vegas and the Last Frontier, opened on US 91, later known as the Strip. The
city's population jumped from 8,500 in 1940 to 20,000 by 1946, the year the
Flamingo Hotel opened.

Built by gangster Benjamin "Bugsy" Siegel, the Flamingo was the first truly
upscale hotel-casino in the state, and it ushered in a new era of lavish Nevada
resorts. Siegel's gangland-style assassination in 1947, allegedly the result of his

*An early-1950s atomic-bomb test on Frenchman Flat at the Nevada Proving Grounds (Nevada Test Site).* —Courtesy Nevada Historical Society

overspending—or skimming—the mob's money building the Flamingo, was also the beginning of Nevada's image as a Mafia-infested state.

In addition to the growth of gambling, the postwar years saw a major buildup of military operations in southern Nevada. In 1950 the United States Atomic Energy Commission designated a huge wedge of land located north of Las Vegas as the Nevada Proving Grounds, later known as the Nevada Test Site. Between 1951 and 1955, the U.S. government detonated forty-five above-ground atomic devices at the site in the interests of maintaining America's lead over the Soviet Union in the race to develop newer and better weapons. Nevadans initially embraced the presence of the test site, but soon concerns about atomic fallout—radiated particles carried by the wind to populated areas—caused the government to conduct the tests underground during the mid-1950s. During the next three decades, hundreds of tests were conducted beneath the desert floor.

By the early 1980s, many of the state's residents were increasingly aware of the dangers of nuclear radiation and troubled by the continued testing. In the mid-eighties the government announced plans to locate a nuclear waste dump at Yucca Mountain in southern Nevada. Concern over the prospect of hundreds of pounds of nuclear garbage being transported on the state's highways and rail lines created much opposition to the plan. An unusual coalition formed to block the dump, including environmentalists, local residents, and hotel-casino owners.

In recent years, state and congressional leaders have performed an amazing contortion that reflects the deeply conflicted feelings most Nevadans have about the test site and the dump: they have managed to stall development of the waste dump while retaining nearly 20,000 jobs at the test site. It remains to be seen how long they can maintain this delicate balancing act.

In the meantime, Las Vegas has continued to grow in population, economy, and political muscle. Since the 1940s, the state of Nevada has placed its bets squarely on the gambling industry and let it ride. Despite occasional slumps, gambling has proved it has more staying power than the state's original economic engine, mining, in spite of increased competition from legal gambling in many other states.

As Max Miller noted in his 1941 book *Reno*:

> In this Nevada the word gambling is a broad term. The word reaches beyond the Methodists' conception of it. Cattlemen are gamblers. Each season in this dry land is a gamble with them. The same with sheepmen, miners, and certainly with prospectors. Not to gamble in Nevada would mean not to be working for a living.

**1**

# INTERSTATE 80: THE EMIGRANT TRAIL

*We have seen more suffering and passed through more hardships since we struck what has been called the beautiful Humboldt, than in all the rest of our journey.*
—Leander Vaness Loomis, 1850 emigrant diary

The Humbug. The Hellboldt. The Swampy. The Muddy. The Barren. The Humboldt River, which explorer John C. Frémont named for his friend, the German naturalist Baron Alexander von Humboldt, has earned a variety of disparaging nicknames over the decades. "Meanest and muddiest, filthiest stream, most cordially I hate you," wrote one Iowa traveler in an 1850 poem about the river, which he penned after surviving the trek. Writer Mark Twain, who spent several years in Nevada, once joked that "one of the pleasantest and most invigorating exercises one can contrive is to run and jump across the Humboldt River till he is overheated, and then drink it dry."

Travelers have long had a love-hate relationship with the Humboldt River, which zigzags for nearly 500 miles across northern Nevada. The Humboldt was perhaps the cruelest joke played on emigrants who sought only to cross Nevada to reach the promised land of California. At first the Humboldt, at the eastern edge of the state, seemed to promise water, food, and grass, and a reliable path to follow. But it proved a fickle companion. It twisted, elbowed, and doubled-back on itself, prolonging the journey. It dried out and disappeared, then reappeared and flooded. And in the end, it did not even take them all the way across the state. Instead, its waters dissolved in alkali flats, the Humboldt Sink. It wore travelers down so much that by the time they reached Forty Mile Desert near modern Lovelock—the worst part of the trip—many were wondering why they ever left Missouri or Indiana or wherever it was they had come from.

Early explorers from Peter Skene Ogden to John C. Frémont believed that the Humboldt was part of the imagined Buenaventura River, a water passage

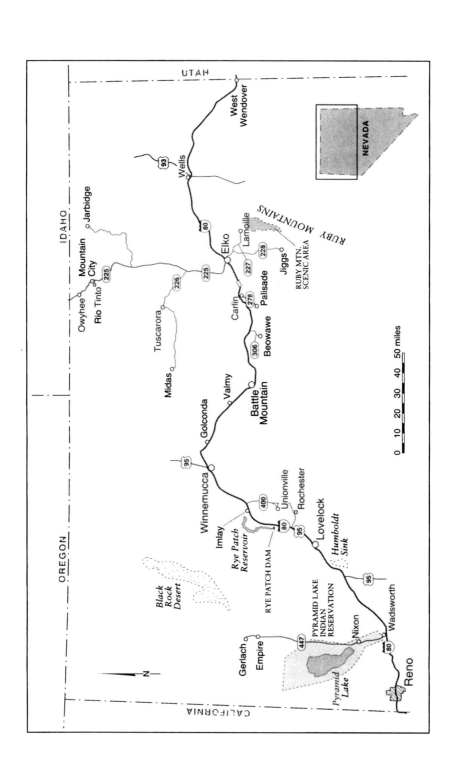

*The Humboldt River near Beowawe, in northeastern Nevada.*
—Courtesy Nevada Commission on Tourism

that was thought to connect the rivers of the American midwest to the Pacific Ocean. Early maps of the American West show such a river stretching from the interior to northern California. It was Frémont who observed in 1844 that the area between Utah's Wasatch Range and the Sierra Nevada was an interior drainage—the rivers did not flow to the sea—and named it the Great Basin.

Nevada, however, would not have developed without the Humboldt River. As the only source of water between the Great Salt Lake and the rivers of western Nevada, it was a lifeline. From 1840 to 1869, the Humboldt was a virtual highway to the West for thousands of travelers. While only about 2,000 emigrants attempted the arduous journey during the 1840s, the discovery of gold in northern California in 1849 unleashed a hoard of fortune seekers. An estimated 44,000 people braved the trek in 1850. Between 1851 and 1860, some108,600 more traveled across Nevada via the Humboldt Trail, which was part of the Emigrant Trail to California.

The new transcontinental railroad, built between 1861 and 1869, incorporated much of the Humboldt route. Of even more importance to the future of Nevada, however, were the new communities the Central Pacific Railroad established to serve as supply points, freight connections, maintenance yards, and switch stations. Almost overnight, the towns of Reno, Sparks, Lovelock, Winnemucca, and Elko bloomed in the desert. Modern-day explorers can follow the Emigrant Trail across northern Nevada on a four-lane highway, Interstate 80.

# I-80
# WEST WENDOVER–ELKO
**109 MILES**

## WEST WENDOVER

In 1845 John C. Frémont and his expedition were the first non-Indians to pass through the area around what is now West Wendover, at the Utah-Nevada line on I-80. While traveling across the bleak Bonneville Salt Flats west of the Great Salt Lake, the expedition party ran low on water. Frémont sent his guide, Kit Carson, ahead to search for a spring. Carson discovered several springs at the base of a large mountain in present Nevada, north of the West Wendover area. He sent up smoke signals from there to lead the expedition to the water. Frémont named this point of reference for his thirsty charges Pilot's Peak.

The community of West Wendover, Nevada, just across the border from Wendover, Utah, began in the 1920s as a gas station on the edge of the

*The Enola Gay monument in West Wendover.*

Bonneville Salt Flats. For years the station was all that greeted motorists as they entered Nevada from the east. When the state legalized gambling in 1931, the station's owner, Bill Smith, opened a small casino and restaurant, the Stateline Club, to offer a taste of Nevada-style hospitality to tourists who had made it across the salt flats. Today the Stateline Casino occupies the site, still owned by Smith's family.

During World War II, the Wendover Air Force Auxiliary Field, which straddled West Wendover and Wendover, Utah, was the scene of top-secret atomic-bomb tests. The *Enola Gay*, the airplane that dropped the world's first atomic bomb on Hiroshima, was hangared here. The remains of the airbase lay in Wendover, Utah.

About three miles west of West Wendover is one of the few places on land where one can see the curvature of the earth. Take the frontage road running parallel to I-80 to the top of a small hill, and see across unobscured miles of flatness the bend in the planet's surface.

## WELLS

Sixty miles west of West Wendover on I-80 is the community of Wells. The Central Pacific Railroad founded the settlement in 1869, when it was called Humboldt Wells because of the presence of dozens of spring-fed ponds. Emigrant diaries often referred to the area as "the wells" because the ponds, deep and naturally round, resembled wells more than springs.

As with most rail towns, Wells's commercial district developed adjacent to the tracks. By the early 1870s, several blocks of saloons, stores, boardinghouses, and hotels had opened on the street directly west of the tracks. Three fires in the late nineteenth century destroyed most of the town, but it was rebuilt each time.

Wells was less resilient, however, to changes in transportation. The old US 40 had passed through the center of the town, but the construction of I-80 in the 1960s shifted traffic a few miles south of the town's heart. Commerce followed the interstate travelers, new businesses sprang up along the new highway, and Wells's downtown faded away. By the early 1990s not a single downtown business remained open. Some boarded-up buildings still bear their signs—the Bullshead Bar, which opened in 1869, and Quilici's, an old-time general store that operated for more than a century.

## METROPOLIS

The site of Metropolis, fifteen miles northwest of Wells, is a little out of the way from the highway. Take I-80 exit 352 west to Eighth Street, turn left and drive along the railroad tracks, then follow the signs.

Metropolis is one of Nevada's few ghost towns that was not formerly a mining town. It was founded in 1909 by the Pacific Reclamations Company, a New York development firm, and has been described as the state's first real-estate scam. The town's promoters lured the unsuspecting with glowing descriptions of northeastern Nevada's long growing season and reliable water supply—despite the fact that the area has a harsh, hostile climate and little water.

To address the water problem, in 1912 Pacific Reclamations constructed a 100-foot dam and a canal system on a tributary of the Humboldt River. The company proclaimed that the water from the dam would support 40,000 acres of cultivated farm land and a modern city of 7,500 residents. The developers opened an office in Salt Lake City and targeted Mormon farmers. Their blueprint showed a town with neat, orderly lots, paved streets, water fountains, streetlights, schools, a hotel, and two parks.

By the end of 1912, they had installed the lots, streets, lights, and sidewalks and developed a four-block business district, including a three-story brick hotel and a two-story brick school. The Southern Pacific Railroad was so impressed with Metropolis that it constructed an eight-mile spur from its main line and built a small depot in the community.

That first year, more than 700 people, most of them industrious Mormon farmers, moved to Metropolis. Residents planted hundreds of acres of crops and ranged dozens of cattle. The town's newspaper even spoke of someday snatching the Humboldt County seat away from Elko. But the town's developers quickly found trouble. In 1913 farmers from Lovelock filed a lawsuit against Pacific Reclamation claiming that the real estate company had not sought approval from state or federal authorities to build its dam. In a dry state like Nevada—where nearly every drop of water is claimed by someone—it was a critical oversight. The courts ruled that Pacific Reclamation was entitled to only a portion of the water behind its dam—enough to irrigate 4,000 acres.

The court decision coincided with the beginning of a three-year drought. Desperate farmers were forced to dry-farm their crops, which proved moderately successful, while many took up dairy farming. Meanwhile, Pacific Reclamation was forced to file for bankruptcy protection, and the company finally folded in 1920.

Some families left Metropolis. Others stayed, and of those a few had success raising wheat and potatoes. Metropolis's run of bad luck, however, was not over. Drought conditions after 1914 were exacerbated by periodic invasions of jackrabbits, which ate most of the crops. At the same time, regular infestations of giant Mormon crickets, which also devoured the fields and even ate the paint off houses, further jinxed the town. By 1925 the Southern Pacific Railroad had removed its track and sold the depot. The elegant Metropolis Hotel burned in 1936 and the post office closed in 1942. Five years later, the imposing brick schoolhouse closed for lack of students.

All that remains today of this would-be agricultural paradise in the sagebrush are a few brick foundations and walls. The ruins seem out of place—Stonehenge-inspired shapes standing strangely in a lonely desert valley. Most

*The former Metropolis School.*

of the old Metropolis School has disintegrated or been removed, but the ornate arch remains, a solitary stone testimonial to the dreams of those who built Metropolis. A stone monument briefly tells the town's story, and a few miles north the illegally built dam remains in the water.

## TOBAR

Another illusory agricultural paradise was the community of Tobar (TOE-bar), eighteen miles southwest of Wells on a marked dirt road off US 93. Only a few concrete foundations remain at the site today.

Tobar was founded as a Western Pacific Railroad construction camp in 1908. The town's name has a rather unusual origin. One of the first businesses to open there was a tent saloon. To advertise the establishment, the owner painted a crude directional sign and nailed it to the side of the railroad station. Others who saw the sign mistakenly thought it was the name of the town—and that is how Tobar got its name.

In 1914 a Salt Lake City real estate broker began promoting the town with slick—and less than truthful—brochures claiming Tobar was an agricultural Garden of Eden that offered "the biggest business opportunities in the West." "Where the Big, Red Apple Grows" touted the ads, and similar outlandish statements recommended the region for growing wheat, potatoes, oats, alfalfa, vegetables, and fruit. By 1915 about 500 people had been persuaded by this hyperbole and settled in Tobar.

In 1918 the U.S. post office changed Tobar's name to Clover City, but the railroad refused to accept the new name, which resulted in some confusion. Finally, in 1921 postal authorities bowed to the railroad's pressure and changed the name back to Tobar.

By any name, Tobar was a failure. Like Metropolis, the town's agricultural potential was wanting. Insufficient water combined with the jackrabbit invasions that began in 1914 led to the town's rapid demise. Most of the farmers were gone by the 1920s. The hotel closed in the 1930s. The railroad left in 1946, and then the Clover Valley Store closed, which was Tobar's last business.

## ELKO

Fifty miles west of Wells on I-80 is the modern-day mining boomtown of Elko. Explorer Peter Skene Ogden was the first nonnative to visit the Elko area, wandering through during a beaver-hunting expedition in 1828. Thirteen years later, wagon trains following the Humboldt Trail frequently set up camp in the region, which had abundant grass and water.

The Central Pacific Railroad founded Elko in late 1868. The railroad selected the site as a railhead and freight terminus because of its proximity to several mining camps, including Tuscarora. The town was reputedly named by railroad official Charles Crocker, who enjoyed naming rail towns after animals. He is said to have added an *o* to the word *elk* to make the pronounciation easier. In early 1869, newcomers raised tents on the lots they bought from the railroad, and the town began to blossom. In March of that year, the Nevada legislature designated Elko the seat of a new county of the same name, thus assuring the town's success.

Elko's first courthouse, a fine, red brick, Greek Revival edifice, was erected on the main boulevard, Idaho Street, in December 1869. In the next year, Elko grew to 2,000 people and boasted a newspaper, the *Elko Independent,* still in publication, and many substantial wood and brick homes. In 1874 Elko became the site of the first University of Nevada campus. The town's remoteness, however, limited its appeal to college students and the university was moved to more populous Reno in 1885.

Ranching became an integral part of the local economy, with large cattle and sheep outfits. By the 1890s, the latter had attracted a large number of Basque sheepherders, known for their excellence as sheepmen. To cater to these newcomers, local Basque entrepreneurs established several boardinghouses in Elko. In addition to shelter, these boardinghouses offered the sheepmen traditional Basque meals and sold Basque newspapers. The inns served as gathering places for the Basques in town, giving them an opportunity to converse in their native tongue, and holiday celebrations and other social events were often held there. The dining rooms at these boardinghouses were open to the public, and many still serve Basque cuisine to this day.

Elko prospered as a transportation hub during the late nineteenth and early twentieth centuries. The town remained an important railroad stop for Southern Pacific and Western Pacific trains well into the mid-twentieth century. In 1920 Elko became a stop on the first transcontinental airmail route.

In the 1990s, substantial gold discoveries in the region have spurred the doubling of Elko's population, currently 30,000. The former rail and cow town has become a late-twentieth-century mining boomtown. Recent changes, however, have not erased the town's sense of history. The streets bear reminders of the town's frontier past. Several homes on Court Street date to the town's earliest days. The Dewar House, at 745 Court, was built in late 1869, shortly after the town was established. The county government offices at Sixth and Court are housed in the former Elko County High School, the first public high school in the state, constructed in 1895.

In the business district, a handful of historic commercial structures are still standing. The Commercial Hotel dates back to 1899 and was the first Nevada casino ever to offer entertainment, in 1941. Of particular note is J. M. Capriola's western shop at Commercial and Fifth, which houses one of the state's oldest and most famous saddle shops. Over the years, the proprietors have taken orders for custom-made G. S. Garcia saddles from many celebrities, including Will Rogers and Sylvester Stallone.

Near the Commercial Hotel is the Pioneer Hotel building, built in 1912, now home of the Western Folklife Center. Since 1984, the center has sponsored the annual Elko Cowboy Poetry Gathering. Elko's gathering was one of the first such events in the modern West. Held in late January, it attracts more than 8,000 people each year.

One of the best places to learn about the region's history is at the Northeastern Nevada Museum at 1515 Idaho Street. In addition to displays of handmade saddles and silver work, Basque clothing, and regional natural history, there is a Pony Express Station made of wood and sod, originally located in the Ruby Valley, on the museum grounds. Perhaps the most unusual item on exhibit is a pair of wooden shoes with cow hooves for soles. The shoes were crafted by a cattle rustler in the 1920s, who hoped that no one would be able to trace his footsteps. The scheme worked until he was caught in the act by two deputies.

## NV 225
## ELK–IDAHO BORDER
### 105 MILES

### RIO TINTO

The site of Rio Tinto is eighty-two miles north of Elko (two miles south of Mountain City) off NV 225. When copper was discovered at Rio Tinto in 1913, few people believed the news. S. Frank Hunt, the prospector who made the discovery, didn't have the funds to properly develop his mine, so he spent years trying to persuade local people to lend him money for the project. He repaid many with paper shares in his mine, which most people promptly discarded as worthless.

In 1932, however, Hunt's mine became the real thing. Digging at the 225-foot level, Hunt and partner Ogden Chase uncovered a rich copper vein. Hunt sold his share at a handsome profit to the Anaconda Copper Company, which developed the mine and constructed a company town with electricity, sewer and water systems, a movie theater, and schools. During the next fifteen years, Rio Tinto generated more than $23 million in copper ore before its mines were exhausted in the late 1940s. After the mine shut down, the town's buildings were dismantled and moved to other communities. Ruins of a schoolhouse are all that remain at the site.

### MOUNTAIN CITY

Visitors to Mountain City, eighty-four miles north of Elko on NV 225, will find a few empty stone and wood buildings mixed with newer structures. Today about seventy-five people live in the town, which survives by providing services to tourists and sports fishers heading to nearby Wild Horse Reservoir.

Chinese miners are credited with making the earliest gold discoveries in Mountain City. After completion of the transcontinental railroad, many Chinese laborers wandered into Nevada in search of work. In 1868 a handful of Chinese prospectors began placer mining in the area. Word of their discoveries attracted other miners, and in 1869 a small camp named Cope was founded. Shortly after, a town site was laid out and named Mountain City.

By the early 1870s, Mountain City had grown to more than 1,000 people and had nearly 200 buildings, from simple, wooden miners' cabins to brick breweries and saloons. A ditch diverted water from the nearby Owyhee River. At its peak in 1871, Mountain City had a post office, a gambling house, a bank, and a dozen hotels. The town began to decline after its ore played out in the mid-1870s. Though it experienced brief revivals in 1898 and 1932, Mountain City never returned to its previous prosperity.

# NV 226
# NV 225–MIDAS
### 67 MILES

## TUSCARORA

In the mid-1980s Horizon Gold Shares, a Denver-based mining company, announced plans to develop a large-scale open-pit gold-mining operation adjacent to the historic mining town of Tuscarora, fifty-two miles north of Elko by way of NV 225, NV 226, and NV 18. Practically overnight a huge hole appeared at the southern edge of the tiny town. When the mining company found more deposits beneath the town itself, the owners decided to try to relocate the hamlet's twenty-odd permanent residents.

But under the leadership of internationally known artist Dennis Parks, who founded a pottery school in Tuscarora in 1966, the town rallied to oppose the mining company. The obvious David-versus-Goliath appeal of the fight attracted national attention, including coverage by major TV networks, and ultimately led to the town's preservation.

Tuscarora got its start in the late 1860s after a local Shoshone Indian showed gold to a trader on the Humboldt River, twenty-five miles to the south. A small mining camp soon grew up near the site. A miner from North Carolina named the camp Tuscarora after an Indian tribe in his home state. By 1869 several hundred miners, mostly from the Austin mining district, 200 miles to the south, were working the area. Joining them were hundreds of Chinese laborers whom the Central Pacific Railroad had laid off when it completed the transcontinental line earlier that year. Many of the Chinese workers dug ditches to bring in water from Six Mile Canyon and upper McCann Creek, a few miles north of Tuscarora.

In early 1871 one miner, W. O. Weed, found new silver reserves on nearby Mount Blitzen, and by July of that year Tuscarora had a post office. Other discoveries accelerated the district's growth, and by 1877 more than 3,000 people lived in Tuscarora, although more than half were transient miners. There was also a fairly large Chinese district on McCann Creek, southwest of the town. But Tuscarora began a slow decline in 1880, as the ore started to run out. The 1880 census reported 1,400 residents. While mining continued to be productive on a smaller scale for the next several decades, by 1915 the town had dwindled to only a handful of optimists.

Today Tuscarora has a number of photogenic ruins. An old brick store with a classic frontier-style facade stands on the main street, its collapsed wooden awning barely hanging over the two windows and doorway. Across the street is an incredibly contorted wooden house, which, though part of its roof has collapsed, somehow maintains a semblance of structural integrity. Just north of the town center, on a hillside, stand the solitary remains of a towering smokestack,

*An abandoned building in Tuscarora.*

once part of a large stamp mill. There are also a dozen former miners' houses and shacks, some renovated and still inhabited, scattered throughout the town. A few of the deserted buildings still contain torn curtains, beds, and other furnishings.

A testament to one of the hazards once posed by the open-pit mine is the pit's uncomfortable proximity to one old wooden house. A dilapidated outhouse stands behind the home less than four feet from a fence surrounding the massive glory hole, which is 800 feet long, 400 feet wide, and 150 feet deep. Not far away, Dennis Parks's Tuscarora School of Pottery, formerly a two-story wooden hotel, displays many of Parks's works, including ceramic plates, cups, bowls, and vases, all made of local clay and other materials found in the area.

## MIDAS

Midas is forty-five miles west of Tuscarora on NV 18, a maintained gravel road. In 1907 gold was discovered in the southeast canyons of the Owyhee Bluffs of northwestern Elko County. Within months a small town was thriving just below the mines.

The camp was originally called Gold Circle, because the gold seemed to encircle the community. But when the time came to acquire a post office, the federal postal officials rejected the name because too many mining camps in Nevada already had the word gold in their names. Midas, the name of the legendary king with the golden touch, was chosen to suggest the same idea. By its first anniversary, Midas had more than 2,000 residents, most living in tents in the gulches below the canyons. A newspaper and several service businesses quickly appeared.

*Built in the early twentieth century, the Midas School now serves as a community center.*

But Midas proved not to have the golden touch. The gold deposits were not as plentiful as originally believed, and within a short time the townspeople began to drift off to work claims in more promising locations. By 1909 only a few hundred prospectors were still mining in the area.

Then Midas had a second boom after 1915, when several new mines opened and the fifty-ton Elko Prince mill was built. The town's remote location, however, made transporting the ore expensive. Despite producing more than $456,000 in gold ore in 1918, the district's peak, operations were only marginally profitable. The community limped along until the mill burned down in 1922.

In 1927 a new, 100-ton plant was built near Midas and mining activity resumed. The mines were productive until the advent of World War II, when materials and supplies became scarce and operations ceased. By 1950 only nine people lived in Midas. In recent decades, however, the town has experienced a modest revival as a retirement community for people from Elko, Carson City, Reno, and Winnemucca, and it has grown to nearly 100 full-time residents.

# NV 227 AND NV 228
# ELKO–JIGGS
**33 MILES**

## LAMOILLE

At the foot of the Ruby Mountains lies the tiny hamlet of Lamoille (la-MOY-al), a pastoral place surrounded by fields dotted with cattle and rolled carpets of hay. Lamoille was settled in the 1860s and may have been named after a French Canadian trapper who built a cabin here in the 1850s. Or local rancher Thomas Waterman may have named it for a town in his native Vermont.

With its magnificent backdrop, Lamoille is one of the state's most photogenic small towns. Of special note is the Presbyterian Church, a beautiful steepled and whitewashed chapel that could belong in Garrison Keillor's mythical Lake Wobegon.

## THE RUBY MOUNTAINS

Twenty miles south of Elko lie the Ruby Mountains, one of the most picturesque ranges in Nevada. With several peaks exceeding 10,000 feet rising above the desert, the Rubies epitomize Nevada's basin-and-range topography. This

*Lamoille's Presbyterian Church.*

*The Ruby Mountains, in the distance.*

majestic range is ninety miles long and as much as sixteen miles wide. The highest peak, Ruby Dome, soars to 11,387 feet. The range is the most heavily glaciated in the state, with about thirty glacial lakes tucked into its many folds and ridges.

The mountains were named after the nearby Ruby Valley, where in the late 1840s or 1850s a group of emigrants allegedly found garnets, though the existence of neither garnets nor rubies here has ever been documented. The name Ruby Valley first appeared in Captain James H. Simpson's 1859 survey of Nevada—although his party did not report finding any garnets—and it was later bestowed on the area's first post office, established in 1862. The Ruby Valley post office, which operated until 1869, was most likely part of an Overland Stage station and military post called Camp Ruby or Fort Ruby.

With or without garnets, few would dispute that the Rubies are one of the gems of Nevada. Ninety thousand acres of the range have been designated a federal wilderness area. Lamoille Canyon Road, which can be accessed from NV 227 at Lamoille, is one of the state's most scenic drives. This twelve-mile road enters Lamoille Canyon on the west side of the range. At the mouth of the canyon there is a public picnic area beside a lovely mountain stream. Interpretive signs at several viewing areas explain how the canyon was carved by glacial processes, point out avalanche sites, and identify other points of interest.

## JIGGS

Jiggs, forty miles south of Elko on NV 228, is the only community in Nevada named after a comic strip. The site was originally a Shoshone settlement. The tribe harvested pine nuts from the piñons in the surrounding mountains, where they also found abundant game.

When a small ranching settlement formed in the early twentieth century, a quarrel arose over what to name the community. At different times it was known as Mound Valley, Skelton, and Hylton. Finally, in 1918 postal authorities selected the name Jiggs from a list submitted by local ranchers. In light of the controversy, it seemed appropriate to name the town after the comic-strip character in *Bringing Up Father* who constantly bickered with his wife.

# I-80
# ELKO–WINNEMUCCA
## 125 MILES

## CARLIN

Carlin, twenty-three miles southwest of Elko on I-80, began life in 1868 as a railroad town. The town was named for William Passmore Carlin, a Civil War union army officer. As with most rail towns, Carlin's original commercial district—much of it now shuttered but still standing—was built along the tracks. The rest of Carlin, however, is booming because of the nearby Newmont gold mine, one of the largest in the world. Several newer restaurants and businesses have sprung up adjacent to the interstate.

## PALISADE

Not much remains of the former railroad town of Palisade, ten miles south of Carlin on NV 278. From the cemetery overlooking the town site, you can hear the rushing waters of the Humboldt River, an occasional train passing through a nearby tunnel, and the wind whispering inside the steep canyon that inspired the town's name.

Palisade was once an important railroad stop—in fact, at one time it served three different rail lines, including the Central Pacific, the Eureka & Palisade, and the Western Pacific. The Central Pacific Railroad surveyed the town in 1870, and within a few years it had grown to more than 300 residents. At its peak, it competed with Elko and Carlin as a major shipping point serving the thriving mining camps of Mineral Hill, Eureka, and Hamilton.

For about three years in the early 1870s, Palisade became notorious for a hoax that the town perpetrated on unsuspecting railroad passengers for its own entertainment. About once a day, the train made a brief stop in Palisade for water and wood. When passengers disembarked to stretch their legs, they would encounter a crowd of angry-looking, armed thugs having a disagreement. A fight would erupt and the toughs would begin shooting at each other. After scurrying back onto the train, the passengers would look back and be horrified to see bodies lying in the street in pools of blood. As the train pulled out, a band of Shoshone would appear and join the battle.

Once the train was out of sight, the "dead" miraculously rose from the street and retired to nearby saloons. The shooters had fired blanks and the blood was from a local slaughterhouse. Sometimes the script changed, and there would be a bank robbery followed by a dramatic gunfight between lawmen and the robbers. Palisade citizens eventually grew tired of the faux carnage, and after an estimated 1,000 performances they discontinued the shootouts.

By 1875 the narrow-gauge Eureka & Palisade Railroad was complete, connecting Palisade to the Eureka mines, about ninety miles to the south. The Eureka & Palisade set up its headquarters in Palisade and shared a depot with the Central Pacific. For the next fifty-five years, the line transported millions of dollars' worth of ore to Palisade, where it was transferred to the Central Pacific line, and after 1910 to the Western Pacific line. But starting in the late 1880s, Palisade experienced a slow decline with the decreasing productivity of Eureka's mines. In 1910 a major flood destroyed much of the town and damaged all three train lines, later rebuilt. A few years later, a fire accelerated the town's demise. By the time the Eureka & Palisade Railroad ceased operations in 1938, Palisade was a ghost town.

Today the remains of about ten structures stand half hidden by the thick sagebrush and tall grass, mostly the ruins of crude miners' shacks. The walls are of concrete or brick, but their wood or sod roofs have collapsed. Other traces of the town's existence are scattered around the site: an old safe, the rusted hulk

*The concrete ruins of a miner's shack in Palisade.*

of an old car, and other assorted junk. The cemetery tells us the most about Palisade. Still maintained by descendents of the town's first residents, it has substantial marble monuments and fine examples of wooden markers, all in remarkably good condition.

There is another reason to visit Palisade besides its historic remains—the stunning Humboldt Palisades. These dramatic cliffs, more than a thousand feet high, rise up to the east of the town. A dirt road parallel to the train tracks leads into the rugged twelve-mile-long canyon.

## BEOWAWE

Beowawe (bee-OH-wah-wee) is a tiny ranching community six miles south of I-80 on NV 306, on the northern lip of the beautiful Crescent Valley. There are several stories behind the town's unusual name. One claims it is an adaptation of the Northern Paiute word for "gate" or "opening," which roughly describes the area's topography in relation to the surrounding mountains. According to another tale, the name means "great posterior" and was first used when a local tribe was frightened by the sight of a particularly stout railroad manager.

About seven miles northwest of Beowawe, via an unmarked dirt road, are the remnants of the Beowawe geysers, a once-famous landmark. One of the geysers reportedly sprayed water more than thirty feet high. But in the early 1960s geothermal springs were diverted for a nearby power plant, and the geysers spew no more.

Four miles south of Beowawe is Gravelly Ford, a notable Emigrant Trail crossing. A large cross near here marks the misleadingly named Maiden's Grave, the burial site of Lucinda Duncan, a grandmother who died while traveling with her family on the trail.

## BATTLE MOUNTAIN

The town of Battle Mountain, seventy miles west of Elko on I-80, gets its name from a bluff where, in the mid-nineteenth century, Shoshone warriors and a wagon party fought on the Emigrant Trail. Or it might have been an Indian raid on a road-building crew. Depends on who is telling the story. Miners settled the area in 1867 after the discovery of substantial silver, copper, and gold deposits. The present Battle Mountain site was developed in the late 1860s as a railroad station.

Battle Mountain now has nearly 7,000 residents and is thriving in the modern gold-mining economy. Interstate traffic and its recently acquired position as seat of Lander County have also helped the town. In addition to gold, this area is known for its beautiful turquoise gems.

The Trail of the Forty-Niners Interpretive Center in Battle Mountain is operated by the Central Nevada Emigrant Trail Association. It commemorates the estimated 200,000 pioneers who traveled the trail between 1840 and 1860. Maps, books, artifacts, replicas of pioneer items, and computer simulations help visitors imagine the challenges of making the 2,200-mile trek from Missouri to California.

## VALMY

Valmy is a tiny roadside stop fourteen miles west of Battle Mountain on I-80. It was named for a famous French battle site as a sly reference to the many battles between local tribes over the springs found here. A railroad stop was established here in 1910 to provide water and fuel for passing trains. The town gained probably its greatest fame in the early 1980s, after rock-music icon Bruce Springsteen posed for an album-cover photo in front of Valmy's 1930s-style gas station and general store (the album was released in Britain). The Valmy Shell station still serves gas and food. The huge smokestacks in the distance are part of Sierra Pacific Power's coal-powered electrical plant.

## GOLCONDA

Twenty-three miles west of Valmy on I-80 is Golconda, population about forty. When large numbers of wagons were crossing Nevada on their way to California, the site of Golconda was a favored stop because of its natural hot springs. Traces of the Emigrant Trail are visible north of the town.

Many scholars believe that it was in the Golconda area, near Emigrant Canyon, where one of the early tragedies of the Donner party occurred. In October 1846 James Reed killed teamster John Snyder during an argument. Reed was banished from the group, while his wife and four children remained with the

*The Valmy gas station and general store appeared on the cover of a Bruce Springsteen album.* —Courtesy Nevada Commission on Tourism

wagon train. Ironically, because of his head start, Reed reached California ahead of the storms that trapped the rest of the party in the mountains, and he later led one of the rescue parties. His family survived.

In 1863 Golconda became the starting point for an ambitious project to carry local water to mines at Mill City through a canal. The French Canal was to be sixty miles long, fifteen feet wide, and three feet deep. Construction was completed as far as Winnemucca—at a cost of $100,000—before engineering errors caused leaking and ended the project.

In 1868 the Central Pacific Railroad established a gold-ore shipping station near the hot springs and named it Golconda after an ancient city in India famous for its great wealth. The ore came from the Gold Run Mining District, about twelve miles south. The railroad company also built a small resort at the springs for the relaxation of weary transcontinental travelers.

Later the Golconda & Adelaide, a narrow-gauge rail built in 1897, transported ore from reactivated mines at Adelaide, about eleven miles south of Golconda. Golconda quickly grew to more than 500 residents and gained a post office and several hotels. The excitement quickly subsided, however, when in 1899 the mine closed due to the marginal quality of the ore and the railroad ceased operations.

About seven years later, new investors reopened the mines, ore mill, and railroad, but operations once again proved unprofitable and all were shut down for good by 1910. In the late 1930s, after hearing about new manganese and tungsten discoveries, speculators built a large chemical plant outside of town to process the ore. But the plant closed at the end of World War II and was

*The Golconda School, now a community hall.*

dismantled in the early 1950s. Mining continues, however, at the Getchell and Pinson Mines, twenty miles north of Golconda.

The original hot springs hotel, which became regionally famous in the early part of the twentieth century, burned in 1961. Today Golconda is a sleepy roadside hamlet with only a handful of businesses. A gray-and-white, red-roofed schoolhouse, constructed just after the turn of the twentieth century, now serves as a community center. Standing guard nearby is the original railroad water tower, a black cylinder on stilts. Less than a mile west of the water tower lie the remains of Golconda's once-famous hot springs, now just a large warm-water pond.

### The Battle of Rabbit Creek

One of the most tragic episodes in Nevada history occurred at Rabbit Creek, just north of Golconda. In February 1911, a dozen Shoshone and Bannock Indians led by a man called Shoshone Mike were accused of murdering four sheepmen in the Little High Rock Canyon area of the Black Rock Desert. Several posses formed to hunt the group. After chasing the band for a month over 200 miles, one of the posses trapped them in a dry creek bed. A fight ensued and eight of the Indians were shot and killed, as was one member of the posse. The four surviving members of Shoshone Mike's band, all children, were taken to Fort Hall, Idaho, where three died of disease and one was adopted.

Historians cite this event as the end of the days when Indians roamed free in Nevada; by the early twentieth century nearly all had been moved to reservations. The battle of Rabbit Creek continues to generate controversy. Some historians believe that the band murdered the sheepherders and mutilated the bodies, while others insist the murderers were cowboys from a local cattle outfit and the Indians robbed and mutilated the bodies later. Cattle ranchers frequently fought with sheepmen in those days. Evidence supports the latter view—the rifles carried by Shoshone Mike's band were not the same caliber as those that killed the sheepmen.

## WINNEMUCCA

At the junction of I-80 and US 95 is Winnemucca (win-uh-MUCK-uh). Trapper Peter Skene Ogden was the first non–Native American to visit this area during his trek through Nevada in 1828. Later the site of Winnemucca was a popular ferry crossing—it was one of the few dependable fords across the Humboldt River—for travelers heading to California.

In 1853 a trading post was established near the river to provide supplies to the emigrants. Within a short time, a small settlement had developed around the post, called Frenchman's Ford because its founders were mostly French. Since the community sat on the Humboldt Trail, the major transportation route across the state, it thrived as a regional shipping center, serving local sheep and cattle ranches.

*Chief Winnemucca.*
—Courtesy Nevada
Historical Society

Nearby gold and silver strikes in the early 1860s, such as the one in Unionville, forty miles to the southwest, boosted the town's fortunes, as it became the gateway to these new discoveries. In 1868 the Central Pacific Railroad, which became part of the Southern Pacific Railroad in 1899, reached the community and renamed Winnemucca in honor of a famous Northern Paiute chief. The railroad brought jobs and served to link the town to distant markets.

Unionville was the first seat of Humboldt County, but after its decline the county seat was moved to Winnemucca, in 1872. A courthouse went up in 1874. Since the railroad ran a mile south of the river and most of the town's established buildings, Winnemucca soon became two communities. Uppertown was the newer section, adjacent to the railroad, while the older, river district was called Lowertown.

For a time, the two districts competed to become Winnemucca's commercial center. Uppertown was the first to get oil streetlights. But eventually the rivalry faded as new development connected the two districts by way of Bridge Street. To ensure continued peace, the new county courthouse (its predessessor had burned down in 1918) was constructed in 1921 on Bridge and Fifth Streets, midway between the two districts.

A second railroad, the Western Pacific Railway, came into Winnemucca in 1909. The Western Pacific built a roundhouse and depot in the town, which became a regional freight center for the railroad. In order to build on level ground, the Western Pacific tracks ran within a few miles of the Southern Pacific's right-of-way for 177 miles along the Humboldt River. At Palisade, the lines were so close that the Western Pacific had to negotiate a crossing over Southern Pacific tracks.

The creation of a national highway system brought Winnemucca's most modern stage of development. Winnemucca's first automobile arrived in 1905. Within fifteen years, the Victory Highway, one of the earliest transcontinental roads, crossed Nevada, passing right through Winnemucca. Once again, the town's location ensured it would not be overlooked as the West developed.

During the early and mid-twentieth century a third commercial district grew up parallel to the Victory Highway, which in the 1920s was renamed US 40. In the 1970s, I-80 was built north of Winnemucca's business center to avoid slowing down traffic, draining off downtown activity.

### The Great Winnemucca Bank Robbery

One of Winnemucca's most enduring legends is the story of how Butch Cassidy and his gang robbed the First National Bank in Winnemucca on September 19, 1900. Cassidy, the Sundance Kid, and other members of their Wild Bunch rode into town, robbed the bank of about $32,000 in gold, and shot it out with authorities before escaping. Later, Cassidy allegedly sent the bank a photograph of himself and his gang, along with a thank-you note for all the money. The robbery became so infamous that for many years the town held an annual Butch Cassidy Days in September.

But the story is not true. There was indeed a robbery that day, but there's no evidence that Butch Cassidy or the Sundance Kid ever set foot in Winnemucca. The tale about the photo is a hoax, says David W. Toll, a Nevada journalist and historian. Toll found records proving that the photo of Butch and his gang came from the Pinkerton Detective Agency to bank owner George Nixon, who was present at the robbery, so that he could identify the participants. Nixon did not finger Butch Cassidy, and he provided less-than-certain identification of the Sundance Kid. Nevertheless, the detectives named both outlaws on their flyers, offering a $6,000 reward for the arrest of the supposed Winnemucca robbers. No one was ever arrested.

### Sarah Winnemucca

The remarkable Sarah Winnemucca was born about 1844 near the Humboldt Sink. She was the daughter of Chief Winnemucca and granddaughter of Captain Truckee, a Paiute leader who had served as a scout for several early wagon trains and for explorer John C. Frémont. Sarah Winnemucca was highly unusual among nineteenth-century Native Americans in that she attended white schools. Her grandfather insisted she be well educated and sent her to live with a white family in Stockton, California. Later she spent three years studying at the Convent of Notre Dame in San Jose. She was fluent in three Indian dialects as well as English and Spanish.

After returning to Nevada, Winnemucca became involved in a dispute with a local Indian agent who was withholding food that was supposed to go to the Paiutes. This began her lifelong crusade against this country's treatment of Indians. In 1870 she wrote to the Commissioner of Indian Affairs, who had suggested that sending the Paiute to a reservation would improve their lives. Winnemucca said:

*Sarah Winnemucca.*
—Courtesy Nevada
Historical Society

Myself and most of the Humboldt and Queen's River Indians were on the Truckee Reservation at one time but if we had stayed there it would have been only to starve. I think that if they had received what they were entitled to from the agents they would never have left there.

On the other hand if the Indians have my guarantee that they can secure a permanent home on their native soil and that our white neighbors can be kept from encroaching on our rights . . . I warrant that the savage as he is called today will be a law-abiding member of the community fifteen or twenty years hence.

Winnemucca was living in southern Oregon in 1878 when she discovered the local Bannock tribe's plan to attack white settlers so they would leave Indian lands. Fearing her people would be drawn into the fight, she rode 233 miles to urge her father and other Paiute not to become involved. While the Paiute did not join the Bannocks in their war, the government still rounded up many of them and sent them to a reservation in Yakima, Washington.

The horrible conditions on the reservation moved Winnemucca to embark on a series of lectures about her people's plight. She succeeded in drawing attention to the issue, and in 1879 she and her family were invited to meet with President Rutherford B. Hayes. In 1883 she conducted a lecture tour in the East and, with the help of sympathetic supporters, published a book about her people's treatment, entitled *Life among the Piutes: Their Wrongs and Claims*, under her married name of Hopkins. It was the first book ever written by a Native American.

Unfortunately, all her activity only made many Indian agents more hostile to the Paiute and to Winnemucca herself. One agent, W. V. Rinehart, went so far as to denounce her as a "common prostitute and thoroughly addicted to the habits of drunkenness and gambling." She responded by gathering commendations from prominent military figures and political leaders familiar with her efforts, which she included in her book.

For much of the rest of her life, Winnemucca continued to give lectures. She would dress in native costume and talk of the injustices experienced by Native Americans. She also briefly ran an Indian school in Lovelock, but it folded due to lack of funding and poor administration. She died in 1891.

### Historic Winnemucca

Winnemucca today has many reminders of its rich and varied history. The oldest building in town is the Winnemucca Hotel at 95 Bridge Street in Lowertown, a modest, two-story wooden structure that opened in 1863. The hotel originally served as a stagecoach stop, post office, and restaurant. It is still a Basque restaurant and hotel. At East Fourth and Melarkey Streets, St. Paul's Roman Catholic Church, built in 1923, is northern Nevada's only Spanish Colonial–style structure. The Martin Hotel, a Basque boardinghouse built in 1913, is a remnant of Uppertown. It remains a popular restaurant, though it is no longer used as an inn. Sadly, one of the town's most beloved historic buildings, the 1907 Nixon Opera House, was destroyed by arson in 1992.

The Humboldt County Museum on Jungo Road has exhibits portraying the region's development. The museum incorporates the former St. Mary's Episcopal Church, a traditional gothic structure built in 1907 and moved to the museum grounds in 1977.

# I-80/US 95
# WINNEMUCCA– WADSWORTH
## 132 MILES

### UNIONVILLE

To get to Unionville, take the NV 400 exit at Mill City and go south about seventeen miles to the signed dirt road, which you follow three miles west. Today Unionville has an assortment of ruins amid a handful of inhabited residences. Among the sights still to be found are a picturesque century-old schoolhouse and the Old Pioneer Garden Country Inn. The latter is a bed-and-breakfast in the rustic 1864 Hadley House.

*Remains of a mining mill in Unionville.*

Before he began writing as Mark Twain for Virginia City's *Territorial Enterprise*, young Sam Clemens made a visit to the mining camp of Unionville to try his hand at prospecting. He arrived in the town during the winter of 1861 and staked several claims. After a few days of digging and mucking, Clemens decided there had to be an easier way to make a living. He lost money in the local mining stock exchange before departing for Virginia City and more lasting fame.

Unionville's silver deposits were discovered in early 1861 by a band of Paiutes. The Indians guided several prospectors from Virginia City to the remote canyon, and a mining district soon developed. When the town was platted, it was named Dixie because most of the miners came from the South. However, later arrivals, during the Civil War, were largely federal sympathizers, so the town's name soon became Unionville.

Within two years nearly 800 people lived in the community, now the seat of newly created Humboldt County. Unionville had a newspaper, a horse-drawn trolley line, a town hall, and a schoolhouse. But its prosperity was short-lived. Although the mines continued to produce into the 1870s, the railroad town of Winnemucca had eclipsed Unionville as the county's largest community and successfully petitioned to acquire the Humboldt County seat in 1872. Not long after, Unionville's businesses and people also began to depart for more prosperous locales.

## IMLAY

Imlay, about twenty-three miles southwest of Winnemucca on US 95/I-80, was once an important stop for pioneers on the Emigrant Trail. The area around Imlay was known then as Lassen (or Lawson) Meadows, where Oregon-bound emigrants turned north onto Lassen-Applegate Trail. Lassen was a rare oasis of grass and water.

In 1908, the Southern Pacific founded the town of Imlay. The railroad built a roundhouse there, and some shops. The town soon had a number of businesses. Several nearby mining camps, such as Unionville and Star City, also used the town, which grew to several hundred people. After the mines in the region closed in the 1920s and the railroad removed its facilities, Imlay began to decline. About 100 people live in the community today.

### Thunder Mountain

Adjacent to Imlay is a strange, three-story-high mound of concrete, rock, glass, and scrap metal known as Thunder Mountain. This unusual folk-art creation was built in the 1960s and '70s by an eccentric desert artist who called himself Chief Rolling Mountain Thunder. Each visit to this weird monument brings a new revelation of something—perhaps a face carved in a wall or an unusual shape formed in the stones—that was not noticed before. The monument incorporates more than 200 individual sculptures of Native Americans,

*The sculpture called Thunder Mountain, by Frank Van Zandt, a.k.a. Chief Rolling Mountain Thunder.*

including Sarah Winnemucca. A portion of Thunder Mountain burned in 1983, but the main structure was saved. It was listed on the Nevada Register of Historic Places in 1992.

Environmental artist Frank Van Zandt (Chief Rolling Mountain Thunder) moved from northern California to northern Nevada in the late 1960s because he believed that the area around Thunder Mountain—an adjacent peak in the Humboldt Range—had spiritual qualities. He worked with incidentally available materials, including bottles, rocks, auto parts, wood scraps, and other found objects. In January 1989, Van Zandt took his own life at age seventy-seven.

## THE RYE PATCH RESERVOIR

The tired, hot, and thirsty pioneers crossing Nevada could only dream of coming to a place like the Rye Patch Reservoir. More than eighty years before the Rye Patch Dam impounded it, emigrants found this stretch of trail between present-day Imlay and Lovelock to be one of the driest, dustiest parts of the trek across Nevada. "It is a perfectly barren land for forty long miles, and it is distressing to hear the complaints of the poor cattle, which are suffering for want of food," wrote Harriett S. Ward in her journal of her 1853 crossing. Today the reservoir covers nearly half of that parched forty miles.

Like the rest of northern Nevada, the Rye Patch region was submerged beneath the waters of prehistoric Lake Lahontan 12,000 years ago. As the lake receded, it left behind sediment that has since been steadily eroded by the Humboldt River. This river channel is why the Rye Patch Reservoir sits nearly 100 feet below the surrounding terrain, nearly hiding the lake from view.

The U.S. Bureau of Reclamation built the Rye Patch Dam in 1936 to store water for the Lovelock area, whose average annual rainfall is only six inches. Rye Patch was named for the large patches of wild rye grass that once grew here, before the cattle brought here in the 1870s ate it all. The dam radically transformed a seasonally wet river bottom into a man-made lake used for boating and fishing.

The Rye Patch State Recreation Area, about twenty-three miles northeast of Lovelock off US 95/I-80, encompasses the reservoir, picnic grounds, and campsites. The reservoir is nearly twenty-two miles long and one-third mile across at its widest point, and it holds up to 40,000 acres of water. It has produced state-record fish, including a fifteen-pound walleye and a thirty-one-pound channel catfish. The concrete dam, at the reservoir's west end, is an impressive piece of construction. Eight hundred feet long and 500 feet wide at its base, it rises 72 feet above the riverbed. A 110-foot spillway handles overflow.

## ROCHESTER

To reach the site of Rochester, take I-80 to the Oreana exit, nine miles south of the Rye Patch Dam, and continue east for three miles, then turn right on a maintained dirt road and drive seven miles to the remains of Lower Rochester. The first whites in the Rochester Canyon area were prospectors from Rochester, New York, in the early 1860s. The first small-scale silver mining proved largely unsuccessful. In 1912, however, prospector Joseph Nenzel found large bodies of silver ore in the canyon, and this sparked a significant boom.

By 1913 more than 2,000 miners were working the area, and a two-and-a-half-mile-long ribbon of miners' shacks, commercial businesses, and other buildings ran down the heart of the canyon. Those who clustered near the top of the canyon formed the town of Rochester Heights. Meanwhile, farther down the canyon grew the larger community of Rochester. At its peak in 1913–14, Rochester had an orchestra, some dance halls, regular freight service, and a 100-ton ore mill.

By 1915, however, Lower Rochester, yet another town site, replaced Rochester as the biggest camp. The upstart had the advantage of being connected to the Southern Pacific rail line by a shortline railroad. Lower Rochester had an aerial tram system to carry ore from the mines to the mill, built in 1917. The mines continued to produce through the 1920s and 1930s, but they were shut down in 1942 because of equipment and supply shortages during World War II.

After the war there were efforts to revive the mines, but none succeeded until the 1980s, when a large-scale gold-mining operation, the Coeur Rochester Mine, opened on the mountain above the canyon. The mine is still in

*A dilapidated building and old headframe hoist in Rochester.*

operation. Today Rochester, which now comprises the entire area, still has a handful of picturesque wooden headframes—tall, derricklike hoists used to bring ore to the surface. Up the canyon, a handful of stone foundations and crumbling wooden miners' shacks peek through the sagebrush.

## LOVELOCK

Lovelock is seventy-two miles south of Winnemucca on I-80. The Lovelock area has long held an important place in the history of Nevada and the American West. The West's earliest explorers, including Peter Skene Ogden and John C. Frémont, passed through the region on their expeditions and noted its abundant grasslands. Later, immigrants to California following the Humboldt River across Nevada stopped here. They called the Lovelock area Big Meadows, where they rested their livestock and restocked their supplies of water and hay before crossing the dreaded Forty Mile Desert.

The first settlers at Big Meadows were James Blake and his family, who in 1861 operated a stage stop and 300-acre ranch. In 1866 George Lovelock, an Englishman, established a large cattle ranch in Big Meadows. Three years later he donated eighty acres to the Central Pacific Railroad for a town site, named Lovelocks. Postal authorities shortened the name in 1922.

*Pershing County's round courthouse, built in 1921, sits in the center of Lovelock.*
—Courtesy K. J. Evans

In the 1860s and 1870s, following the completion of the transcontinental railroad, Lovelock grew into a shipping center for many nearby mining towns, such as Unionville, Oreana, and Rochester. By the early twentieth century, however, mining activity in the region had slowed, and farming and ranching became more important to Lovelock. The town's most prominent resident during this time was John G. Taylor, owner of one of the American West's great cattle empires. At one point, Taylor's holdings included more than 60,000 head of sheep and 8,000 cattle. He owned 130,000 acres of grazing land and leased another half million acres.

Today Lovelock remains a quiet agricultural community. Its economy is based on cattle ranching and crops such as barley, wheat, oats, and alfalfa. As it did more than a century ago, the town serves as a stop for travelers needing rest and refreshment while crossing Nevada on I-80.

Lovelock has a number of buildings worth seeing, including the Pershing County Courthouse at Main and Central Streets, one of only two round courthouses in the country. This structure was designed by Reno architect Frederick J. DeLongchamps, who designed many public buildings in early-twentieth-century Nevada. The Marzen House Museum, just west of downtown on old US 40, carries an extensive collection of antique farming equipment and pioneer-era furnishings.

### *Lovelock Cave and the Redheaded Giants*

Twenty miles south of Lovelock, on the southeast edge of the Humboldt Sink, is Lovelock Cave. The cave's excavation in 1924 was one of the West's first major archaeological digs. It yielded important Native American artifacts, including prehistoric tule-duck decoys. An early dig at this cave was also the source of one of Nevada's most intriguing miscalculations.

In the 1920s and 1930s, John T. Reid, a mining engineer and amateur anthropologist who had close ties to the local Northern Paiute, uncovered several prehistoric skeletons. By his measure, these people had stood about seven feet, seven inches tall, and one was nine feet, six inches. The hair remaining on some of the skulls was a brownish red. The discovery appeared to give substance to a traditional Paiute legend about redheaded giants who once lived in the Humboldt Sink area. According to the Paiute, these people were vicious and cruel, and possibly man-eaters. They tormented the Paiute until the tribe retaliated, chasing the giants into the Lovelock Cave and killing most of them.

Reid died in 1948, and the Nevada Historical Society bought his papers and artifacts, including the bones. The bones were misplaced, however, so Reid's analysis of the skeletons went unchallenged for several decades. In 1977, the bones were found and reanalyzed. Newer technologies revealed that Reid had mismeasured the leg bones. The skeletons proved to be of average or slightly below-average height. The hair color was from red ochre paint used on the bodies—a common burial practice among Great Basin tribes.

## THE FORTY MILE DESERT

The worst part of pioneer travel through Nevada was crossing the Forty Mile Desert, a barren stretch that begins southwest of Lovelock and skirts the Humboldt Sink. From the sink, California-bound travelers could choose between two routes of roughly equal distance: one west to the Truckee River, and the other continuing south to the Carson River at Ragtown, near Fallon. Neither had much water or grass, and both were equally hard to traverse.

In 1858 William A. Wallace, a reporter at San Francisco's *Alta California* newspaper, wrote of his own trek across the Forty Mile Desert on the Ragtown route. There were thousands of acres of "leafless and lifeless, white arid plains without water, upon which the sun glares," he reported, with "heaps of bones" from dead animals, "ten thousand tons" of wagon irons, and enough ox chains to stretch all the way to Salt Lake City, all strewn along the trail. Wallace continued:

> This forty miles is the terror of the whole route, and no wonder. These bleaching bones and rusty irons are evidences the sight of which makes one wish to hurry on, and not feel safe until they no longer greet the eye. I never saw a desert before, and I do not wish to see another.

## WADSWORTH

The community of Wadsworth, fifty-nine miles south of Lovelock on I-80, can trace its existence back to prehistoric times, when it served as a seasonal village for the nomadic Paiute. Explorer John C. Frémont camped in the vicinity on January 16, 1844. In 1854 traders established a post at the site, first known as the Big Bend of the Truckee River, then later, Drytown. The trading post served as an important supply point for wagon trains traveling Emigrant Trail.

In 1868 the Central Pacific Railroad established a division point on the site and plotted the town of Wadsworth, named for James Samuel Wadsworth, a Union army officer who had died in the Battle of the Wilderness in May 1864. Wadsworth was a thriving railroad town until 1905, when railroad officials relocated the maintenance shops from there to Sparks because of a realignment of the route.

# NV 447
# WADSWORTH–BLACK ROCK DESERT
**85 MILES**

## OLINGHOUSE

The little-known mining town of Olinghouse is nestled in the Pah-Rah Mountains, nine miles northwest of Wadsworth via NV 447 and a maintained dirt road. While the community never grew very large, it produced sufficient "color" (gold) to support nearly continuous mining from its first strike in 1859. The area's earliest miners were stray prospectors dispersing from Virginia City in hope of discovering the next Comstock Lode. A few headed north toward the Black Rock Desert, picking up occasional veins and traces of minerals along the Pah-Rah Range.

Prospecting in the area continued sporadically for the next thirty-five years. The first significant activity began in 1897 in the White Horse Canyon, three miles north of Olinghouse. Despite these findings, the larger mining companies remained skeptical about the district's potential. The hundred or so independent miners working the veins were able to recover a few dollars a day.

A post office opened in 1898 and a small business district developed over the next decade, during which the town got its current name. Elias Olinghouse was a Wadsworth cattle rancher with a large summer ranch operation in the eastern Pah-Rah Range. Originally called Ora, the town took Olinghouse's name since he had claim on most of the land around there.

In 1907 the town's fortunes began to look up, as investors seeking to strike another Tonopah or Goldfield started pouring money into almost any Nevada mining camp that showed the slightest promise. The investors built several mills, as well as a rail line to connect the mines to the mill. Within a year,

*An old mine
shaft in
Olinghouse.*

however, the boom was over and Olinghouse returned to its sleepy ways. The mill and railroad were dismantled, and once again only a few dozen miners remained, surviving but never getting rich.

Today, there's a modern open-pit gold-mining operation north of town. Olinghouse itself remains quiet. A few modest wooden cabins, most inhabited, line the canyon, along with some interesting mill ruins and a few abandoned mine shafts, reminders of the town's astonishingly brief glory days.

## NIXON AND THE PYRAMID LAKE INDIAN RESERVATION

Sixteen miles north of Wadsworth and a mile south of Pyramid Lake on NV 447 is the small community of Nixon, the center of the Pyramid Lake Paiute reservation. The town, established in August 1912, was named for U.S. senator George S. Nixon of Nevada. Nixon today is a peaceful rural community with several hundred residents.

The Pyramid Lake Indian Reservation encompasses 322,000 acres, including Pyramid Lake and the communities of Nixon and Wadsworth. It is the largest reservation in Nevada. President Ulysses S. Grant signed the proclamation establishing the reservation in 1874. Between 400 and 700 Paiutes have historically occupied the site. John C. Frémont noted a fairly large settlement with several grass huts there in his 1843–44 expedition report.

# PYRAMID LAKE

Pyramid Lake is the largest remnant of ancient Lake Lahontan, the giant inland sea that once covered much of Nevada. It lies thirty-three miles north of Reno and is part of a closed water system that begins in the Sierra Nevada. The lake is the outlet of the Truckee River, which flows down from Lake Tahoe.

Pyramid Lake is a haunting place. Extraordinary rock formations, often cloaked in shadows, give the lake an almost otherworldly presence. It is easy to understand why Pyramid Lake is the subject of many Paiute legends. According to the Indians, the lake's distinctive pyramid-shaped rock is a symbol of the spearhead used by the Great Father, who thrust it upward to ward off a lengthy drought.

Near the Pyramid, on the lake's southeast shore, are several stone "bubbles"—large, mushroom-shaped rocks, hollow in the center and large enough to climb into. Just south of the bubbles is the Great Stone Mother and Basket, a remarkable natural stone statue of a hooded Indian woman seated with an open basket next to her. One Stone Mother legend says she was so filled with grief when some of her children were driven away by their evil siblings, she cried until the lake filled with her tears. Her basket remains empty, awaiting their return.

Perhaps no part of the lake captures its weird geological nature as much as the north shore. You can access the north shore from NV 445. Less developed than the west shore, this is a place of great contrasts—serene yet strangely unsettling, with its many unusual formations. Here, beside a stretch of shore appropriately named Enchanted Beach, are the Needles, a group of rocks that resemble cathedral spires. These magnificent towers, like all the stone formations at Pyramid Lake, are made of tufa (TOO-fuh), a limestonelike substance of calcium carbonate. Adjacent to the Needles is the lake's most impressive geyser, which spews a continuous stream of scalding water fifteen feet into the air. Near a smaller geyser, a mile west of the Needles, small hot springs bubble from cracks in the rocky shore and pour steaming rivulets into the lake.

On the north shore, it is easy to visualize a time when the lake was the domain of the Cui-ui Eaters, the indigenous Paiute clan. The cui-ui (pronounced kwee-wee) fish was an important part of the tribe's diet and economy. Biologists believe that this rare fish first appeared more than 2 million years ago. The cui-ui, with its distinctive external skeleton, is listed as an endangered species, although the population at Pyramid Lake has increased in recent years.

Another fish, the cutthroat trout, has also struggled to survive at Pyramid Lake. John C. Frémont remarked in 1844 that Pyramid Lake teemed with large fish and that "their flavor was excellent—superior, in fact, to that of any fish I have ever known." But in the 1920s, a government water project redirected the flow of the Truckee and Carson Rivers to the Lahontan Reservoir, reducing the water in Pyramid Lake and damaging its cutthroat population. Pyramid Lake's once-thriving fishing industry, which reached its zenith in 1925 with a world-

*Tufa formations at Pyramid Lake.*

record forty-one-pound cutthroat, was gone by the late 1930s. The lake's salinity level became so high that by 1943 there were no native cutthroat trout left at all.

Fortunately, cutthroat were found in Walker Lake, several hundred miles south, and hatchlings were reintroduced to Pyramid in the 1980s. In addition, the Truckee-Carson-Pyramid Lake Water Rights Settlement Act of 1990 settled nearly a century of disagreements regarding water use at the lake. As a result of the legislation, fresh water from the Truckee River is again flowing into Pyramid Lake, and the fish have resumed their traditional spawning runs.

### The Pyramid Lake War

While there were occasional skirmishes between Indians and emigrants during the settlement period in Nevada, most were minor. The most significant hostile outbreak occurred in 1860. On May 7, four white men from a Carson River trading post called Williams Station (near present-day Fallon) kidnapped two young Paiute women. Word quickly reached a band of visiting Bannock who, ironically, were in the area to participate in a council to discuss what to do about the influx of whites. The Bannock warriors, along with several Paiutes, rescued the women and burned the station, killing the four white men.

News of the attack inflamed white settlers, few of whom cared about the facts. In Virginia City, residents formed a citizen militia of 105 men to seek revenge. On May 10 the hastily organized assemblage of miners, businessmen, and retired military officers, led by Major William Ormsby of Carson City, marched northeast toward Pyramid Lake, where a large group of Paiute were known to live. The volunteer militia made no attempt at surprise, but did not expect to meet much resistance.

The Pyramid Lake Paiute, who had not been involved in the Williams Station incident, saw the advancing war party and prepared for battle. However, at the urging of their war leader, Numaga, the Indians first agreed to negotiate for peace. Numaga, the son of Chief Winnemucca, believed his people could not win a war with the whites, who vastly outnumbered the Indians.

On May 12 Numaga sent a small group of riders with a white flag to meet the militia and arrange a meeting. The eager citizen army, however, began shooting

*The Paiute war leader Numaga.* —Courtesy Nevada Historical Society

at the Indians and chased them into a narrow ravine. Unbeknownst to the militia, Numaga had amassed his warriors on either side of the depression. In the subsequent battle, seventy-six volunteer soldiers, including Major Ormsby, were killed, and nearly all of the rest suffered injuries.

News of the slaughter heightened the tensions. A second, larger military force quickly organized to put down the Indian insurrection. With weeks of the first Pyramid Lake battle, a total of 549 volunteers, under the command of Colonel Jack Hays, joined a group of 207 regular army soldiers from California to seek revenge on the Indians. The group engaged the Paiute at the mouth of Pyramid Lake on May 31, 1860. This time results were not a surprise—approximately 160 Indians dead and only 2 white casualties. Following the hostilities, the U.S. government established a series of small military posts across Nevada to protect settlers and guard the developing transportation routes.

## EMPIRE

In all of Nevada, Empire, sixty-nine miles north of Wadsworth on NV 447, comes closest to still being a company town. Pacific Portland Cement Company established the community in 1922 when it discovered large gypsum deposits in the area. The town's name comes from the company's brand of gypsum products. Over the years, the town has grown in lockstep with the gypsum plant's fortunes. Today about 200 people live in Empire, most working for U.S. Gypsum, current owner of the plant.

## GERLACH

Six miles north of Empire on NV 447 is the tiny settlement of Gerlach, the closest community to the Black Rock Desert. Frémont camped here in 1843 and is said to have bathed in the natural hot springs near the town, which he named Boiling Springs. The Western Pacific Railroad established Gerlach in 1909 as a station on its main line. It was named for the Gerlach Land & Cattle Company, part of the large Gerlach & Waltz Ranch, founded in the late nineteenth century by Louis Gerlach, now gone.

Today Gerlach consists of about three dozen houses and trailers, a couple of small motels, and a high school whose average graduating class is about six students. The town's main landmarks are the 1909 water tower, listed in the National Register of Historic Places, and Bruno's Country Club, a diner and lounge noted for its huge handmade ravioli.

## THE BLACK ROCK DESERT

The Black Rock Desert is a V-shaped alkali flat of nearly a million acres fifteen miles northeast of Gerlach on NV 34. This desert was one of the most difficult stretches of the Applegate Trail, a northbound turnoff from the Emigrant Trail to California named for its blazer, Jesse Applegate. Many pioneers

*A small boy wanders across the dry playa of the Black Rock Desert.*

took it as an alternative to the Oregon Trail because it avoided the need to travel on the often treacherous Columbia River.

The Applegate route began at Lassen Meadows, along the Humboldt River. It went through Antelope Springs and entered the Black Rock Desert at its northeastern edge. Travelers used the triangle-shaped Black Rock Mountain as a guidepost for the journey. From there, they followed the base of the Black Rock Range, surviving the inhospitable desert by moving from spring to spring. Many of these springs, however, were sulphurous and sickened all who drank from them.

More recently, because of its vast hard surface, the Black Rock Desert has been the site of several land-speed records, including the breaking of the sound barrier on October 13, 1997. Andrew Green of England made the run in the rocket-powered Thrust SSC car. Two days later, Green duplicated the feat and set the official world land-speed record with two runs averaging 763.035 miles per hour. The runs generated a soft sonic boom, as most of the noise was absorbed by the desert floor.

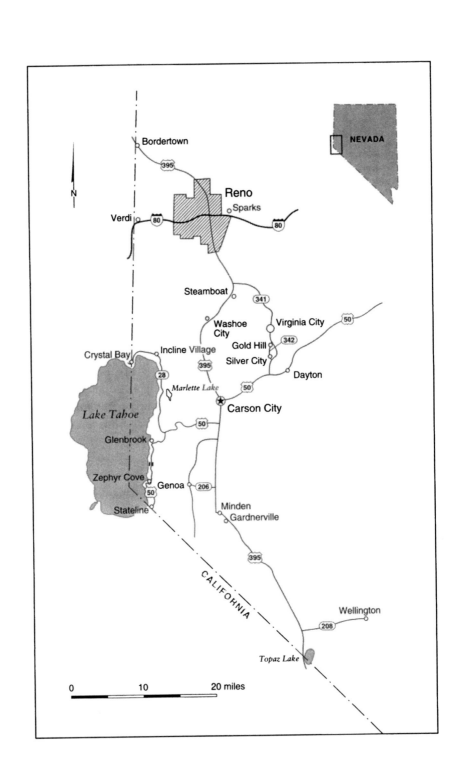

## 2

# RENO AND THE LAKE TAHOE AREA

*Reno sits here upon a river-meadow with her back against the High Sierra and her face toward the Great Desert—and does not care what people say of her.*

*Reno has not cared for fifty years. Sixty years.*

*She neither affirms nor denies.*

*Her living depends on mystery. Her living depends on having people talk about her.*

—Max Miller, *Reno*

Reno still depends on having people talk. But its reputation is only a secondary attraction. The city's resorts and its proximity to Lake Tahoe and the Sierra Nevada are what bring in its 5 million visitors every year. But while gambling and tourism may drive Reno's modern economy, the city came into being for a far more prosaic reason—it had a bridge. A toll bridge over the Truckee River appeared shortly after the Comstock Lode discovery in 1859, built to serve those headed to the mines in Virginia City. The little rest stop before the bridge grew into Reno.

The Truckee Meadows, the valley where Reno is situated, was home to the Paiute for centuries. The first non-Indians to visit the Truckee Meadows were the Murphy-Townsend-Stevens party, one of the earliest California-bound wagon trains to cross Nevada, in the fall of 1844. Led by Martin Murphy, John Townsend, and Elisha Stevens, the group of fifty emigrants followed the Humboldt River across Nevada to Big Meadows. There they encountered a Paiute they called Chief Truckee because that was how his name sounded to them. Chief Truckee told them of a river to the west that flowed from the mountains. They headed to the river, which they named for their Indian guide, and then into the Truckee Meadows.

After passing through the future site of Reno, the party continued west into the Sierra Nevada. Upstream from present-day Truckee, California, the group divided, with some following the Truckee River to its source at Lake Tahoe before continuing to California. The others headed to what is now called Donner Lake, which they named Truckee Lake.

While both halves of the Murphy-Townsend-Stevens party eventually reached their destination, the Donner tragedy in 1846–47 caused most emigrant groups traveling to California in the summer of 1847 to avoid the Truckee River route. But after James Marshall struck gold in northern California in 1848, tens of thousands of fortune hunters crossed Nevada, resurrecting the Truckee River route.

Nevada might have remained a series of way stations for travelers heading elsewhere if not for the 1859 discovery of the Comstock Lode, the American West's largest and most significant gold and silver deposit. Virtually overnight, the mining camp of Virginia City sprang up at the site. Before long there was a bridge across the Truckee River for miners going south to Virginia City, and the crossing place would eventually become known as Reno.

# I-80
# WADSWORTH–RENO
## 30 MILES

### SPARKS

Sparks sits just on the eastern edge of Reno on I-80. When the Southern Pacific Railroad sought to relocate its Wadsworth switching yard, it considered Reno but decided to build east of there because land was cheaper. A passenger station and freight yard opened on the new site in 1905, and soon the community of Sparks developed around the railroad facilities. Many railroad employees either moved their homes from Wadsworth or built new homes north of the railroad yards on lots the company sold. At first the new town was called East Reno, then Harriman, after E. H. Harriman, the rail line's owner. But Harriman decided in 1904 to rename the community Sparks, for sitting Nevada governor John Sparks.

For the next five decades, the railroad remained the town's biggest influence. When the railroad relocated the yards to Roseville, California, in the 1950s, Sparks was forced to redefine itself. In 1955 a restaurateur from Idaho, Dick Graves, opened the Sparks Nugget, a coffee shop and casino. The property prospered under the leadership of Graves's general manager, John Ascuaga, who later bought out Graves. By the 1990s John Ascuaga's Nugget, as it is now known, had become one of western Nevada's largest hotel-casinos, with 1,980 rooms. It is currently Sparks's biggest employer, with more than 2,500 workers.

In 1960 Sparks profited from the passage of the state's freeport law, which encouraged warehousing and light industry by lowering taxes. Since then,

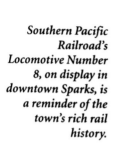

*Southern Pacific Railroad's Locomotive Number 8, on display in downtown Sparks, is a reminder of the town's rich rail history.*

hundreds of thousands of square feet of warehouse and industrial space have gone up in Sparks.

### Historic Sparks

The former Sparks Courthouse, at 820 Victorian Avenue, is now the Sparks Heritage Museum. The building, erected in 1931, houses many historic photographs depicting the town's railroad days. Railroad artifacts include uniforms, steam whistles, dining trays, and an extensive collection of railroad lanterns.

Across the street from the museum is the restored Glendale School, built in 1864 and moved to downtown Sparks in the 1980s. It is the oldest schoolhouse in the state and had the longest continuous operation, closing its doors in 1958. Among its alumni were U.S. senator Pat McCarran of Nevada, who served from 1933 to 1954. The school was originally located in the tiny community of Glendale, east of Sparks's borders at the time. Glendale eventually became part of Sparks.

Adjacent to the Glendale School is Locomotive Number 8, built in 1907. The ten-wheeler, retired in 1954, was one of the last steam locomotives regularly used by the Southern Pacific Railroad. Attached to this engine are several antique Southern Pacific train cars, including a 1911 Pullman that President Harry Truman used on his successful whistle-stop campaign in 1948. Nearby is the original Sparks depot, now the Sparks Information Center and Chamber of Commerce.

## RENO

In 1859 entrepreneur Charles W. Fuller constructed a crude wooden toll bridge over the Truckee River, roughly where Virginia Street now crosses the river in downtown Reno, to serve the increasing traffic to Virginia City. He

Reno Twenty Years Ago, *painted in 1881 by Cyrinus B. McClelland, noted nineteenth-century Reno artist. It depicts Reno founder Myron C. Lake and Chief Winnemucca at Lake's Crossing in June 1862.* —Courtesy Nevada Historical Society

also erected a rest stop made of logs. After a short time, the place became known as Fuller's Crossing.

Two years later Fuller sold the bridge and surrounding land to Myron C. Lake, who promptly built a more substantial bridge as well as an inn and re-named the settlement Lake's Crossing. As the owner of the only bridge in the Truckee Meadows that crossed the Truckee River, Lake was able to charge high tolls—one dollar for each loaded wagon, fifty cents for a horse and buggy, and ten cents for a man on foot. This soon made him wealthy. He invested his profits in other endeavors—a livery stable, a grist mill, and a kiln. He also purchased more land in the Truckee Meadows and began raising cattle.

Lake also benefited from the construction of the transcontinental railroad. To ensure the railroad would pass through his property, Lake deeded 400 acres to Charles Crocker, superintendent of the Central Pacific Railroad, who sur-veyed and plotted the land. In return, Crocker agreed to build a depot at Lake's Crossing and to auction the subdivided lots to home builders, thus ensuring the development of a community. He also gave 127 lots back to Lake.

On May 9, 1868, the railroad auctioned the lots, and Crocker named the new community Reno, after Civil War hero General Jesse Lee Reno. For the next fifteen years, Reno profited from its proximity to the Comstock Lode. In 1872 the Virginia & Truckee Railroad linked Virginia City to Reno, which be-came the region's transportation hub because it was already established on the Central Pacific line.

When Virginia City's mines began to peter out in the late 1870s and early 1880s, Reno's fortunes—and, indeed, all of Nevada's—also waned. But the discovery of substantial gold and silver deposits in Tonopah and Goldfield at the turn of the century helped revive Nevada's economy. Even though Reno was hundreds of miles from the mines, it also benefited from the improved financial picture.

By this time Nevada was also gaining a national reputation as a place where certain vices, such as gambling, were tolerated—and Reno was ready to cash in. There was a flourishing red-light district, and the state's lax, no-questions-asked divorce law, requiring only a six-month residency, granted the city even further opportunities to profit from Nevada's forbidden-fruit image. While other states generally required proof of infidelity, cruelty, desertion, or the like to petition for a divorce, Nevada laws were extremely liberal. Nevada judges granted divorces on nearly any ground, including incompatibility—essentially an early form of "no-fault" divorce.

Reno's future as America's divorce capital was assured when the wife of William Ellis Corey, president of U.S. Steel, came here to "take the cure," as they called it in 1905. Laura Corey wished to end her marriage of twenty-two years because her husband had taken up with a young actress. Not only did she get her wish, but her stay in Reno exposed her husband's scandalous affair, which newspapers throughout the country were only too happy to cover.

Reno now had a new mother lode. In addition to its proximity to populous California, Reno, the largest city in Nevada at the time, had hotels, lawyers, and other infrastructure in place that made it convenient to get a divorce there. Soon, the world's rich and famous—and plenty of regular folks—were coming to Reno for the cure. Obtaining a Nevada divorce was even called "getting Reno-vated."

Not surprisingly, there was a backlash, particularly from the nation's religious community. In 1913 the Nevada legislature grew tired of the state's sullied reputation and increased the residency requirement from six months to one year. But this devastated Reno's economy, and two years later the legislature changed it back. Soon other states were trying to get in on the divorce action and loosened their divorce laws, too. The Nevada legislature ended up lowering the residency requirement to three months in 1927, then to six weeks in 1931, just to stay competitive.

Also contributing to the city's irreverent reputation was the staging of the 1910 world heavyweight boxing championship fight between Jack Johnson and Jim Jeffries in Reno. San Francisco had been the planned locale, but promoters were forced to go elsewhere after that city's officials caved in to intense pressure from antiboxing forces. At the time, legal prizefights were relatively new to America—in 1897 Nevada became the first state to legalize professional boxing. The sport drew considerable opposition from church groups and others who believed it was brutal and inhumane. After San Francisco dropped out, Reno stepped forward with an offer to build a stadium to host the Johnson-Jeffries fight.

The bout was shamelessly billed the "Battle of the Races" since Johnson, the reigning champion, was black, and Jeffries, a retired former title holder, was white. Johnson was a controversial figure because he was married to a white woman and had an appetite for expensive clothing, jewelry, and automobiles. Supporters of Jeffries referred to him as "the Great White Hope."

The match was to have forty-five rounds, but it ended in the fifteenth, after Jeffries conceded. Johnson, who was younger, quicker, and stronger, had mercilessly pounded the older, out-of-shape former champion. Later, the formerly undefeated Jeffries said he should never have agreed to the fight. The event thrust Reno into the national spotlight.

Today the city continues to promote itself with big events and exotic attractions. Many of the activities that made Reno infamous still go on there, if not as controversially. From its inception, Reno has had a knack for giving people what they want.

### The West's First Train Robbery

It was nearly midnight on November 4, 1870, when the Central Pacific Railroad's Atlantic Express slowed for a brief stop in Verdi, five miles west of Reno. The conductor stepped out onto a flatbed car for a bit of fresh air, then noticed that the bell cord had been cut. He turned to head back to the engine when he found himself facing three men in black masks. In the engine compartment, two more figures, similarly dressed, climbed over the tender's woodpile, dropped into the compartment, and, with their guns drawn, ordered the engineer to slow the train.

The men brought the engineer to the door of the mail car and knocked on the locked door, then whispered for the engineer to give his name to the guard inside. The door opened and the guard found himself staring down at several gun barrels. The outlaws quickly looted the car of nearly $40,000 in gold and escaped into the night on horseback. The next day, Nevada newspapers were filled with stories about the first train robbery in the western United States.

Since the culprits left no obvious clues to their identities, the thieves may have gotten away with the crime except that one of the gang became nervous when a local deputy sheriff began questioning people at the hotel where he was staying. Rather than attempt to lie, he hid in an outhouse with his loot. In his panic he fled the privy, leaving $120 in gold coins behind. Lawmen quickly captured him and eventually caught his partners. The authorities recovered all but $3,000 of the gold. Legend holds that the thieves hid the missing money in Six Mile Canyon near Virginia City, but no one ever found it.

### The Birth of Blue Jeans

In the fall of 1870, a woman needing a pair of pants for her husband, a woodcutter, visited Reno tailor Jacob Davis. She told Davis that the ready-made pants in the general stores were too small and not sturdy enough for her husband. When Davis asked for the man's measurements, he was astonished to learn that the man's waist was 56 inches, his thighs were 29 inches around, and his calves were 21 inches.

Davis agreed to sew the pants in three days and began searching his shop for a suitable material. He had just received a large shipment of white cotton canvas, called number seven duck, which he normally used to make tents. It was stiff and difficult to sew, but he decided it was the only fabric strong enough for the job. To reinforce the pocket corners, the tailor used copper rivets— usually used for fastening leather straps to horse blankets.

The durable pants were an immediate success, and Davis soon could not keep up with the demand from farmers, miners, and of course woodcutters. In 1873 Davis moved to San Francisco and became partners with his fabric supplier, Levi Strauss. The two patented the rivet design and switched to a more flexible, blue cotton-twill material known as *serge de nimes*, made in the town of Nimes, in southern France. Later the name was shortened to denim. Davis prospered as the company's factory manager and eventually sold his interest in the pants to Levi Strauss, whose name became forever linked with the blue denim pants.

### George Wingfield: King of Nevada

Few have controlled the state of Nevada as completely and for as long as did George Wingfield. Born in Arkansas in 1876, Wingfield was raised on a ranch near Lakeview, Oregon. He arrived in Nevada in the late 1890s, working as a cowboy in the Winnemucca area. He also became quite good at poker, an avocation he would pursue the rest of his life.

In 1899 Wingfield invested his gambling earnings in a saloon and other property in the booming mining camp of Golconda, 180 miles east of Reno. His business was moderately successful for the next two years, but he nearly lost everything when Golconda's mines failed. About this time, Wingfield became close friends with banker George S. Nixon of Winnemucca. The Wingfield-Nixon association would ultimately prove extremely profitable for both parties.

Wingfield relocated to Tonopah in 1901, at the start of its great mining boom. He recognized the area's potential and began investing in real estate and, later, mining ventures. In 1902 Wingfield and Nixon established the successful Boston-Tonopah Mining Company to oversee several of Wingfield's claims. Subsequently Wingfield pursued many other partnerships in mines and banks in central Nevada, including the Goldfield Consolidated Mines Company, which at one time controlled nearly all the mines in Goldfield.

In 1908 Wingfield moved to Reno, where he played real-life Monopoly by expanding his mine holdings, buying and building hotels, and taking control of Nevada's banks. His economic muscle—he was generally considered the state's richest man—allowed him to exert considerable influence on politicians of both parties, and he eventually became the most powerful political figure in the state.

*George Wingfield.*
—Courtesy Nevada Historical Society

At one point, the state leaders of both the Republican and Democratic parties had offices in Wingfield's Reno National Bank building and shared the same telephone number. This at least created the impression that Wingfield controlled both parties. With Nevada's bipartisanship strategy, both major parties cooperated to keep one Republican and one Democratic senator in Washington so that the state would get proper patronage no matter which party was in the majority. Thus business interests such as Wingfield's benefitted regardless.

Wingfield's power began to wane in the 1930s with the advent of the Great Depression. The federal government took over his failed banks. In November 1935, Wingfield filed for bankruptcy and liquidated his assets, and in the late 1930s he returned to mining to restore his fortunes. He invested in the Getchell Mine, near Golconda, which proved to be one of the state's most productive gold mines, and he was able to recover control of his hotel properties. While he never regained the kind of influence he once had in Nevada, he was able to recoup his wealth. When he died in 1959, at age eighty-three, his estate was valued at more than $3 million.

### E. E. Roberts

One person who came to embody Reno's live-and-let-live philosophy was Edwin Ewing Roberts, mayor of the city from 1923 to 1933. Roberts was born on December 12, 1870, in Sutter County, California. He earned his teaching credentials at California's state normal school in San Jose and taught in Hollister, California, in the early 1890s.

Roberts first came to Nevada in 1897 to see a heavyweight boxing championship match between "Gentleman Jim" Corbett and Bob Fitzsimmons in Carson City. He liked Nevada and soon accepted a teaching job in the small community of Empire, a lumber-milling town east of Carson City. Two years later he passed the Nevada bar exam and was immediately elected Ormsby County district attorney, a post he held for the next decade.

In 1910 Nevadans elected Roberts as their lone representative to the U.S. Congress. While Roberts served in Washington, his daughter Hazel met and married Baseball Hall of Famer Walter "Big Train" Johnson, who pitched for the Washington Senators. Roberts served four terms as a representative before losing his race for the U.S. Senate in 1918. For the next four years, Roberts practiced law in Reno, specializing in divorce. He once boasted that he had won more than 2,000 divorce cases.

*Mayor Edwin Ewing Roberts of Reno.* —Courtesy Nevada Historical Society

Politics once again beckoned, and in 1923 Roberts was elected mayor of Reno, then a town of about 15,000 people. He had campaigned on a pledge to reopen the segregated red-light district on the east side of town, which the previous city administration had closed the year before. (Nevada law at the time gave cities the option of legally permitting prostitution.) Residents began to question the decision to close the district after prostitutes began plying their trade all over town.

As mayor, Roberts made headlines with his public statements articulating his libertarian philosophy. "It's all nonsense trying to regulate people's morals by law," he asserted in a speech in 1931. "For eight years I've been trying to make Reno a place where everybody can do as they please, just so they don't interfere with other people's rights." This was the same year the state of Nevada scandalized the nation by legalizing gambling and enacting a six-week residency requirement for divorce.

In another 1931 campaign speech that gained national attention, Roberts, who was running for a third term as mayor, not only defended Nevada's legal gambling, prostitution, and divorce, but condemned Prohibition as unenforceable. "The only way to put bootleggers out of business," he said, "is to place a barrel of good corn whiskey on every downtown street corner, with dipper attached, and signs inviting passersby to help themselves to all they want, free of charge."

Not surprisingly, Roberts's attitude horrified many national Prohibition groups and church leaders, who roundly condemned him. But Renoites loved it, and they reelected their feisty mayor in a landslide. Roberts died in office in 1933.

### The Mystery of Roy Frisch

On Friday evening, March 22, 1934, banker Roy Frisch went to a movie. What happened next has been the subject of conjecture ever since. At the time, Frisch was living with his mother and two sisters at 247 Court Street in downtown Reno. Frisch's mother recalled that about 7:45 P.M., Frisch walked to the Majestic Theater, several blocks from his house, to see the film *Gallant Lady*. He watched the movie and departed the theater between 9:45 P.M. and 10:15 P.M. A friend recalled encountering Frisch at the corner of Sierra and Court Streets. From there, Frisch walked up Court Street toward his house.

He was never seen again.

The next morning, Frisch's mother discovered he had not slept in his bed. Puzzled, she called his office and his friends before contacting the Reno police. The police searched for Frisch's body in old mine shafts and vacant buildings. They followed any lead, even checking out a headless body found in San Francisco Bay. Despite these efforts, as well as extensive publicity about the disappearance and a $1,000 reward, Frisch never turned up. Finally, in 1941 he was declared legally dead.

*Roy Frisch's house.*

What makes the Frisch mystery so intriguing is that Frisch was the cashier at the Riverside Bank and an advisor to Nevada financier and political boss George Wingfield, who owned the bank. At the time of the disappearance, federal law-enforcement officials were investigating Wingfield for his association with two Reno gamblers and con men, William J. Graham and James C. McKay. Authorities believed that Graham and McKay were involved in a national horse-racing fraud and an insider stock-trading scam, and they thought the con men were laundering the money through the Riverside Bank.

In 1933 Frisch had testified before the grand jury that indicted Graham and McKay. The court scheduled an arraignment for April 2, 1934, with Frisch as the government's prime witness. Frisch had also been asked to appear before a federal committee investigating the failure of several other Wingfield banks.

A number of theories have been floated to explain what happened to the banker. One of the most popular says that outlaw Lester Gillis, a.k.a. George "Baby Face" Nelson, a friend of Graham and McKay, murdered Frisch and either buried him near Spanish Springs, north of Sparks, or stashed the body in a mine shaft. In the 1990s a story circulated that Frisch was buried in George Wingfield's backyard at 219 Court Street, only two doors down from Frisch's own house. Reno police, however, did not feel there was sufficient evidence to warrant digging up the yard.

### Walter Van Tilburg Clark

One of Nevada's best-known writers was Walter Van Tilburg Clark, author of *The Oxbow Incident*. Born in Maine in 1909, Clark came to Nevada at the age of eight, after his father, Walter E. Clark, was appointed president of the

University of Nevada in Reno. The younger Clark attended Reno schools and in 1934 graduated from the University of Nevada with a master's degree in medieval literature. He enjoyed teaching and spent much of his life as a literature and creative-writing instructor, including twelve years at the University of Nevada.

Clark wrote fiction and nonfiction about the West, particularly Nevada. Between 1940 and 1949, he published three novels, *The Oxbow Incident, City of Trembling Leaves,* and *Track of the Cat,* all of them memorably drawn against the Nevada landscape. In Clark's work, place is a character, not mere background. *The Oxbow Incident* and *Track of the Cat* were made into movies in the 1940s.

Despite winning critical acclaim for his books, Clark ceased to write novels after 1949. For the next two decades, he restricted his output to occasional magazine articles, poems, and short stories. By way of explanation, he once wrote, "[Teaching is] an occupation I respect so much that it's kept me from doing . . . as much writing as I should have." In 1962 he embarked on an ambitious undertaking—editing fifty-five volumes of journals by Alf Doten, a nineteenth-century Virginia City newpaperman. Clark completed this project just before his death in 1971.

### Historic Reno

Reno has changed considerably since its heyday as the country's scandal city, but reminders of its early days are sprinkled throughout the community. In 1908 the famed Reno architect George W. Ferris designed the McKinley Park School, at 925 Riverside Drive, in the classic Spanish Mission style. Nearby is the Dow House–Glass Gallery at 935 Jones Street, built in 1907–8. In the 1930s this Queen Anne–style home was a popular rooming house for divorce seekers. In 1911 Prince Hawkins, one of the heirs to John Mackay's fortune, built the Hawkins House at 549 Court Street, an elegant colonial-style mansion. Architect Elmer Grey, who later designed the Beverly Hills Hotel, designed the home.

Downtown, the former Masonic Hall–Reno Mercantile Company building at 98 West Commercial Row, built in 1872, is the oldest standing commercial structure in the city. From 1895 to 1970, the upper floor served as the Mason's hall while the ground floor was the Reno Mercantile and later a pawn shop. Not far from downtown is the Court Street neighborhood, site of several impressive homes, including the 1907 George Wingfield House at 219 Court. This two-story neoclassical house is on the National Register of Historic Places.

A few blocks east of the Wingfield House, the Washoe County Courthouse remains one of Reno's grandest civic structures. Completed in 1911, it was designed in the neoclassical style by Frederick J. DeLongchamps, the state's most prominent architect during the first half of the twentieth century. In addition to dozens of houses, government buildings, and post offices,

*The Washoe County Courthouse.*

DeLongchamps designed no fewer than seven Nevada courthouses, all built between 1911 and 1922. The Virginia Street Bridge, adjacent to the Washoe County Courthouse, was built in 1905 and is the oldest functioning bridge in Reno.

### Reno's Famed Arch

One of Reno's most recognizable sights is an illuminated steel, plastic, and neon arch with the words "Reno, the Biggest Little City in the World." Over the years, Reno has had at least six different commemorative arches. The first one, a temporary constuction erected atop the Virginia Street Bridge in 1899, welcomed home Nevada troops returning from the Spanish-American War. In 1914 the city erected another temporary arch over Virginia Street to greet visitors passing through on their way to the Panama-Pacific Exposition in San Francisco. A third arch was temporarily installed over the city's main street in June 1920 to promote the Reno Rodeo.

In October 1926 the city constructed a more substantial, steel arch for an exposition celebrating the completion of the Lincoln and Victory highways, the nation's first transcontinental roads, both of which passed through Reno. This time, the arch was not removed. Instead, city leaders held a contest for a new slogan to put on it. The $100 prize attracted thousands of entries, including one from a Sacramento man who suggested "the Biggest Little City in the World." While not the most original suggestion—the slogan had been used before during boxing matches and promotional events—it won the prize.

*From the 1930s to the early 1960s, this arch spanned Virginia Street in the center of Reno.*

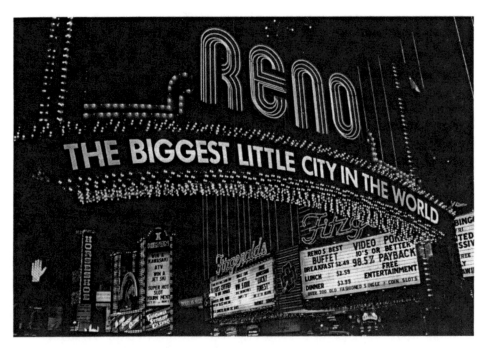

*The second arch to feature Reno's slogan, "the Biggest Little City in the World," lit up the town from 1964 to 1987.* —Courtesy Reno News Bureau

In June 1929 the arch with its new slogan was lighted. The slogan was revised in 1934 because some residents thought it sounded old-fashioned, but the words were restored the following year, this time in neon letters. This version of the arch stood over Reno for the next twenty-eight years, appearing on postcards, in movies and books, and in a thousand tourist snapshots.

In 1964 a new, plastic-and-steel arch replaced the old one, but it still bore the "Biggest Little City" slogan. The deposed 1930s version languished in a city park for two decades before it was renovated and erected over Lake Street in downtown Reno, adjacent to the National Automobile Museum. In 1987 the city replaced the 1960s version with the present Reno arch and donated the old one to Willits, California.

### University of Nevada, Reno

In 1885 the University of Nevada relocated from Elko to Reno after the original site proved too remote to attract many students. Morrill Hall, the first building erected on the new campus in 1886, was named for Senator Justin S. Morrill of Vermont, author of the 1862 Land-Grant College Act. The act provided land for public universities, including the University of Nevada and many other state colleges in the country. The university restored Morrill Hall in the 1970s to use as offices.

Two buildings, Lincoln Hall and Manzanita Hall, date to the 1890s. The campus's design, with buildings bordering an open quadrangle, was modeled after Thomas Jefferson's design for the University of Virginia. Stanford White, who also created New York's original Madison Square Garden, was the architect of "the Quad."

*Morrill Hall at the University of Nevada, Reno.*

White also designed the Mackay School of Mines building, completed in 1908 and restored in the 1990s. This building houses the DeLa Mare Library of mining-related materials and the W. M. Keck Museum, a mining museum. In front of the Mackay building stands a bronze statue of Comstock millionaire John Mackay, the school's namesake. Sculptor Gutzon Borglum, who later carved Mount Rushmore, completed the statue in 1908.

### The Nevada Historic Society

North of the university is the Nevada Historic Society, at 1650 North Virginia Street. Founded in 1904, the society is Nevada's oldest museum. Over the years, it has accumulated an unequaled collection of historic books, documents, photographs, and other Nevada artifacts. The society has an exceptional library, unsurpassed photo archives, and exhibits that offer an excellent overview of the state's history.

The museum houses Native American artifacts, such as willow baskets crafted by the legendary Washo basket-maker Dat-so-la-lee. Displays illustrate early exploration of the state, the discovery of the Comstock Lode in Virginia City, and the emergence of Nevada's ranching industry. A comprehensive display of antique gambling devices and slot machines, including a Liberty Bell, the first three-wheel gaming device, are also of interest.

## US 395
## BORDERTOWN–TOPAZ LAKE
### 81 MILES

US 395 passes through Nevada's earliest-settled and most historically interesting region, the southwest corner. The route hugs the eastern edge of the Sierra Nevada and demarcates the rugged mountains from the high desert of the Great Basin. The highway enters Nevada from California at Bordertown, sixteen miles northwest of Reno, then passes right through Reno itself, and exits at Topaz Lake, sixty-five miles south of Reno.

### STEAMBOAT SPRINGS

Steamboat Springs is about seven miles south of Reno on US 395. Early emigrants named it for the way steam rose from cracks in the ground, in the puffing and blowing manner of a steamboat. In the early 1860s a doctor named Ellis built a hospital and bathhouses on the site.

In 1871, the Virginia & Truckee Railroad established a terminal at Steamboat Springs, which became an important shipping point for materials bound for nearby Virginia City. The settlement grew to include an elegant hotel that catered to the area's most prominent citizens. The end of Virginia City's mining boom in the 1880s, however, also marked the end of Steamboat Springs. Fire later destroyed the buildings. Today a small private resort occupies the site.

## WASHOE CITY

About fifteen miles south of Reno, at the north end of Washoe Valley on US 395, are the remnants of Washoe City, once the largest town in Washoe County. In 1864 Washoe City was a thriving community of more than 4,000 people. When Nevada became a territory in 1861, Washoe City was named the seat of newly created Washoe County.

The town began in the late 1850s as a supplier of lumber and water to the Comstock silver mines in nearby Virginia City. By 1861 Washoe City was the center of commerce for sawmills, farms, and several quartz mills. Dozens of freight wagons traveled daily between Virginia City and Washoe City. The wagons, loaded with food and timber for the mines, returned brimming with ore for milling. In 1863 the town built its first courthouse and jail. By then there was also a school, a small hospital, and meeting halls for the Masons and Odd Fellows.

Unfortunately, the town's glory years were short-lived. In 1869 many of Virginia City's mines shifted their milling operations to facilities along the Carson River. The timber companies had exhausted Washoe Valley's supply of trees and moved on to the thickly forested slopes around Lake Tahoe. The community's decline accelerated after 1872, when the Virginia & Truckee Railroad linked Virginia City to Reno. The line, which passed through the center of Washoe City, meant the end of the freight-wagon business.

Not surprisingly, Washoe City's fall coincided with Reno's rise. Even the town's newspaper moved to Reno in 1868. Two years after that, Washoe County's citizens, mostly living in the Truckee Meadows, voted to relocate the county seat to Reno. Washoe City supporters unsuccessfully appealed to the courts to overturn the election results, but in May 1871, the Nevada Supreme Court ruled the transfer legal and appropriate. Angry, the remaining 800 Washoe City residents attempted to secede from Washoe County and join Ormsby County (now part of Carson City), but the effort failed.

The courthouse was dismantled in 1873, and in 1888 the magnificent Masonic Hall was abandoned and later collapsed. The most substantial structure still standing in Washoe City today is a stone-and-brick building adjacent to a residential subdivision at the north end of Washoe Valley. About two-thirds of this building is original; the brick wall on the north side is new. The only other significant remains are the headstones in the Washoe City Cemetery on US 395.

## WASHOE VALLEY

Washoe Valley is intersected by US 395 and encompasses Washoe Lake. In the region's mining heyday, the valley's once-lush forests of pine trees provided wood for the industry while the lake provided water. Later, the Washoe

Valley became an attractive place for the wealthy to build country estates. Today the valley is home to many affluent families.

### Will James

Famed western artist-writer Will James called Nevada home at several points in his life. He was born in Canada in 1892 and arrived in Nevada in 1910. For several years he drifted through eastern Nevada, taking on ranch work wherever he could find it. After attempting to start his own herd by means of a "long rope" in November 1914, James was convicted of cattle rustling and sentenced to a term at the Nevada State Prison in Carson City. After his parole in April 1916, he resumed life as a saddle bum. During this time, James honed his skills as an artist, living the stories that would one day make him famous.

In 1920 James began selling sketches to *Sunset* magazine. He also married Alice Conradt of Reno that year. Within two years he had become a regular contributor to *Scribner's* magazine, the *Saturday Evening Post,* and *Redbook.* His first book, *Cowboys North and South,* was published in 1924. A year later *The Drifting Cowboy* came out. He wrote his most famous book, *Smoky, the Cowhorse,* in 1926, and in 1934 Hollywood made it into a movie. A second film version of *Smoky* came out in 1946, and a third in 1966.

At the time he wrote *Smoky,* James and his wife were living in a four-room cabin they had built in Washoe Valley, ten miles north of Carson City. The book's success allowed James to sell his Washoe Valley cabin and purchase a large ranch in southeastern Montana in 1927. He never lived in Nevada again. James wrote and illustrated twenty-six books and dozens of magazine articles during his lifetime. He died on August 28, 1942.

### Eilley Orrum Bowers: The Washoe Seeress

Eilley Bowers was born Allison Orrum in 1826 in Scotland. At the age of fifteen, she married a Mormon missionary and traveled to the United States, settling first in Illinois, then in Salt Lake City. Following the Mormon custom of the day, her husband, Stephen Hunter, took several more wives once they had settled in Utah. Eilley was uncomfortable with polygamy and divorced her husband, then married Alexander Cowan in 1853.

The Cowans purchased 300 acres in Washoe Valley. In 1857 Alexander, also a Mormon, decided to go to Salt Lake City, and rather than go to Utah, Eilley divorced him. She moved to Johntown, a mining camp south of present-day Virginia City, where she opened a boardinghouse for miners and acquired a handful of mining claims from boarders unable to pay their debts.

In 1859 Eilley married one of her boarders, Lemuel "Sandy" Bowers, and the two combined their mine holdings. Among them was what turned out to be the site of one of the Comstock's earliest major gold and silver strikes. Within a short time, Eilley and Sandy Bowers had become Nevada's first mining millionaires. In 1864 the couple began building a huge stone mansion on Eilley's acreage in Washoe Valley. It was one of the most magnificent homes in the state, and the couple loved to entertain. Over the next four years, they spent lavishly on the finest clothing, furniture, and collectibles.

Unfortunately, Sandy Bowers died suddenly of silicosis (black lung disease) in 1868, at the age of thirty-five—and he died broke. Eilley discovered that her husband had invested much of their money in unprofitable mining ventures. Despite her best efforts, including an attempt to operate the mansion as a resort, Eilley lost her fabulous home in the early 1870s. Tragedy struck again in 1874 when her adopted daughter, Persia, died at the age of twelve.

In 1875, following her many misfortunes, Eilley set up shop in Virginia City as "the Washoe Seeress." She had become intrigued by the occult in Salt Lake City. She owned a crystal ball and had occasionally made predictions for friends. As the Washoe Seeress, she survived by practicing this arcane art for nearly a decade, until the decline of the Comstock Lode caused her customers to vanish. In the 1880s she moved to San Francisco, where she worked in various jobs, including operating a small boardinghouse, as she had done so many years before. In 1898 she went to a rest home in Oakland, where she died in 1903 at age seventy-seven.

The Bowers Mansion had its own fate to meet. After Eilley sold it in 1876, the mansion passed through several owners and became increasingly run-down over the years. In 1903 Reno entrepreneur Henry Rider purchased it and operated it as a resort for locals. Rider sold it in 1946 to the Reno Civic Club and Washoe County for use as a park. But it was not until the 1960s, when Washoe County voters approved a bond to finance it, that the house was restored to its original condition.

*The Bowers Mansion.*

Today the beautifully rebuilt Bowers Mansion stands as a symbol of the old Comstock wealth. Some of the Bowerses' original furnishings are on view in the house, including a piano and Sandy Bowers's silver inkwell. Close by the house are the graves of Sandy, Eilley, and Persia Bowers. The mansion is eight miles north of Carson City via US 395 and NV 429, and tours are offered daily.

## CARSON CITY

Thirty miles south of Reno off US 395 is Carson City, one of Nevada's oldest communities. In November 1851, Frank and Joseph Barnard, George Follensbee, W. L. and Frank Hall, and A. J. Rollins established a small trading post for travelers on the Emigrant Trail. They called the post Eagle Station after Frank Hall shot an eagle flying above the store and mounted the bird's body over the doorway.

Eagle Station traded hands several times during the next few years before Carson City trader John Mankin purchased it and the entire Eagle Valley. In 1858 Mankin sold his holdings to Abraham Curry, B. F. Green, J. J. Musser, and Frank Proctor. The new owners platted a town site and named it Carson City for frontier scout Kit Carson, who had explored Nevada with John C. Frémont.

Abraham Curry eventually bought out his partners and became an energetic promoter of his community, which prospered as a supply point for miners working in nearby Virginia City. In addition to selling lots, Curry built

*Abraham Curry, founder of Carson City.* —Courtesy Nevada Historical Society

houses, toll roads, and several commercial businesses, including the Warm Springs Hotel, two miles east of the town center. Confident that Nevada would become a state, Curry set aside ten acres of land in the middle of his settlement and offered to donate it as a site for the state capitol when the time came.

When Congress created Nevada Territory in 1861, Curry offered his hotel free of charge as a meeting place for the territorial legislature. Carson City thus became the seat of the territorial government. And because of Curry's land donation, the Nevada legislature designated Carson City the capital when Nevada became a state in 1864. That same year, the state purchased the Warm Springs Hotel from Curry and converted it into the Nevada State Prison, with Curry serving as the first warden.

In 1866 the federal government commissioned Curry to build a branch mint to produce gold and silver coins from ore mined in Virginia City, and Curry was named superintendent of the mint. The stone building was completed in 1869, and Curry began minting coins the following year. But he resigned later that year and in 1872 began work on a large housing-and-repair facility in Carson City for the Virginia & Truckee Railroad, which initially ran from Virginia City to Carson City. He completed the nearly 10,000-square-foot stone structure in 1873.

Despite having made thousands of dollars from his various business ventures during his lifetime, Curry made more bad decisions than good and died penniless in October 1873.

### The Battle for the Capital

While Abraham Curry may have been certain that Carson City would become the state capital when he set aside land in the late 1850s, it did not happen without a debate. Even before Nevada became a state, there was controversy over where to place the seat of power. Genoa was an early contender. In 1857 Genoa was the site of the first public forum to discuss forming a territory separate from Utah, and it served as the site of the first territorial convention in 1859, where attendees established a renegade provisional government for Nevada.

In 1864, the small mining camp of American City, later known as American Flat, a mile west of Gold Hill, made a handsome financial bid to become the capital. American City's boosters were so eager for their town's success that they offered $50,000 to the territorial government if it would choose to locate the capital there. The offer was rejected.

During the capital debate, Carson City's cause was aided by William Stewart, an influential Carson City attorney who later became one of Nevada's first U.S. senators. Stewart cunningly won support from other Nevada communties by offering to make them county seats. Immediately after Carson City was picked, officials from Lander County, in central Nevada, protested by opposing the authorization of building funds. They thought Austin would be a better site because, in the words of Lander County's state senator D. W. Welty, Carson City was "a swamp" and a "mud hole."

Even once the capital was established in Carson City, its future was not certain. Senator Stewart, once Carson City's advocate, later tried to move the capital to Winnemucca. It was the late 1880s and Stewart was concerned about Nevada's depleted mining resources and the resulting severe depression. His idea was to expand Nevada's population base by annexing portions of the politically weaker territories of Idaho and Utah. He recommended that Winnemucca, because it would be in the center of the new state, become capital. But his proposal was shelved after President Grover Cleveland and, not surprisingly, residents of Idaho and Utah Territories objected.

### The State Capitol

The state capitol was completed in 1871 and is one of the oldest buildings in the city. It is also one of the most interesting. Architect Joseph Gosling of San Francisco designed it in the form of a Grecian cross, accented by Corinthian, Ionic, and Doric styles. Peter Cavanaugh & Sons of Carson City constructed it of stone from a quarry at the Nevada State Prison. An annex was added to the rear of the building in 1905, and the north and south wings were expanded in 1914–15.

*The Nevada State Capitol.*

A comprehensive exhibit, "The Story of Our Capitol," is housed in the old senate chambers on the second floor. Elsewhere on display are the original Utah and Nevada Territory seals, as well as historic photographs and documents. Among the items shown is the telegraph that relayed the official Nevada state constitution to Washington D.C. on October 8, 1864, which at the time was the longest and costliest telegram ever sent. A copy of the November 2, 1864, edition of the *New York Herald* is also on view, with its headline announcing the creation of Nevada as America's thirty-sixth state.

### Hannah Clapp

The black, wrought-iron fence around Nevada's capitol is perhaps the most obvious and lasting reminder of the role Hannah E. Clapp played in the history of Nevada. Clapp was born near Albany, New York, in 1824. After graduating from a local teachers college, she taught in Michigan and was one of the first instructors at Michigan Female College.

In 1859 she joined her brother Nathan and his family on a wagon train to California. Along the way the party stopped in Salt Lake City, where they met some Mormons. Clapp wrote to friends that she was appalled and angered at the treatment of Mormon women, saying they were treated like "miserable slaves." She even claimed to have had an audience with Brigham Young to voice her concerns, though there is no record of the meeting. These sentiments were the first indication of Clapp's feminist leanings.

Clapp settled in Vacaville, California, for several months before heading to Carson City to take a job as a nanny and teacher for a local family. She

*Hannah E. Clapp.*
*—Courtesy Nevada*
*Historical Society*

immediately saw the need for schools in Nevada and in 1861 organized the Sierra Seminary, a private coeducational school and the first legally chartered school in the state. By the next year, the school had become such big news that Mark Twain, then a reporter at the *Territorial Enterprise*, visited during exams and penned a glowing report. He later recast this story for the "examination evening" scene in his book *Tom Sawyer*. Many years later, in the fall of 1877, Clapp, along with her close friend and partner Eliza Babcock and fellow teacher Annie Martin, opened the first kindergarten in Nevada.

In 1875 Clapp, a savvy investor, was the low bidder for the contract to supply materials for an iron fence at the new state capitol. After reading a newspaper notice requesting bids for the fence materials, she contacted wrought-iron manufacturers and put together a competitive bid of $5,550, which was $350 lower than the next-lowest proposal. Though she was a well-known member of the community, having lived in Carson City for ten years, it was nevertheless unusual for a woman to be awarded such a contract. She fulfilled its terms and made a $1,000 profit.

In 1887, at the age of sixty-three, Clapp was appointed preceptress (dean of women) and professor of history and English at the University of Nevada, newly relocated to Reno from Elko. She was the first female faculty at the university and was also in charge of supervising the women's dormitories and managing the school library. She retired fourteen years later.

Clapp was devoted to the cause of women's rights, and she is sometimes credited with being Nevada's first lobbyist because of her efforts to win voting rights for women. When she died in 1908, the *Reno Gazette-Journal* wrote, "It is doubtful if any single individual has had a wider influence in the forming days of Nevada than Miss Clapp."

### The Fight of the Century

In January 1897 Nevada became the first state to legalize boxing. Almost immediately after the bill was signed into law, promoters announced a bout in Carson City between James J. "Gentleman Jim" Corbett, the reigning heavyweight champion of the world, and Robert Fitzsimmons, holder of the world middleweight title. The event, scheduled for St. Patrick's Day 1897, was heavily promoted as the "Fight of the Century."

Nevada was roundly criticized throughout the country for legalizing boxing, which detractors called inhumane. Editorials, including a few in Nevada newspapers, condemned the state for permitting the fight. One Philadelphia paper opined that Nevada's statehood had been a "grave mistake" and wished there was a constitutional provision that would allow it to be absorbed by a more "self-respecting" state. Perhaps because of the great controversy, Nevada's first legal prizefight drew more than 6,000 spectators—twice the population of Carson City. Filmmakers documented the event using three kinetoscope cameras, making it the first motion picture filmed in the state.

*The world middleweight title bout between James J. "Gentleman Jim" Corbett and Robert Fitzsimmons, March 17, 1897.* —Courtesy Nevada Historical Society

The heavyweight champ, Corbett, won the early rounds, including a knockdown in the sixth. But as the fight continued, Corbett tired. It ended in the fourteenth round when Fitzsimmons knocked Corbett out with a hard blow to the pit of his stomach. Despite protests from Corbett's corner that he had been delivered a low blow, officials declared Fitzsimmons the winner.

### Historic Carson City: The Kit Carson Trail

In 1991 a group of city agencies led by the Carson City Convention and Visitors Bureau developed the Kit Carson Trail, a 2.5-mile walking tour through Carson City's historic neighborhoods, to promote the capital city's history. Like Boston's Freedom Trail, the Kit Carson Trail follows a bright blue line painted on the sidewalks. On the trail are the State Capitol; the former U.S. Mint, built in 1869 (now the Nevada State Museum); St. Teresa of Avila Catholic Church, completed in 1871; St. Peter's Episcopal Church, opened in 1868; the First United Methodist Church, erected in 1865; and the First Presbyterian Church, built in 1864. This last is the oldest church building still in service in the state, while the Methodist Church houses the state's oldest religious congregation, established in 1859.

The blue line also leads into the city's historic residential neighborhoods. Walking tourists can see dozens of striking homes once inhabited by prominent Nevada citizens. The houses range from modest—such as the 1862 Smail House at 512 North Curry Street, considered a fine example of Greek Revival architecture—to elaborate, like Henry M. Yerington's Victorian mansion at 512 North Division Street, built in 1863 and once the home of the superintendent of the Virginia & Truckee Railroad. The Bliss Mansion, at 710 W. Robinson,

*The Bliss Mansion is one of more than fifty
historic buildings on the Kit Carson Trail.*

a fifteen-room home built in 1879 by lumber magnate Duane L. Bliss, is now a bed-and-breakfast inn.

The Krebs-Peterson House, at 500 North Mountain Street, is a classic Victorian built in 1914 by Ernest Krebs Sr., a prominent surgeon, and later owned by state controller Edward Peterson. The two-story home was a set in the movie *The Shootist,* John Wayne's last film. The sandstone Stewart-Nye residence, at 108 N. Minnesota, was built in 1860 for William Morris Stewart, Nevada's first U.S. senator, and was sold in 1862 to James Nye, Nevada's only territorial governor.

One of the most significant buildings on the trail is the Orion Clemens House, at 502 North Division Street, built in 1863 by the first and only secretary of Nevada Territory. Orion Clemens was the older brother of Samuel Clemens, better known as Mark Twain. Samuel, who began his literary career at Virginia City's legendary *Territorial Enterprise* newspaper, occasionally stayed at Orion's house in 1863 and 1864.

Also of particular historical interest is the G.W.G. Ferris House, at 311 West Third Street, built in 1869. Famed agriculturist George Washington Gale Ferris built this home and resided there for many years with his family. Ferris's son, G.W.G. Ferris Jr., became a successful Chicago architect and invented the Ferris Wheel.

### Lone Mountain Cemetery

Carson City's Lone Mountain Cemetery, on the corner of Roop Street and Beverly Drive, has many notables from Nevada history interred there: Abraham Curry, Carson City's founder; Henry M. Yerington, superintendent of the Virginia & Truckee Railroad and namesake of the town of Yerington; five of Nevada's governors; Abe Cohn, a Carson City businessman who became famous for selling baskets made by the famous Washo basket maker Dat-so-la-lee; Hank Monk, a stage driver immortalized by Mark Twain for a white-knuckle ride that Monk once gave to Horace Greeley, the famed editor of the *New York Tribune*; and Jennie Clemens, daughter of Orion Clemens and Twain's niece, who died of spotted fever in 1864 at age nine.

### Nevada State Museum

The Nevada State Museum, set in the historic U.S. Mint building in the heart of Carson City, is a treasure house of Nevada history, culture, and natural history. A coin press from the mint and samples of nearly every coin produced there are on display, along with elegant silver dishes, bowls, and silverware made from Comstock silver for the U.S. Navy.

*Lone Mountain Cemetery contains the graves of many of Nevada's pioneers.*

*The historic U.S. Mint building now houses the Nevada State Museum.*

The natural history exhibit shows native birds, reptiles, fish, and almost every other creature that has walked, crawled, hopped, slithered, or glided across the Nevada landscape. The prehistoric Nevada display has a reconstructed skeleton of the largest mammoth ever found in North America. This massive beast of 17,000 years ago stood thirteen feet high at the shoulder and is here posed in a simulated mud bog next to the bones of a 25,000-year-old horse. A life-size diorama of a Paiute Indian camp includes a typical sagebrush-and-grass hut, handmade baskets, and other items. Figures represent tribal members performing daily tasks such as grinding pine nuts, a staple of their diet.

The museum exit passes through a reconstructed ghost town. This mock mining camp has the standard ghost-town buildings—newspaper office, assay office, general store, and, of course, saloon. An automated old prospector and his mule guide the tour, describing life in a nineteenth-century Nevada mining camp. A replica of a mine of the era, with typical square-set timbers and mining equipment, ends the tour.

The Inyo Number 22 is one of the many restored Virginia & Truckee
Railroad locomotives displayed in the Nevada State Railroad Museum.
—Courtesy Nevada State Railroad Museum/Daun Bohall

## Nevada State Railroad Museum

Over the years, Nevada has been the home of sixty-nine major and minor
rail lines. The Nevada State Railroad Museum, at the south end of town (2180
South Carson Street), is devoted to the preservation and study of these lines.
Its primary focus is on the Virginia & Truckee Railroad; most of the museum's
collection of engines and cars are from the V & T. The state purchased the
trains in 1974 from Paramount Pictures, which had acquired them in 1937
when the railroad was in financial trouble.

The museum's collection includes the Inyo Number 22, an 1875 wood-burn-
ing Baldwin 4-4-0 locomotive. The engine was one of five of its type that the
V & T purchased in the 1870s to pull passenger cars from Reno to Virginia
City. Also called "the Brass Betsy" because of its elegant brass trimmings, the
Inyo ran for more than fifty years. It appeared in a number of movies, including *Union Pacific* in 1938 and *The Virginian* in 1946. In 1969 it was refurbished
to resemble Central Pacific Railroad Engine Number 60, the Jupiter, and taken
to Promontory Point, Utah, as part of a National Park Service ceremony com-
memorating the centennial of the completion of the transcontinental railroad.

Another piece of rolling stock on display is the V & T Caboose Number 9,
built in 1873. Originally a twenty-two-passenger car, the railroad rebuilt the
Number 9 as a coach for sixty people in 1891 and later used it as a crew car.
Like the Inyo, it was sold to Paramount and appeared in films before it was retired
in the late 1950s. In 1971 the state purchased the caboose and restored it.

Coach Number 4 is the oldest piece of V & T equipment in the museum. Built in 1872 in San Francisco, it was one of the original sixteen passenger cars the railroad bought. Its interior is paneled in laurel, redwood, and maple, with elaborate brass lamps and overstuffed chairs. Like the others, the Number 4 appeared in many films.

On an adjacent track, the Dayton Number 18 resembles the Inyo but is an even rarer locomotive. The Central Pacific Railroad in Sacramento built it in 1873 for plowing snow; it is one of only two of its type still in existence. It used a huge curved plowing blade hooked to its nose to clear the tracks of snow. The Dayton, like the Inyo, was also used at the Promontory Point centennial celebration in 1969. It was repainted to look like Union Pacific Railroad Engine Number 119.

The museum relocated several historic railroad buildings to its grounds. Among them are the restored Wabuska depot and a nineteenth-century railworker cottage. There is also a reproduction of a square water tower from the nineteenth century. On special occasions the museum offers rides on some of the antique rolling stock.

### Stewart Indian Museum

The Stewart Indian Museum and Trading Post, at 5366 Snyder Avenue, sits on the grounds of the former Stewart Indian Boarding School. The museum, founded in 1982, tells the story of the boarding school and celebrates the history, crafts, and traditions of Native American people.

The school's story began in the 1880s, when Nevada's superintendent of public instruction, C. S. Young, recommended to the U.S. Bureau of Indian Affairs and the Nevada state legislature that an Indian industrial school be established. Nevada was not formally educating most Native Americans at that

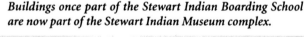

*Buildings once part of the Stewart Indian Boarding School are now part of the Stewart Indian Museum complex.*

time. In 1887 the state legislature authorized the creation of an Indian school and the bonds to pay for it, provided the federal government agreed to operate it.

Nevada's U.S. senator William Stewart guided the corresponding federal legislation, including congressional funding, to approval. The Clear Creek Indian Training School, as it was originally known, was built on 240 acres south of Carson City and opened on December 17, 1890. It was later renamed in honor of Senator Stewart.

On opening day, the school had a superintendent, W. D. C. Gibson, three teachers, and thirty-seven students from the Paiute, Washo, and Shoshone tribes. Within a month, more students had arrived, bringing the enrollment to ninety-one by January 1, 1891. In its first decades, the school was operated much like a military academy, with rigid schedules and military-style uniforms. Academic classes consumed the first half of each day, followed by vocational training in sewing, harness- and shoemaking, leatherwork, blacksmithing, carpentry, masonry, printing, and other skills. The school produced Nevada's first Native American newspaper, the *Indian Advance*, in 1899.

The Stewart Indian Museum's Hall of Fame highlights two of the areas in which Stewart students excelled—athletics and music. The school's athletes competed in football, track, basketball, boxing, and baseball. Stewart won several state championships, including the 1916 football title, the 1966 A-conference basketball championship, and seven consecutive AA cross-country championships in the 1970s. The school's award-winning band, organized in 1896, performed in competitions and at special events, including the National Music Festival in Long Beach, California, in 1940.

In addition to educating Native Americans from Nevada, the Stewart facility served Indian students from all over the country. In the late 1940s the school became part of a special program for Navajos, and by the mid-1950s, most of the students were of Navajo descent. The federal government closed the school in 1980, deciding to phase out Indian boarding schools. They sold the land to the state of Nevada, which deeded three of the buildings to the nonprofit Stewart Indian Museum.

Stonemasons who had been trained at the school constructed the museum building and the more than one hundred surrounding structures, using rough-cut, multicolored local stone embedded in dark mortar. This building style is known in Carson City as the Stewart Indian School style of architecture, but it was actually copied from a church in Arizona that then-superintendent Frederick Snyder had admired in the 1920s. The first school building of this design was completed in 1923.

## Kings Canyon Road

Kings Canyon Road may not look like much today. It is just a narrow, rutted dirt road heading west from Carson City into the mountains. But it is one of the region's most storied routes. Long before the arrival of white settlers, a

Washo Indian trail crossed over the mountains between Lake Tahoe and the Carson City area. In the 1850s, fortune seekers heading to the goldfields of California used the route. Among the earliest settlers in the area was Dr. Benjamin King, for whom the canyon was named.

Kings Canyon Road was first known as the Lake Bigler Toll Road. John Bigler was a California governor, and his was one of the earliest names given to Lake Tahoe. Engineer Butler Ives constructed the toll road in 1863. A business group needing a route to bring timber from Lake Tahoe to Virginia City's mines financed the project, which included an extensive system of flumes and log chutes. Later, the route became part of the historic Lincoln Highway, America's first transcontinental road. The land at the base of the canyon, which belonged to a Basque family named Borda, was once a sheep ranch. In the late 1990s the Bordas donated their ranch to Carson City so Kings Canyon Road could be kept open to the public.

To find this historic road from downtown Carson City, head west on King Street. The pavement ends after about four miles, and the next eleven miles are passable only with a four-wheel-drive vehicle with high clearance.

## GARDNERVILLE AND MINDEN

The twin communities of Gardnerville and Minden are about fifteen miles south of Carson City on US 395. Lawrence Gilman, a land developer and hotel owner, established Gardnerville in 1879 after purchasing a seven-acre tract from rancher John M. Gardner, for whom he named the town. Gilman moved the former Kent House from the Genoa area to his land and turned it into the Gardnerville Hotel, adding a blacksmith shop and a saloon. Because the town was in the heart of the fertile hay and grain country of the Carson Valley and roads linked it to the mining towns of Bodie and Aurora to the south and Virginia City to the north, Gardnerville soon became the region's commercial center.

Minden began with the Dangberg family, who had extensive land holdings in the Carson Valley by the 1890s. In 1905 the Virginia & Truckee Railroad and H. F. Dangberg Land & Livestock Company, operated by the sons of pioneering western Nevada rancher Henry Fred Dangberg Sr., established Minden to serve as the southern terminus of the railroad. The town was named after the German birthplace of Henry Dangberg.

The Carson Valley Museum and Cultural Center, at 1477 US 395 in Gardnerville, occupies the former Douglas County High School building. This 1915 structure, designed by Nevada architect Frederick J. DeLongchamps, played a key role in the development of Douglas County. In 1906, when Minden and Gardnerville were both trying to take the county seat from Genoa, a deal was cut—Minden would get the county seat and courthouse and Gardnerville would get a high school.

The high school soon became an important part of Carson Valley life. It hosted the first county fair and attracted large crowds for sporting events and student plays. In 1958, however, the building was no longer large enough for the growing student population. The town built a new high school behind the old one, which was converted to a junior high school. In the mid-1980s, more stringent earthquake standards almost doomed the old school. It was declared unsafe and there was talk of tearing it down. But in 1988 the Carson Valley Historical Society acquired the structure and raised enough funds to renovate it and establish the museum and cultural center.

The museum's exhibits include historic photos and artifacts, a replica of a Basque sheep camp, an art gallery, and a display of handmade Washo Indian baskets. In the basement is the Early Day Telephone Display Room, filled with antique telephone equipment. There is also reconstruction of several early twentieth-century Carson Valley businesses, including a newspaper office.

## WELLINGTON

Wellington is eight miles east of US 395 on NV 208; the exit for NV 208 is about two miles north of Topaz Lake. This tiny agricultural community in the Smith Valley is best known as the home of the 126-year-old Wellington Mercantile. The red barn-style structure was constructed in 1873 and was known then as Hoye's Store, after owners John and Mary Hoye. In its first years, it also served as a stage stop for the line that operated between the Carson Valley and the mining camps of Bodie and Aurora.

The town itself goes back to 1860, when Jack Wright and Leonard Hamilton built a bridge over the West Walker River and opened a stage station. In 1863 Daniel Wellington purchased the bridge and station, which took his name. He added a house, a livery stable, and a hotel. A small community grew around Wellington's outpost, including the Wellington Mercantile and the Wellington Hotel. The latter, built in 1875, has undergone extensive remodeling over the years and is now called the Heyday Inn. Wellington's quaint one-room schoolhouse, built at the turn of the twentieth century, now houses a local museum.

# NV 206 (JACK'S VALLEY ROAD)
# GENOA–NV 88

### 12 MILES

## GENOA

There is debate among historians about whether Genoa or Dayton should be considered the state's first settlement. But while Dayton sprang up as a mining camp, Genoa's founders constructed sturdy wooden homes and brick commercial buildings, some of which still stand today. Therefore, the general

*Historic buildings line the main street in Genoa.*

consensus is that Genoa, fifteen miles south of Carson City on NV 206 (also called Jack's Valley Road), is the state's oldest continuously settled town.

In 1850 a group of Mormon traders led by Joseph DeMont and Hampton S. Beatie arrived in the Carson Valley. Beatie and another associate, Abner Blackburn, constructed a crude, roofless building to serve as a trading post for Emigrant Trail wagon trains. A year after that post was abandoned, another Mormon, John Reese, established a new post about fifty yards south of the earlier one and called it Mormon Station. In 1855 Mormon elder Orson Hyde, the first probate judge for western Utah (now Nevada), formally named the site Genoa because he said it reminded him of the Italian city where Columbus was born. However, unlike its Italian namesake, Nevada's Genoa is pronounced "Juh-NO-uh."

The trading post quickly developed into a small but important farming community for western Nevada. In 1857 Brigham Young recalled all his western followers to Salt Lake City because of a dispute with the federal government. Most of the Mormons abandoned their homes and farms or sold them for token payments. This ultimately led to land disputes, and in 1862 Orson Hyde, who found his Carson Valley land confiscated by non-Mormons in his absence, is said to have placed a curse on the residents in hope of frightening them into paying for the property. The town survived the curse and for a time was the center of activity in the region.

As the Mormons were departing Genoa in 1857, the remaining residents, still officially living in Utah Territory, petitioned Congress to create a new territory for Nevada. The residents desired some type of stable government, particularly since Utah Territory officials were preoccupied with their feud with the federal government. A public meeting was held at Gilbert's saloon in Genoa on August 3, 1857, to discuss the territorial initiative. The movement temporarily faded, however, after the Mormon Church resolved its differences with Washington and new officials came in to oversee the interests of residents in western Utah Territory.

In 1858 the territorial government designated Genoa the county seat for Carson County, Utah. Western Utahans, however, remained unsatisfied with the territorial governance and once again began to discuss establishing a separate territory. Genoa hosted a territorial convention in July 1859, where the conveners approved plans for a provisional government. In an election held later that year, residents voted in Issac Roop of Susanville (now part of California) as governor. The federal government did not recognize this provisional government, however. When the federal government finally created Nevada Territory in 1861, the territory named Genoa the seat of Douglas County, a role Genoa continued when Nevada became a state in 1864.

In 1858 Genoa became home of Nevada's first printed newspaper, the *Daily Territorial Enterprise*—previous Nevada papers had been handwritten. The paper later moved to Virginia City, where it became one of Nevada's most famous newspapers. From 1860 to 1861, Genoa was a stop on the famous Pony Express route and a rest station for travelers on the Overland Stage. By the mid-1860s, however, Virginia City and Reno had eclipsed Genoa in importance. Within twenty years Genoa claimed only a few hundred people and a handful of businesses. In 1916 the agriculture community of Minden, which had a rail connection, replaced Genoa as the county seat.

Several fires over the years destroyed much of the original town. According to local lore, in 1910 one of the worst fires started after a resident of the county "poor farm" lit a pan of sulfur under his bed to rid it of bedbugs and the mattress caught on fire. Whatever the cause, the fire burned half the business district, including the struggling Mormon Station trading post, which had recently been used as a chicken coop and a pig barn. But despite setbacks, Genoa has survived.

### Snowshoe Thompson

Every time snow blankets the Sierra Nevada, skiers should thank Jon Torsteinson Rui, better known by his anglicized name, John "Snowshoe" Thompson. Prior to Thompson's arrival in the region in the mid-1850s, no one in these parts had ever strapped on a pair of wooden slats and slid down a hill.

Thompson was born in Norway in 1827. His family came to America when he was ten years old and settled in the Midwest. In 1851 Thompson joined the thousands of people heading to California to mine for gold. After several fruitless years of mining in the Sierra Nevada, he settled in the Sacramento area to farm. Then he heard about a lucrative postal contract to carry mail from Placerville, California, to Genoa, a tiny hamlet in what was then Utah Territory.

Thompson had a plan for how to carry the mail—he would create a pair of long, wooden skis, called snowshoes in his day. They were like those he had used as a child in Norway. He applied for the job using the name John A. Thompson because he felt his real name was unpronounceable to most non-Norwegians. Worried he would not be hired unless he appeared eager, he showed up carrying his handmade, twenty-five-pound oak skis, which were ten feet long and an inch and a half thick. History does not tell us if he impressed the postmaster, but he got the job because he was the only applicant.

Thompson began his 180-mile round-trip over the mountains on January 3, 1856. It took him three days to reach Placerville, but he made the return trip in an amazing forty-eight hours. Word of his accomplishment traveled fast, and within a short time Thompson was a Nevada legend. Most incredible was the fact that Thompson often carried a pack loaded with 80 to 100 pounds of mail and assorted packages. He even carried, over several trips, much of the machinery and printing equipment used to produce Virginia City's famous *Territorial Enterprise*.

Thompson delivered the mail in small towns throughout the Sierra for nearly two decades and gave new life to the cliché about mailmen making their rounds in rain and snow and gloom of night. Yet Thompson was rarely paid for his Herculean services. In 1874 he petitioned the U.S. Congress for back pay but was turned down—despite traveling all the way to Washington D.C. to make his appeal—because he had never signed a contract.

Over the years, Thompson taught dozens of people how to glide across the snow, introducing the sport of skiing to the Sierra Nevada region. Thompson died in 1876 and is buried in the Genoa Cemetery, a mile north of town.

### Sam Brown: Outlaw

In early Nevada, law enforcement was virtually nonexistent. One of the worst bullies was a gunman named Sam Brown, who frequently terrorized residents of Virginia City, Carson City, and the Carson Valley. While the record is spotty, historians believe he killed his first man in Texas, shot another in Mariposa, California, and murdered three men in the California mining camp of Fiddletown. In February 1859, Brown shot and killed William Bilboa in Carson City; this was his first Nevada victim.

Other fatal encounters followed, including a stabbing in a Virginia City saloon. It was alleged that after Brown pulled his knife out of his victim, he wiped it clean on his pant leg, then lay down on a billiard table and fell asleep. Brown generally preyed on "safe" victims—drunk, unarmed loners without friends to seek revenge.

On July 6, 1861, Brown attended a friend's trial in Genoa, where he hoped to intimidate the jurors with his presence. He attempted to enter the courtroom with his weapons, but was accosted by one of the attorneys, who stripped him of his gun. Angry about the rough treatment he had received, he retrieved his gun and rode a few miles south to Henry Van Sickle's ranch and inn. For no apparent reason—other than perhaps simple meanness—he fired a shot at Van Sickle, who was standing on his front porch. The rancher fled inside, pursued by Brown. The outlaw, however, was unable to find Van Sickle, so he climbed on his horse and rode north to Carson City. Van Sickle grabbed a shotgun and rode after him.

The rancher soon caught up to Brown and fired his shotgun, knocking Brown from his horse but leaving him unharmed. Brown returned fire. Van Sickle reloaded his shotgun and began stalking his assailant, finally catching him. "I got you," Van Sickle reportedly said just before he fired. "And I kills you." A jury later acquitted Van Sickle of murder, ruling that Brown's death "served him right."

### Historic Genoa

Many historic buildings and homes grace Genoa. The Genoa Bar, at the corner of Main and Mill Streets, was built in the 1850s and is reputedly the oldest "thirst parlor" in the state. At Main and Carson Streets stands the former home of William J. "Lucky Bill" Thorington, a prominent Genoa landowner who was hanged in 1858 for allegedly harboring a horse thief, although some believe that the real reason was that he was a polygamist. Thorington's brick Victorian, built in the mid-1850s, was later owned by Judge D. W. Virgin, the first district attorney of Douglas County.

Between the Thorington House and the Genoa Bar is the renovated Raycroft Depot, a portion of which was built in the 1850s. The original building, buried within later additions, once served as law offices for Senator William Stewart and Judge Virgin, and later as a newspaper printing plant, butcher shop, and stagecoach depot.

In 1947 the site of the old Mormon Station became a state park, with a replica of the old trading post. Interpretive exhibits tell the story of the town's history. Near the park is the Kinsey House, one of the oldest homes in the state. Stephen A. Kinsey, one of the original Mormon Station settlers and the first postmaster in the Carson Valley, built the two-story structure in 1856.

Across from Mormon Station State Park is the "Pink House," so called for its bubble-gum-colored exterior. John Reese, founder of Mormon Station, constructed the two-story home in 1853, at a site a few blocks west of where it now rests. Local merchant J. R. Johnson moved the house in 1865. It became another home of Judge Virgin in 1884 and was later the residence of his daughter, Lillian Virgin Finnegan. Today a popular restaurant occupies the Pink House.

A splendid two-story brick courthouse on the corner of Main and Fifth Streets, built in 1865 but abandoned when the county seat was lost, was used as a school from 1916 to 1956. In 1966 the town converted it into a regional museum. Exhibits re-create the original jail and a blacksmith shop and display an assortment of Native American baskets and crafts, as well as a large collection of paintings by Hans Meyer-Kassel, a German-born artist who painted many Nevada scenes in the 1940s and 1950s.

## WALLEY'S HOT SPRINGS

Walley's Hot Springs Resort, a mile south of Genoa on NV 206, was created in 1862 by David and Harriet Walley. In its early days the spa catered to miners from nearby Virginia City, who needed a place to soak away the aches and pains of their daily labors. Built at a cost of $100,000, the resort had eleven baths, a ballroom, and gardens. The Walleys advertised the thermal waters as a cure for "rheumatism and scrofulous affections [*sic*]."

With the decline of the Comstock mines, Walley's lost much of its clientele. The owners sold it in 1896 for $5,000 and it functioned as a hotel until 1935, when it burned down. Subsequent owners have renovated and rebuilt the resort over the years, and today it has six pools and cottages with private baths.

## MOTTSVILLE AND SHERIDAN

Mottsville and Sheridan were among the handful of small settlements that sprang up on the western edge of the Carson Valley along the Emigrant Trail. Mottsville was named for Hiram Mott, an early Carson Valley rancher. His family was among the earliest to settle in Nevada. Little remains of the town except the Mottsville Cemetery, one of the state's first cemeteries, established in 1857. The site of Mottsville is six miles south of Genoa on NV 206.

A few miles farther south on NV 206, a historical marker notes the site of Sheridan. The town was founded as a general store for travelers in 1855 by Moses Job, the namesake of Job's Peak, the tall mountain west of the town site. For a brief time in the 1870s, Sheridan was the largest community in the Carson Valley, but by the late 1890s it had begun to decline, and by the mid-twentieth century it had disappeared.

### Ben Palmer

One of the earliest residents in the Carson Valley was Ben Palmer, who claimed 320 acres of grassland near Sheridan in 1853. Palmer was Nevada's first African American landowner. He had worked as a drover and arrived in the area with his sister Charlotte and her family. Charlotte and her husband, David Barber, who was white, settled on 400 acres adjacent to Palmer. Shortly after arriving, Charlotte gave birth to a son, Benjamin, the first non-Indian born in Nevada.

Within a few years, Ben Palmer was one of the most successful cattle ranchers in the Carson Valley. By 1857 he was one of Douglas County's largest taxpayers, and the value of his land holdings ranked tenth in the county. In 1857 Palmer drove 1,500 head of cattle from Seattle to the Carson Valley.

Despite the fact that many early Nevada laws discriminated against non-whites—for instance, they could not vote—Palmer was highly respected by his neighbors. After 1870, when Nevada extended voting rights to nonwhite men, Palmer registered to vote and twice served on a county grand jury. Palmer died in 1908 at age eighty-two. He is buried beside his sister, her husband, and their seven children in the Mottsville Cemetery.

## NV 341 AND NV 342
## US 50–VIRGINIA CITY

### 8 MILES

### SILVER CITY

Silver City is three and a half miles south of Virginia City at the mouth of Devil's Gate. Almost since men first discovered silver and gold in nearby Gold Canyon, Devil's Gate has had a reputation—only partly deserved—for trouble. The gate stands between twin reefs of craggy dark rock jutting from the surrounding canyon walls, almost meeting in the center. NV 341 somehow squeezes through the lava-rock formation. Miners blasted a wider passage through Devil's Gate in the mid-nineteenth century to accommodate wagons.

Devil's Gate's ominous name was further tarnished in the late 1850s and early 1860s, when the narrow passage became a hideout for highwaymen. J. Ross Browne, a noted journalist, wrote in 1860 of the "unhallowed character of the place." Dozens of newspaper reports of the day mention thieves relieving people of their valuables as a toll through the gate.

Later there was an official toll station at the gate. Since the passage offered the easiest way to reach Virginia City, thousands of newcomers trudged through the gate's narrow opening on their way to the boomtown. Despite the many unflattering reports about the area, by 1860 Silver City had cropped up at the gate. Browne vividly describes the hustle and bustle of the town, with its bawdy saloons, frail wooden shacks, and miners of every ethnicity crawling over the hillsides in search of silver:

> The deep pits on the hill-sides; the blasted and barren appearance of the whole country; the unsightly hodgepodge of a town; the horrible confusion of tongues; the roaring, raving drunkards at the bar-rooms, swigging fiery liquids from morning till night; the flaring and flaunting gambling-saloons, filled with desperadoes of the vilest sort; the ceaseless torrent of imprecations that shocked the ear on every side; the mad speculations and feverish thirst for gain.

Perhaps because Silver City never gained the acclaim and attention of Virginia City, only a few of its historic buildings survive. While the community does not have a large commercial district like Virginia City, it does have a post office, the Hardwick House bed-and-breakfast (located in a former icehouse), and a large cemetery.

## GOLD HILL

The community of Gold Hill, a former mining town in the shadow of Virginia City, shares much of the history of its more famous neighbor. In the late 1850s, both towns were the site of major gold and silver discoveries that were part of the Comstock Lode. In 1859 Gold Hill began as little more than a few dozen miners camping under trees or living in crude wooden shacks. But within a few years, Gold Hill rivaled Virginia City in wealth and population. By the early 1870s, it had 8,000 residents and was an important stop on the Virginia & Truckee Railroad line. It was also home of one of the most respected newspapers in the state, the *Gold Hill News*.

As with Virginia City, Gold Hill's decline began in the late 1870s when the mines played out. By 1882 the newspaper had moved to Idaho and most residents had drifted away. In 1943 Gold Hill lost its post office. Several hundred people live in Gold Hill today.

While many of Gold Hill's buildings have disappeared over the years, mostly victims of fires and neglect, enough of the town remains to provide a glimpse of its once-thriving past. The old Virginia & Truckee Railroad depot still sits on a flat near the north end of town. Constructed in 1872, the wooden frame building was used until the Virginia City portion of the V & T ceased operating in 1936. In recent years, the depot was partially restored to serve as the

*The Gold Hill Depot.*

ticket office for the revived V & T Railroad, which renewed service as a tourist rail between Gold Hill and Virginia City in 1990.

Down the canyon from the depot is the former Bank of California building, which dates back to 1862. The stone-and-red-brick structure is one of the few surviving commercial buildings from Gold Hill's early days. Since the bank closed in 1879, the building has housed a variety of businesses, including a pool hall and an art gallery. Next door to the bank is the Gold Hill Hotel, one of the oldest hotels in the state. The original stone facade was constructed in 1859. The two-story wooden section in the rear is a newer addition, built in the late 1980s.

Up the hill from the hotel are the picturesque remains of the Yellow Jacket mine's shaft and headframe (hoist), built in 1937. The Crown Point Mill, which processed ore from the Yellow Jacket and Crown Point Mines in the 1930s, stands adjacent to the hotel. Across NV 341 from the ore mill is the green stone foundation of the Rhode Island Mill. Dating to 1862, it was one of the first stamp mills in Gold Hill.

## VIRGINIA CITY

Arguably, there would not be a Nevada without Virginia City, twenty-four miles south of Reno on US 395 and NV 341. It is only because of the discovery of the Comstock Lode that Nevada is not simply eastern California or western Utah. The first hint that there might be something worthwhile in the canyons of western Nevada's Virginia Range came from itinerate miners who drifted into the area after failing to strike it rich during California's gold rush. Between 1851 and 1858, a small community of prospectors worked in Six Mile Canyon and Gold Canyon, northwest of the present town of Dayton. Using the region's limited water, they crushed and washed gravel and rock, eking out a few dollars' worth of gold each day.

All that changed with the discovery of the Comstock Lode in about 1856. Historians believe that brothers Hosea Ballou Grosh and Ethan Allan Grosh found it. For two or three years, they had been regularly prospecting in Gold Canyon and, like the other miners working in the region, encountered a sticky, bluish mud that interfered with the process of extracting gold. But unlike the other miners, who threw away the mud, the Grosh brothers suspected it contained silver. Letters they wrote to friends and family mentioned finding a "monster ledge" of silver, indicating that they knew what they had found.

Unfortunately, both men died before ever having a chance to exploit their discovery. In August 1857, Hosea, age thirty-three, swung a pick into his foot. Since there were no doctors in Nevada at the time, he was not able to have his injury properly treated and died of blood poisoning two weeks afterward. Three months later, Ethan, thirty-one, attempted to cross the Sierra Nevada in early winter. He became trapped in a blizzard and later died from untreated frostbite that had become gangrenous.

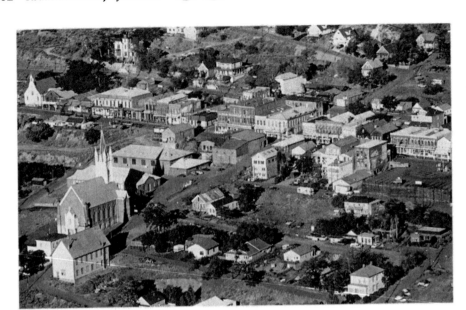

*A view of Virginia City, "Queen of the Comstock."* —Courtesy Nevada Commission on Tourism

Early in 1859 Patrick McLaughlin and Peter O'Riley, who were later joined by Henry Comstock and others, claimed the discovery of the Comstock Lode. Like much of Nevada's early history, the details are cloudy, but it appears that McLaughlin and O'Riley were working near the top of Six Mile Canyon when they encountered some crumbly, bluish black rock. They did not immediately recognize that it was nearly pure silver but found enough gold to make the site worth working. The gold, however, proved difficult to separate from the black rock, which turned to a sticky mud when mixed with water.

Shortly after staking the claim, the two were visited by Henry Comstock, who insisted that the site was part of a larger mining claim he owned. McLaughlin and O'Riley agreed to make Comstock and his friend Immanuel "Manny" Penrod partners in the claim. Word of the promising discovery spread, yet many miners preferred to work in parts of the canyon where the gold was easier to extract.

The four continued prospecting along the promising seam, which grew thicker as they dug deeper. In June 1859 a Truckee Meadows ranch hand, B. A. Harrison, took samples of the rock to an assayer in Placerville, California, where he was told that it had a yield of $876 per ton in gold—and an amazing $3,000 per ton in silver! News of the discovery soon raced throughout northern California, and many miners who had come too late to benefit from California's gold rush headed to Nevada.

Meanwhile, miners working in the vicinity of the McLaughlin-O'Riley strike began organizing a more formal mining district. By August 1859 the region had been named Ophir, and the site of the McLaughlin-O'Riley discovery was called the Ophir Mine. McLaughlin, O'Riley, Comstock, and Penrod soon sold their rights to the mine because they did not have the resources to develop it. As historian Ronald M. James notes, the lode irrevocably changed the region's population as "a new society of outsiders [with the money to develop the claims] had replaced the original ragtag band."

Between 1860 and 1864, Virginia City experienced a series of booms and busts as new discoveries sparked brief periods of prosperity, followed by the inevitable lean times after the veins petered out. In 1864 a new force known as the Bank Crowd began to exert influence on Virginia City. The Bank Crowd included William C. Ralston and Darius Ogden Mills, owners of the powerful San Francisco–based Bank of California; William Sharon, the bank's representative in Virginia City; and investor Alvinza Hayward.

Under Sharon's direction, the Bank of California began lending money to the owners of Virginia City mines and mills at rates lower than those of other financial institutions. The bank's offers came at a time when the Comstock mines had entered a lull, so that many mine and mill owners eagerly accepted the deal. Unfortunately, the economic situation did not immediately improve, and many found themselves unable to make their loan payments. Sharon mercilessly foreclosed on properties, and within four years he had acquired

*John Mackay, one of the "Silver Kings," owned some of the most productive mines in Virginia City in the 1870s.* —Courtesy Nevada Historical Society

control of virtually all of Virginia City's most productive mines and mills. It was quite a swindle.

In 1869 the Bank Crowd began construction of the Virginia & Truckee Railroad to connect Virginia City to the Central Pacific Railroad at Reno. Completed in 1872, the railroad further cemented the bank's control over Virginia City. Now, not only did it own the mines and mills, but the means of getting the ore to market.

The Bank Crowd's stranglehold on the Comstock mines remained intact until 1872, when a group of four Irishmen—John Mackay, James Fair, William S. O'Brien, and James C. Flood—outmaneuvered Sharon to gain control of the bank's Hale & Norcross and Kentuck Mines. The four also acquired the Consolidated Virginia Mine, which proved to be one of the most productive Comstock properties. All four men became extremely wealthy—they were known as the Silver Kings—and effectively ended the Bank Crowd's near-total control over mining in Virginia City.

Ultimately, the Comstock Lode proved to be one of the richest mining strikes in U.S. history. Estimates vary, but between 1860 and 1880, Virginia City's mines produced between $320 million and $750 million in gold and silver.

### Virginia City's Namesake

Among the earliest prospectors working the Comstock Lode—he had been working the site even before the lode was discovered—was James "Old Virginny" Finney (or Fennimore—his name shows up several different ways in history books), who is generally credited with naming Virginia City. A popular anecdote is that an inebriated Finney—who hailed from Virginia—was walking down one of the steep hills of the mining camp that had grown up around the Comstock Lode when he stumbled and broke a bottle of whiskey. Rather than mourn the loss of the precious liquid, he used the opportunity to christen the settlement Virginia City.

Most historians, however, believe the community was named by others. One account maintains that in September 1859, local miners held a meeting during which they agreed to dub the town in honor of Old Virginny. The colorful story about the whiskey bottle did not appear in print until 1876, nearly fifteen years after Finney died.

### Philipp Deidesheimer and Square-set Timbering

Virginia City owes much of its mining success to a German-born engineer named Philipp Deidesheimer. In 1851 Deidesheimer arrived in California hoping, like tens of thousands of others, to profit from the gold rush. He was hired as a mine superintendent in the northern California mining camp of Georgetown. Soon he gained a reputation as an inventive mining engineer who could find solutions to nearly any problem.

In 1860 William Sharon asked Deidesheimer to solve a vexing problem affecting the Ophir Mine in Virginia City. The Ophir was so rich in ore that in some places the veins were more than sixty feet wide. Some stopes had become so large that dangerous cave-ins were common.

Deidesheimer agreed to study the problem, though he had never seen nor heard of ore bodies so enormous. After inspecting the Ophir, Deidesheimer engineered a method of constructing mine shafts, which he named square-set timbering, that he believed would greatly improve the stability of the mines. Deidesheimer's idea was to build a network of individual square frames, each independent of the others, so if one frame collapsed, it would not drag the others down after it. Also, the square design was inherently stronger than conventional parallel timbering, which usually involved haphazardly wedging timbers from ceiling to floor and wall to wall.

Square-set timbering revolutionized the mining industry and greatly improved the safety of underground mining. Deidesheimer chose not to patent his design but rather encouraged other mines to use the technique to improve miner safety. While others became very rich using his engineering breakthrough, Deidesheimer's main reward was being placed in charge of the Ophir Mine.

In the early 1870s, Deidesheimer invested all his money in mining stock. Unfortunately, the mining market crashed in 1875, and he went bankrupt. In the early 1880s he left Virginia City for Sierra City, California, where he experienced modest success with a mining property he acquired. He remained in California until his death in 1916.

### Camels at the Comstock

In the 1850s the U.S. Army was experimenting with camels for carrying freight in the Southwest. They found camels perfect beasts of burden in the hot, dry region: they could eat almost anything, go for days without water, and carry heavy loads. In 1861 some enterprising souls brought nine camels to Virginia City to haul salt, which was used in processing silver ore, to the mines from interior Nevada's salt flats. The camel-packing operation proved profitable for several years, until salt deposits were discovered near the Carson River, closer to Virginia City.

Meanwhile, in 1864 Samuel McLeneghan purchased several camels, which he housed in a stone barn in Dayton. The camels carried firewood from the Carson River to Virginia City. McLeneghan also found buyers for the camels' hair, which was braided into excellent bridles and ropes.

The camels, however, frightened horses and mules, who upon encountering them would buck and try to run away. Following a few mishaps, Virginia City passed an ordinance banning camels from the streets during daylight hours. By 1875 the Nevada state legislature had banned the animals from public roads. While some ignored the law, the ban effectively ended the camel-transport business in Nevada. Some camel owners moved their animals to Arizona, but many simply turned them loose. People reported seeing wild camels in Nevada as late as 1936.

### *The* Territorial Enterprise

Nevada historian David W. Toll described the nineteenth-century staff of Virginia City's *Territorial Enterprise* as "a Murderer's Row of frontier Western journalists." Founded in December 1858 in Genoa—it was Nevada's first regularly published newspaper—the *Enterprise* moved to Carson City in November 1859 and then to its final destination, Virginia City, in November 1860.

Shortly after the paper came to Virginia City, journalist Joe Goodman became part owner and editor of the paper. Goodman was a gifted editor and writer who had founded the *Golden Era*, a San Francisco monthly. He hired a talented crew of journalists during his thirteen years at the helm, including associate editor Rollin Daggett, who later served as a Nevada congressman, and two reporters named Dan De Quille and Mark Twain.

De Quille, whose real name was William Wright, was born in Iowa in 1829 and came West in the late 1850s. His first stop was California, where he worked as a miner and a journalist. In 1860 he moved to Silver City, Nevada, where he tried his hand at prospecting before coming to Virginia City as a reporter for the *Enterprise*. In 1862, Mark Twain joined the staff, and the two partnered on stories for about a year.

During the time De Quille and Twain both worked at the *Enterprise*, De Quille was considered the superior talent, despite bouts with alcohol. In 1867 he wrote of meeting a man from the Pahranagat (paw-RAN-uh-gut) region of eastern Nevada who showed him half a dozen pebbles that were almost perfectly round. The man called them "traveling stones." De Quille wrote that when the man set the stones in a circle on the floor, the writer witnessed the rocks move toward one another, "like a bunch of eggs in a nest."

This fantastic story—in fact a fabrication—was reprinted in newspapers all over the world. Soon De Quille was flooded with letters from people begging to see the incredible rolling stones of Pahranagat. Promoter P. T. Barnum wired De Quille with an offer of $10,000 if the journalist could coax the owner of the rocks into having them perform under Barnum's big tent.

Twelve years later, De Quille finally tired of the story and in 1879 wrote a brief article recanting his amazing tale. "We are now growing old and we want peace," he wrote. "Therefore we solemnly affirm that we never saw or heard of any such diabolical cobbles as the traveling stones of Pahranagat." But many refused to believe his retraction and accused him of lying in order to keep the performing rocks for himself.

De Quille worked on and off at the *Enterprise* for nearly forty years. He was frequently dismissed for drunkenness but would return, temporarily rehabilitated. In 1897 he retired to Iowa and died less than a year later.

Twain's stint at the *Enterprise* was considerably briefer but no less memorable. Twain arrived in Nevada in August 1861 with his older brother, Orion Clemens, who had been appointed secretary of Nevada Territory. Twain lived off and on in Carson City with his brother in between short turns as a

*Mark Twain.*
—Courtesy Nevada
Historical Society

prospector. During one of these prospecting forays, in Aurora, Twain began sending humorous letters about the hard-luck life of a miner, which he signed "Josh," to Joe Goodman at the *Enterprise*. In July 1862 Goodman offered him a position at the paper. For the next twenty-one months, Twain honed his writing skills there, covering among other things Nevada's territorial legislature in 1862 and 1864.

It was at the *Enterprise* that Twain began using his pen name. There are several stories about the origin of the pseudonym. According to Twain scholar George J. Williams III, the name can be traced to one of Twain's hangouts, John Piper's Old Corner Saloon. In his 1993 book *On the Road with Mark Twain in California and Nevada*, Williams writes that when Twain went to the bar, "he ordered drinks for himself and his pal and asked [Piper] to 'mark twain,' meaning, mark two drinks on [his tab]." The expression became the reporter's nickname. Williams asserts that Twain began using it as a pen name in a dispatch from Carson City on January 31, 1863. The more common story is that Twain took his name from a phrase that Mississippi riverboat pilots used as a warning of shallow waters.

Twain departed Virginia City in May 1864. Some claim he left after challenging a rival newspaperman, with whom he had been carrying on a lively debate in the pages of their respective publications, to a duel. When his offer was accepted, Twain was forced to sneak out of town under cover of night to avoid the conflict. Others believe he simply grew tired of Virginia City and decided to move to the much larger and more interesting metropolis of San Francisco. When he left, Twain allegedly vowed never to return to Nevada. However, he came back on lecture tours in 1866 and 1868.

### The Great Fire of 1875

For the first decade and a half of its existence, Virginia City had avoided the kind of major fire that was common in frontier communities built mostly of wood. On October 26, 1875, however, a fire started in the basement of a Virginia City boardinghouse and quickly spread. There had been no rain for nearly six months, so the town was a tinder box. Strong winds fanned and scattered the flames. Within hours, nearly the entire city was on fire, including many of the mines. Thirty-three city blocks burned to the ground during the conflagration. Insurance companies later estimated more than $10 million in damages to the city.

Fortunately, Virginia City's mines were still flush, and the town was able to rebuild immediately. The year after the fire, Virginia City's population peaked at 23,000. By 1878, however, the mines' output had begun to slump, and within two years Virginia City's boom was over.

### Lucius Beebe and Virginia City's Café Society

In 1948 *New York Tribune* society columnist Lucius Beebe and his companion, Charles Clegg, came to Virginia City to research the Virginia & Truckee Railroad for a book they were writing about America's short-line railroads. The debonair Beebe, who often dressed in top hats and long coats, said later that he was impressed with the old mining town because it had a ratio of one saloon for every twenty men, women, and children. As an openly gay man in the staid 1950s, he was also attracted by the town's moral tolerance. Plus, Nevada had low taxes. Beebe and Clegg soon purchased a nineteenth-century house on A Street in Virginia City, renovated it in a style that Clegg described as "Victorian vulgarity," and added extensive gardens and a six-car garage for their collection of classic automobiles.

Virginia City proved an invigorating change for the two. They collaborated on sixteen books during the next twelve years. In 1952 they revived the *Territorial Enterprise*, the legendary nineteenth-century Virginia City newspaper. The two recruited impressive contributors to the paper, including Nevada novelist Walter Van Tilburg Clark, Pulitzer Prize–winning historian Bernard De Voto, and Smithsonian folklorist Duncan Emrich. Within two years, the lively and literate publication had more than 6,000 subscribers from around the world.

Beebe and Clegg's activities revived Virginia City. Entrepreneurs renovated dilapidated old storefronts. Residents spruced up aging Victorian homes with new paint and trim. The attention that Beebe and Clegg attracted to Virginia City produced a dramatic increase in the number of tourists heading to the historic mining town—which mortified Beebe, who resented the intrusion. Meanwhile, Virginia City had also gained national exposure from being featured, albeit in a highly fictionalized way, in the popular television western *Bonanza.*

In 1960 Beebe and Clegg sold the *Territorial Enterprise* and moved to Hillsborough, near San Francisco, though they kept their house in Virginia City. Beebe's health was beginning to decline from a lifetime of excessive eating and drinking, and he died of heart failure in 1966. Clegg sold the Virginia City house in 1978 and remained in Hillsborough until his death a year later.

### Historic Virginia City

Today's Virginia City is a popular tourist destination with its wooden sidewalks and historic buildings, many of which are open to the public. For instance, "the Castle" on South B Street is an impressive mansion built between 1863 and 1868 by a mining superintendent with a taste for finer things. The home, open in the summer, boasts Italian marble, Czechoslovakian rock crystal, silver doorknobs, and black-walnut paneling.

Other noteworthy historic structures include Piper's Opera House on the corner of B and Union Streets, built in 1885, and St. Mary in the Mountains Catholic Church, on the corner of Taylor and E Streets, erected in 1877. Virginia City's main boulevard, C Street, is lined with saloons, shops, and museums that cater to visitors.

# US 50
# CARSON CITY–STATELINE
### 26 MILES

## LAKE TAHOE

It is easy to see why Mark Twain once called Lake Tahoe "the fairest picture the whole earth affords." Nestled in a deep depression at 6,229 feet elevation in the Sierra Nevada, Tahoe is one of America's most beautiful and photogenic alpine lakes. At twenty-two miles long and twelve miles wide, it is also the largest alpine lake in North America.

Lake Tahoe began to take shape about 25 million years ago when the region underwent severe upheavals and a huge trough formed along a fault in the Sierra Nevada. Later, volcanoes shook the area and massive lava flows blocked the southern end of the trough. Then, 8,000 to 9,000 years ago, a gigantic glacier moved into the region from the south. When the glacier finally melted, it filled the trough with water and a lake was born.

The Washo tribe, who lived in the Lake Tahoe region for thousands of years, had another explanation for the creation of the lake. According to their legend, a character known as Damalalii the Weasel captured a water baby—a small gray creature with long dark hair. Damalalii scalped the magical water baby, who became very angry and began to flood the entire area. The weasel soon realized that the only way he could avoid drowning would be to return the water baby's scalp, which he did. The water receded and left behind Lake Tahoe.

The first non-Indian to see Lake Tahoe was explorer John C. Frémont, who viewed the lake from the top of Red Lake Peak in February 1844, on his second expedition to explore the West. Though it was winter, Frémont's party persisted through the snowpacked Sierras, determined to reach Sutter's Fort in California. From his vantage point Frémont was nearly fifteen miles south of the lake, but he was impressed by its beauty. He named it Bonpland, after the famous nineteenth-century French botanist Aime Jacques Alexandre Bonpland. In 1852, however, the lake was renamed Lake Bigler, in honor of California governor John Bigler. But when Bigler, a Confederate sympathizer, fell into disfavor in the 1860s, the name Lake Tahoe was adopted.

There are several different theories about the origin of the name Tahoe. One claims it is Washo for "big water in the high place." Deke Castleman asserts in his book *The Nevada Handbook* that the Washo name for the lake was *Da-ow-a-ga*, meaning "edge of the lake," and that this is generally considered the forerunner of the name Tahoe. James H. Simpson, who led an expedition across Nevada in 1859, wrote the name of the lake as *Ta-hou*, which he said was Washo for "sea." Henry De Groot, author of an 1876 history of Virginia City, wrote that the lake was called *Tah-hoe-ee*, translated as "big lake or water."

There is also a Washo legend that says the lake was named after a young brave who fought and killed a terrible monster, called the Ong, that lived in the lake. According to the tale, the Ong had an evil-looking human face, giant wings, webbed feet, and massive armored scales that could not be pierced by spears or arrows. The creature lived at the bottom of the lake but would surface periodically to search for humans on which to feast. The young man, who was named Tahoe, hoped to prove his courage by slaying the monster. He allowed the beast to capture him and managed to kill it by shooting poisoned arrows into its mouth. In gratitude, the tribe's chief gave Tahoe his daughter in marriage and named the lake after the young hero.

### Lake Tahoe's Development

Trader Martin Smith established the Tahoe Basin's first post at the present site of Meyers, south of Lake Tahoe, in 1851, but the surrounding area remained a remote wilderness for another decade. In the early 1860s, the need for wood for Virginia City's mines spurred rapid development of a timber industry here. Within a short time, investors had built roads and way stations around the lake, constructed sawmills, and removed millions of board feet of lumber from the surrounding slopes.

In 1873 Henry M. Yerington, one of the owners of the Virginia & Truckee Railroad, and industrialist Duane LeRoy Bliss established the Carson & Tahoe

*Emerald Bay on Lake Tahoe.*

Lumber & Fluming Company. The company soon developed a complex network of sawmills, flumes, chutes—even a railroad—to remove wood from Lake Tahoe. By 1895 the company had harvested approximately 50,000 of the total 51,000 acres of forested land on the Nevada side of the lake. Fortunately, the federal government planted new trees in the basin, and now, a century later, the lake is forested again.

Vacationing Californians discovered Lake Tahoe's natural assets in the late nineteenth and early twentieth centuries. Several rustic yet luxurious resorts opened at the lake, including the Tallac Hotel on the southwestern shore and the Tahoe Tavern near Tahoe City. In 1896 the two-hundred-passenger steamer *Tahoe* began shuttling passengers around the lake. It operated until 1940.

In the 1920s some of America's richest citizens adopted Lake Tahoe and built summer homes there. Among the most opulent residences are Vikingsholm, a Scandinavian-inspired mansion at Emerald Bay; Valhalla, a massive lodge near Richardson Bay; Thunderbird Lodge near Incline Village, built in 1939 by San Francisco multimillionaire George Whittel; and Fleur du Lac, California industrialist Henry J. Kaiser's stone compound on the lake's west side. The Kaiser retreat appeared as the Corleone family's summer house in the film *The Godfather Part Two*. Lake Tahoe's famous south-shore hotel-casinos did not appear until after World War II, when developers improved the roads leading to the lake and casinos took over the Nevada side of the California-Nevada border.

### Mark Twain at Lake Tahoe

In 1861 Mark Twain made two trips to Lake Tahoe. His first visit, in late August, was brief, but in September he returned with his friend Tom Nye and camped for three weeks near what is now Glenbrook. This was the visit he wrote of in *Roughing It*, his book about his years in Nevada. "Three months of camp life on Lake Tahoe would restore an Egyptian mummy to his pristine vigor and give him an appetite like an alligator," wrote Twain. He also wrote of Tahoe's remarkable purity:

> So singularly clear was the water that when it was only twenty or thirty feet deep the bottom was so perfectly distinct that the boat seemed floating in the air! Yes, where it was even eighty feet deep. Every little pebble was distinct, every speckled trout, every hand's-breadth of sand . . . so empty and airy did all spaces seem below us, and so strong was the sense of floating high aloft in mid-nothing-ness, that we called these boat excursions "balloon voyages."

## GLENBROOK

The historic settlement of Glenbrook, just off US 50 on the shores of Lake Tahoe, was founded in the spring of 1860 by Captain Augustus W. Pray, N. E. Murdock, G. W. Warren, and Rufus Walton. The four claimed squatters' rights to the land, including a lush meadow on Lake Tahoe's eastern shore and thick pine forests on the property's other three sides. A small stream running through the meadow inspired the name, originally written as two words.

The four men started a small farm on the property. The following year, Pray and partners Charles R. Barrett and John D. Winters formed the Lake Bigler Lumber Company. They built a small sawmill that soon produced more than 10,000 board feet a day. By 1862, Pray had bought out his partners and acquired nearly 700 acres at Glenbrook. A year later, however, he sold 45 acres of land back to Winters, who built the settlement's first hotel, the Glen Brook House. The following year Pray built the Lake Shore House, Glenbrook's second hotel. As a further attraction he added a miniature steamer ship, the *Governor Blaisdel*, to ferry tourists around the lake.

In 1870 William Sharon and other Bank of California investors, collectively known as the Bank Crowd, acquired 200 acres of land at Glenbrook, including the Glen Brook House. Over the next few years, the Bank Crowd extensively expanded lumber operations at Glenbrook. In 1874–75 additional investors built the Lake Tahoe (Narrow Gauge) Railroad between Glenbrook and Summit Camp, a logging camp above Spooner Lake. While less than nine miles long, the line played an important role in Lake Tahoe's lumber business and ran for twenty-three years. But Glenbrook's lumber operations finally closed in the early 1890s, after decimating most of the trees on Lake Tahoe's slopes.

## CAVE ROCK

Heading south on US 50 from Glenbrook, you will pass through the Cave Rock Tunnel. Cave Rock formed about 5 million years ago during the great volcanic upheaval that created Lake Tahoe. In his California survey report of 1855, George H. Goddard described Cave Rock as a "Legendary Cave." The

*Lake Tahoe's Cave Rock, source of many Washo legends.*

legend belonged to the native Washo people. They said the Great Spirit formed the cave when Lake Tahoe rose high and threatened to drown the Washo, who lived near a tremendous rock. The Great Spirit thrust his spear into the rock and made a cave where the water could drain.

In another version of the legend, the "cruel and evil" Paiute, traditional enemies of the Washo, tried to conquer and enslave the tribe. The God of the World came to the Washo's rescue by creating the cave and imprisoning the Paiute inside of it. There God transformed the evil ones into demons who were afraid of the lake and so could never leave the cave. Their cries and moans can sometimes be heard coming from Cave Rock. This particular legend may have evolved from the many stories in which the cave is the site of fierce turf battles between the Washo and Paiute tribes over who could fish and hunt at Lake Tahoe.

These days one can only imagine what Cave Rock once looked like because it was turned into the Cave Rock Tunnel in the early part of the twentieth century. Construction crews dug a 200-foot passage through the back of the cave and blasted a parallel tunnel through adjacent rock. You can see the rough rock of the original cave walls along several hundred feet of the west (southbound) tunnel.

To the immediate west of the tunnel are remnants of the original Lake Bigler Toll Road, a privately financed road around Lake Tahoe's east shore that once circled Cave Rock. In the mid-1860s the Lake Bigler Toll Road Company constructed the one-mile road, costing about $40,000, along the west face of the rock. At the time, this was the most expensive stretch of road between Placerville, California, and Washoe City. A quarter mile or so of the road still exists, including some hand-chiseled stone buttresses. At the westernmost point, a now-collapsed 100-foot trestle bridge extended the road out over the lake. Look down at the rocks and water below and you will understand why the tunnels were built.

On the north side of Cave Rock, below the tunnel at the waterline, there are several shapes in the rock face, and they have names. The Lady of the Lake is a fifty-foot-tall profile, complete with eyelashes. There is also the Gorilla Profile on the upper curve of the rock. On the south face of the cave are several smaller caves set in the granite. A fairly large one sits above the median between the north and southbound traffic lanes. On some days you can hear the wind whistling through the caves—or perhaps it is the faint wailing of the demons.

## ZEPHYR COVE

Andrew Boynton Gardinier, a French Canadian who homesteaded 160 acres on Lake Tahoe's east shore, established the settlement of Zephyr Cove, three miles south of Cave Rock on US 50, in 1862. Gardinier built a small hotel, the Zephyr Cove House, and prospered by catering to travelers between California and Virginia City. But by 1870, traffic had dwindled and he sold his holdings to Captain Augustus Pray, who wanted the property's timber. Pray closed the hotel and later leased it out as a residence. The property changed owners several times over the next few decades before becoming part of George Whittell's land holdings in 1938.

More recently, Zephyr Cove has become the site of a popular resort and restaurant. The Zephyr Cove Resort caters to snowmobilers in winter, and in fair weather tourists gather on the dock at the cove to board the *M.S. Dixie II* paddle wheeler and the *S.S. Woodwind* trimaran for excursions on the lake.

## STATELINE

South Lake Tahoe's casino district on the California border, in the town aptly called Stateline, began to develop in the late 1940s after Harvey Gross, a Sacramento meat wholesaler, and his wife, Llewellyn, opened the Wagon Wheel Saloon. It was a one-room log cabin with three slot machines, six stools at a counter, and a couple of pool tables. Gross, who sold meat to many of the small casinos near the California-Nevada border, believed that the area had great potential as a gambling destination catering to northern Californians looking for a weekend getaway.

In 1960 Gross erected the lake's first high-rise building, an eleven-story, 200-room hotel-casino that became known as Harvey's. Gross's success encouraged William F. Harrah, who owned Harrah's hotel-casino in Reno, and builder Del Webb, who constructed Bugsy Siegel's Flamingo Hotel in Las Vegas, to also build casinos at South Lake Tahoe.

Stateline today has larger and more modern versions of many of the original hotel-casinos. Harvey's now has 740 rooms and a Hard Rock Cafe, while Harrah's includes an eighteen-story hotel tower. Del Webb's property, originally called the Sahara Tahoe, is now the Tahoe Horizon, under different ownership. A fourth major hotel property, Caesar's Tahoe, a sister property of Caesar's Palace in Las Vegas, opened in 1980.

### Friday's Station

A man known as "Friday" Burke established Friday's Station in 1860. This charming two-story hotel in Edgewood, which is now a golf course a half mile north of Stateline, also served as a Pony Express station. Famed rider "Pony Bob" Haslem was among those headquartered there. You can see the elegant former hotel, restored as a private residence, from US 50.

# NV 28
# US 50–Crystal Bay
### 18 MILES

## MARLETTE LAKE

Nestled in the mountains 1,800 feet over Lake Tahoe is an artificial body of water known as Marlette Lake. Magnates Henry M. Yerington and Duane Bliss created the lake in the late 1860s by building a small earthen dam across the Marlette Basin. By the 1870s, Virginia City needed more water than it had, so Yerington and Bliss agreed to sell water from Marlette Lake to the Virginia & Gold Hill Water Company, supplier to the Comstock mining communities. They doubled Marlette Lake's capacity with the construction of a larger, dirt-and-masonry dam and built a thirty-two-mile-long network of flumes and pipes that fed Virginia City 6.6 million gallons of water every twenty-four hours.

Today, visitors can reach Marlette Lake, off the northeast side of Lake Tahoe just east of NV 28, on foot from the Lake Tahoe Nevada State Park parking lot at Spooner Lake. From there a marked trail leads north about five miles to Marlette Lake. It is a popular place to hike and mountain bike. The abandoned flume from the lake to nearby Incline Village is one of the most heavily traveled mountain-bike trails in the Sierra Nevada.

## INCLINE VILLAGE

The town of Incline Village sits along NV 28 near the northernmost tip of Lake Tahoe. In the late 1870s and 1880s, Incline Village was the site of a remarkable steam-powered cable railway, the Great Incline Tramway. It hauled

*Marlette Lake.*

logs nearly 4,000 feet up the steep slope of Incline Summit, where flumes then carried the logs down to Washoe Valley. Walter Scott Hobart's Sierra Nevada Wood & Lumber Company owned the tram system and purchased or leased nearly every square foot of timberland on the northeast shore of Lake Tahoe.

The lumber company operated the tramway until they had stripped the surrounding mountains of their trees in the mid-1890s. Then the mill machinery and other equipment were relocated to the California side of the lake and the facility was renamed Hobart Mills. In seventeen years, the Incline facility processed more than 200 million board feet of lumber, most used as underground supports in the Comstock mines. In the 1950s housing developers established Incline Village near the old lumber operation.

### Ponderosa Ranch

Nestled on a hillside at the south end of Incline Village is the Ponderosa Ranch, a faithful re-creation of the set used in the popular 1960s television show *Bonanza.* The ranch, built a few years after the show began airing, was in fact sometimes used as a location for filming exteriors for the series.

Now a western-theme park with hayrides, barbecues, and mock shoot-outs, the Ponderosa Ranch is more than simply a backdrop. Owners Bill and Joyce Anderson designed an idealized western town, including a Main Street lined with frontier-style storefronts. There are horse-drawn carriages, thousands of rare antiques, and one of the world's largest collections of antique farm equipment. The Church of the Ponderosa is a popular wedding venue, and the general store is filled with *Bonanza* souvenirs.

## CRYSTAL BAY

Contrary to popular belief, Crystal Bay, on the north end of Lake Tahoe at the California border, was not named for Lake Tahoe's famed clarity. It was named after George I. Crystal, the owner of a lumber company who acquired large tracts of forest on the northwest shore of Lake Tahoe in the 1860s. In the 1870s lumbermen Seneca Marlette and Gilman Folsom purchased Crystal Bay and transported logs out of the basin via the Great Incline Tramway. By the mid-1890s the area's timber resources were gone, and the camp at Crystal Bay was abandoned.

### Cal Neva Lodge

In the 1920s Crystal Bay became a resort community with the opening of the Cal Neva Lodge, a rustic log structure that straddled the California-Nevada state line. At first it was used as a guest house, and later it became a casino. In 1928 Norman Biltz, a Lake Tahoe real estate promoter who by the early 1930s owned 45,000 acres on Lake Tahoe, bought the Cal Neva. Two years later Biltz sold the lodge to Reno gamblers Bill Graham and Jim McKay.

A mysterious fire destroyed the Cal Neva in 1937—there were rumors that Graham and McKay wanted the insurance money—but Biltz immediately rebuilt it and sold it to Sanford "Sandy" Adler, a Reno casino owner. Adler created the club's famous Indian Room, also called the Wigwam Room, and began offering big-name entertainment.

In 1955 entrepreneur Bert "Wingy" Grober acquired the Cal Neva. Grober had previously operated a successful steak house in Miami and over the years had befriended many celebrities, including the Kennedy family and singer Frank Sinatra. The Cal Neva became a popular hangout for show-business personalities and politicians. In 1960 Grober sold the lodge to Sinatra, who remodeled the property and persuaded many of his entertainment-industry friends to perform. But the Nevada Gaming Control Board revoked Sinatra's gaming license in 1963 because of his personal association with organized-crime figures.

Since then, the nine-story Cal Neva has changed hands many times. Today, Chuck Bluth owns the lodge, which has retained much of its rustic charm. With its log exterior, stone vestibule, and stone flooring, it is still a popular North Lake Tahoe resort.

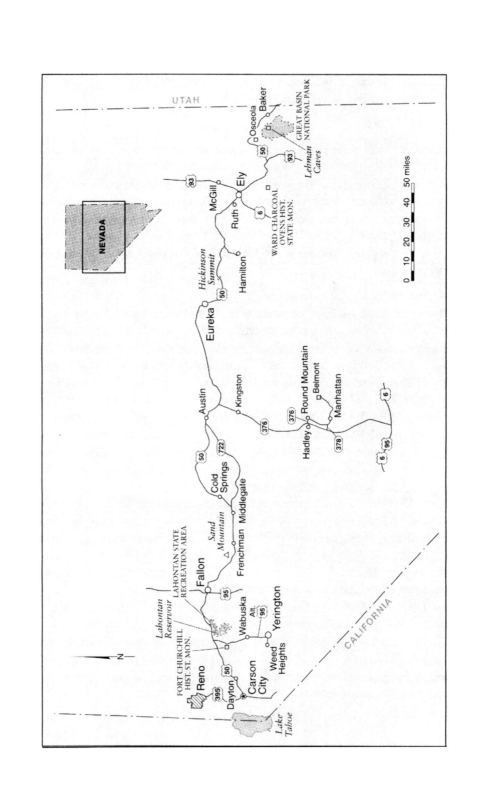

## 3

# US 50: The Loneliest Road in America

*"It's totally empty,"* says an AAA counselor. *"There are no points of interest. We don't recommend it." The 287-mile stretch of US 50, running from Ely to Fernly [sic], Nev., passes nine towns, two abandoned mining camps, a few gas pumps and an occasional coyote. "We warn all motorists not to drive there," says the AAA rep, "unless they're confident of their survival skills."*

—Life magazine article, "America the . . . ,"
describing US 50 in Nevada as America's "Loneliest Road," July 1986

*Life* magazine had it wrong. US 50 isn't lonely—it just looks that way because everything is so spread out. This main highway bisecting Nevada is one of the most scenic and historically significant roads in the state. This route has been in use since 1859, when Captain James H. Simpson of the U.S. Army Topographical Corps led a group of sixty-four men—including scientists, guides, mapmakers, and illustrators—across central Nevada.

Simpson's expedition was looking for a shorter wagon route for the U.S. military between Camp Floyd, south of Salt Lake City, Utah, and Genoa, Nevada. The existing route across Nevada followed the meandering Humboldt River; a more direct route would help bring the West closer to the rest of the country.

The Simpson expedition was a thorough scientific effort to map and explore the Great Basin. The party made detailed maps of the area and kept complete records of the flora, fauna, and geology, as well as noting the Native Americans they encountered. Two artists, H. V. A. von Breckh and J. J. Young, recorded a number of scenes of Nevada in watercolor during the course of the journey. These are the earliest known pictures of the state.

The expedition reached Dayton, near Genoa, on July 11, 1859. In the report, Simpson casually mentions seeing a gambling hall and an opium den there and hearing about promising gold discoveries in Gold Canyon. Simpson's

*US 50 in Nevada, "the Loneliest Road in America."*

notation about Gold Canyon was one of the earliest references to what became known as the Comstock Lode. In Carson City, Simpson had dinner with
Major William Ormsby. After reaching Genoa, he received a guided tour of the
Sierra Nevada and Lake Tahoe from Snowshoe Thompson, the skiing mail
carrier who was the first to deliver a regular route across the mountains.

Simpson's return trip was a bit more challenging because he made the journey during the hottest part of the summer. Simpson found that now, unlike
during his westbound trip earlier in the season, water and grass were not plentiful. Despite the difficult circumstances, the expedition recrossed the state
without incident and Simpson returned to Washington.

Simpson's new trail across central Nevada was several hundred miles shorter
than the route California-bound emigrants had previously traveled. And it
proved of even greater value about a year later, when the Pony Express followed this route. Later, the Overland Mail & Stage Company incorporated
much of the former Pony Express route and many of its stations.

In 1862, shortly after the Pony Express ceased its operations, William Talcott,
a former express rider, discovered silver in the Toiyabe Mountains of central
Nevada. Within a short time, thousands of prospectors had flocked to the area
and established the town of Austin. Because of its abundant grass and water,
Austin also served as an important rest stop for emigrants heading to California.

Many now followed the newer Central Overland Trail, as Simpson's route was known, rather than travel on the longer, more circuitous Humboldt Trail.

While much of the Overland Trail traffic moved north when the transcontinental railroad opened in 1869, the route remained a lifeline from the 1870s to the 1890s for many central Nevada communities, including Eureka, the White Pine Mining District, Hot Creek, Belmont, and Berlin. Several rail lines were built through central Nevada during the 1870s and 1880s, but all ran in a north-south direction. Those going east and west still used the trail as a wagon road.

In 1912 what had been the Overland Trail became part of the Lincoln Highway, America's first transcontinental road. Its builders incorporated existing roads when possible and developed linking roads where they did not exist. Initially, much of the route was not paved. Distinctive signs of red, white, and blue marked the highway the entire way.

As part of the public-relations effort to promote automobile travel, the *Complete Official Road Guide of the Lincoln Highway* series first appeared in 1916. The guides reassured travelers about towns, services, and amenities along the route while reminding them of the challenges of the past:

> As one speeds over the Lincoln Highway in his modern automobile, it is hard to realize the slow moving oxen, painfully dragging the cumbersome "prairie schooner" of '49, the women and children riding inside the canvas covered body, the stifling heat, the dust of the desert rising in choking clouds, the attacks by Indians, the want of water and sometimes food and all the suffering and yearning, . . . an almost interminable journey which now is made from coast to coast in twenty days with nothing but enjoyment from one end to the other.

Now that's a ringing endorsement.

The guides also instructed travelers that although supplies could usually be found along the route, there was one exception—Nevada. West of Salt Lake City, motorists were urged to carry provisions including a slab of bacon, three cans each of various fruits and vegetables, four loaves of bread, two pounds of rice, ten pounds of potatoes, a dozen boxes of matches, and much more.

In 1919 the federal government decided to promote transcontinental travel by sending a convoy of seventy-two military vehicles, carrying 280 officers and enlisted men, across the Lincoln Highway. Among those making the journey was Captain Dwight D. Eisenhower, a member of the Tank Corps, who many years later wrote of the trip:

> I wanted to go along partly for a lark and partly to learn. To those who have known only concrete and macadam highways of gentle grades and engineered curves, such a trip might have seemed humdrum. But it had never been attempted before and in those days we were not sure that it could be accomplished at all.

The convoy made the journey from Washington D.C. to San Francisco in sixty-two days, only about four days behind its original schedule. Along the way, they rebuilt sixty-five bridges, ballasted narrow roads, and filled hundreds of potholes and washouts. Upon completing the trip, the convoy's commander, Lieutenant Colonel Charles W. McClure, pronounced the Lincoln Highway "entirely unsuited" for heavy traffic and said his troops had reached California only "by pushing, shoving and by the will of God."

A subsequent military report stressed the need for developing a high-quality interstate highway system. It was not until 1956 that Congress approved the Interstate Highway Act, which appropriated $129 billion for a national highway network. Interestingly, the legislation was signed into law by President Dwight D. Eisenhower, who, of course, had firsthand knowledge of the need for better roads.

The Lincoln Highway lost its unique identity with passage of the 1925 Federal Aid Road Act. This legislation replaced the use of colorful names with a numbered system, and the Lincoln Highway became US 50, a transcontinental route that stretched 3,073 miles from Ocean City, Maryland, to Sacramento, California.

US 50 earned a degree of notoriety—and a new nickname—in 1986 when *Life* magazine designated the Nevada portion of the route as "the Loneliest Road in America." While *Life* was probably just taking a little poetic license in its description of this remote stretch of road, the folks living along the way were initially annoyed by the characterization. Then, in concert with the Nevada Commission on Tourism, they decided to embrace the idea and developed a tongue-in-cheek "Highway 50 Survival Kit" as well as T-shirts, bumper stickers, pins, and other geegaws with the "Loneliest Road" legend.

Several communities changed their usual promotions to capitalize on the "lonely" theme. Eureka became "the Loneliest Town on the Loneliest Road." Fallon boasted it had "the Loneliest Museum on the Loneliest Road." And the Churchill County Telephone Company placed a solar-powered telephone near Sand Mountain with a sign proclaiming it "the Loneliest Phone."

# US 50
# BAKER–ELY
### 62 MILES

## BAKER

Baker, five miles south of US 50 on NV 487, is a quaint, quiet community with a year-round population of about sixty-five. Its two biggest industries are cattle and catering to tourists, most of whom are passing through on their way to Utah or Great Basin National Park. Baker was named for George W. Baker, one of the earliest settlers in the region. It was founded in the 1890s to serve area ranchers and miners and visitors to nearby Lehman Caves.

Along NV 488 from Baker to Great Basin National Park, playful folk-art sculptures sit on the fenceposts lining the road. Such objects as a skeleton on a bicycle, a grave with cowboy boots, and decorated cowboy hats—called "post-impression art" by the locals—brighten the way.

## GREAT BASIN NATIONAL PARK

On October 27, 1986, Congress created Great Basin National Park. The entrance is five and a half miles west of Baker via NV 488. It is the only national park dedicated to the ecology and natural history of the Great Basin. Within the park are seven of the eight Great Basin ecosystems, from the sagebrush-desert zone—with its jackrabbits, sagebrush, and cacti—to the treeless-alpine zone, home of golden eagles, ravens, holmgren buckwheat, and the endangered Nevada primrose. The park's 77,109 acres, in the Snake Range, encompass the second-highest point in Nevada (the 13,063-foot Wheeler Peak) and the state's only glacier.

Efforts to create the park began in the 1920s. Over the next six decades, however, local ranching and mining interests, fearful that a park would inhibit their ability to make a living, successfully fought numerous federal legislative

*Fence art by the Permanent Wave Society can be found roadside from Baker to Great Basin National Park.*

initiatives. But in the early 1980s, mining, heretofore eastern Nevada's primary source of jobs, virtually ceased, and local residents became more receptive to tourism—including the creation of a new national park—as it became an economic necessity.

The park's most popular attraction is Lehman Caves, among the most richly decorated limestone caverns in the country. Underground streams carved the caves over millions of years. The water dissolved the limestone, and the liquified calcium carbonate slowly precipitated into the stalagmites, stalactites, helictites, coral, and circular palettes you see today.

Absalom Lehman, a local farmer, discovered the caves in 1885. Lehman had attempted mining in both California and Australia with little success before settling near Baker to grow food for nearby mining camps. One day he found an opening in the mountainside above his ranch. Curious, he climbed inside

*Stands of ancient bristlecone pine near the base of Wheeler Peak in Great Basin National Park.*

with a candle lantern and discovered an extensive series of underground chambers. Lehman began taking visitors into the caves and even constructed a wooden staircase so they would not have to climb down a rope to view his fabulous find. In 1922 the caves were declared a national monument and came under the supervision of the National Park Service.

Great Basin National Park also has groves of bristlecone pine trees, some nearly 4,000 years old. Sadly, on August 7, 1964, while the groves were under the jurisdiction of the U. S. Forest Service, the world's oldest bristlecone pine was cut down, felled at the request of Donald R. Currey, a doctoral candidate at the University of North Carolina. The forest service gave him permission to cut the tree so he could study a cross section of the trunk and—ironically—determine its age. Because of the crooked way that bristlecones grow, it was difficult to get an accurate reading from a core sample. No one realized the significance of the tree Currey had chosen to study until it was too late. The tree, nicknamed Prometheus, turned out to be about 5,000 years old. Since then scientists have learned to cross-index multiple samples to determine the age of bristlecone pine trees.

The park's remaining bristlecones, while not as old, are also impressive. These gnarled, twisted giants possess great character and dignity. A developed trail leads to one of the largest groves, near the base of Wheeler Peak.

*Osceola Ditch*

Within Great Basin National Park, west of Lehman Caves, are remnants of one of eastern Nevada's most ambitious projects—the Osceola Ditch. In 1872 prospectors discovered gold south of Sacramento Pass, north of today's park boundary, in what would become the town of Osceola. Five years after the initial strike, miners uncovered extensive placer fields nearby. The town boomed, but organizers soon found that a lack of water limited their ability to develop the district, as placer mining requires water to wash the gold from the gravel.

In the 1880s work began on an eighteen-mile canal to capture water from streams at Wheeler Peak. At a cost of more than $250,000, three hundred laborers dug a 600-foot tunnel and built miles of wooden flumes to transport the water. While the ditch was the first successful hydraulic operation in the state, its usefulness was limited by the region's short summers and by leaks in the flumes from harsh winter freezes. By 1900 the ditch had deteriorated so much that it was abandoned. You can still see the ditch bed and find occasional pieces of weathered wood at the site.

## OSCEOLA

The turnoff from US 50 for the ghost town of Osceola is about fifteen miles northwest of Baker. From there take Osceola Road west about five miles to the site. Osceola was named for a Seminole chief. A gold strike there in 1872 spawned the town. It reached its peak in the mid-1880s, when it had more than 500 residents as well as electric lights—it was one of the few towns in Nevada at the time to have electric power—and the first telephone in White Pine County. Following several fires in the late 1880s, the town began a gradual decline. By 1900 the population had dwindled to about 100.

There were a number of unsuccessful attempts to revive Osceola's mines over the years, including a major effort in 1925. A fire destroyed most of the remaining buildings in the 1950s. The Osceola Cemetery, on a hill overlooking the town site, and a handful of ruins are about all that remain. Nevertheless, Osceola has the distinction of being the longest-lived placer mining camp in Nevada.

## THE WARD MINING DISTRICT

The still-active Ward Mining District is eighteen miles south of Ely, taking the signed dirt road west from US 50. In the summer of 1872, teamsters William Ballinger and John Henry discovered a rich silver outcropping while in search of their grazing bulls. Their discovery became the Paymaster Mine, which soon attracted hundreds of fortune seekers, and the camp grew into the town of Ward. Within three years, Ward had more than 1,000 people, the largest community in eastern Nevada. It was named for B. F. Ward, who with his two partners laid out the town site.

Ward's population peaked in 1877 with 2,000 residents, and the town was large enough to support two newspapers, a Wells Fargo office, a city hall, and a large business district. By 1880, however, the town was in a serious tailspin. The mines began shutting down and only about 250 residents remained. Promising discoveries at Cherry Creek, seventy miles to the north, had lured away many Ward miners. A fire destroyed many of the town's buildings, including the city hall and the school, in 1883. Two years later, only one business remained open in the struggling camp and the population had dwindled to twenty-five. In subsequent years, miners reworked the mines from 1910 to 1920, and again in the 1930s and in the 1960s.

Today, although Ward itself is gone, the area is again being actively mined. The ruins of old Ward are closed to the public, but the cemetery, one mile east, does have a handful of historic wooden and marble headstones for viewing. You can also visit the nearby Ward Charcoal Ovens, fascinating remnants of the old mining days.

### The Ward Charcoal Ovens

Six beehive-shaped charcoal ovens, constructed in 1876 to produce charcoal for the smelters, are the Ward Mining District's most enduring structures. The kilns, three miles south of the site of Ward via Cave Valley Road, are made of native rock. They stand thirty feet high and twenty-seven feet around at the

*The Ward Charcoal Ovens.* —Courtesy Nevada Department of Transportation

base. Each could hold thirty-five cords of piñon wood stacked in layers. The dome shape allowed for easy ignition, and the heat was controlled by opening and closing small vents at the base. Operation of the massive ovens shut down in the early 1880s, when Ward's mines played out.

Over the next century, these intriguing stone structures were used for a variety of purposes, including as stables and informal shelters for itinerate sheepherders and cowboys. The Nevada Division of State Parks acquired the kilns in 1969 and designated the Ward Charcoal Ovens Historic State Monument.

## TAYLOR

East across the wide Steptoe Valley from Ward was a mining community named Taylor. Prospectors discovered silver in Taylor Canyon in 1872, but it was not until 1880 that the district became active. In 1883 Taylor's mines produced $250,000 in ore, and the camp swelled to nearly 1,500 residents. But the silver waned after 1885, and within a decade the town was nearly empty.

The town of Taylor has disappeared, but miners have worked the district's mines nearly continuously over the years. In the early 1980s, Silver King Mines Inc. of Salt Lake City opened a $10 million mine, mill, and processing facility.

## ELY

In eastern Nevada, all roads lead to Ely. It sits in the shadow of the Schell Creek Range, at the confluence of three major highways—US 50, US 93, and US 6—and has long been the region's commercial center.

Ely was founded in 1870 following the discovery of rich mineral deposits in the area, including gold, silver, and copper. The town was originally known as Murray Creek Station and was little more than a stage stop with a few cabins. In 1878 its name was changed to honor Smith Ely, president of Selby Copper Mining and Smelting Company, which had built several smelters in the community. The Nevada legislature designated Ely the seat of White Pine County in 1887.

While miners first prospected for gold and silver, by the early twentieth century they had discovered that the region was flush with copper. In 1903 mining investor Mark Requa formed the White Pine Copper Company and began purchasing mines in the region. Two years later, after several more significant acquisitions, he pooled his assets and created the Nevada Consolidated Copper Company. The company controlled an estimated 26 million tons of copper reserves.

The company extracted copper ore from large pits near Ruth, five miles west of Ely. The largest was the Liberty Pit, which began as an underground mine in 1906 and grew into a manmade canyon that measured over a mile long, ⅝ mile wide, and nearly 1,000 feet deep by the time it closed in 1967. Once the ore was mined, it was loaded on railroad cars and carried 15 miles, going east through Ely, then north to the town of McGill, where it was smelted. The processed material, called blister copper, was then sent 140 miles north to the Southern Pacific line at Cobre, 39 miles east of Wells.

Ely enjoyed a period of relative prosperity lasting nearly eighty years—considerably longer than most mining communities. The Kennecott Copper Corporation purchased Nevada Consolidated in 1958 and continued operations until 1979. Regional smelters had produced more than 5 billion pounds of copper by 1963, and they made more money than was made from the Comstock Lode. You can still see the copper pits' massive tailing mounds from US 50 west of Ely.

Today Ely is a bustling town of 5,300 people. The historic Hotel Nevada, on the corner of Aultman and Fifth Streets, is the tallest building in Ely at six stories. Constructed in 1908, it remains one of the liveliest places in town, with dancing and a casino. The White Pine Public Museum, at 2000 Aultman, is jammed with historical photographs and artifacts including antique cowboy gear, Shoshone arrowheads, early-twentieth-century furniture and china, and railroad and mining equipment.

### East Ely

Of special historical interest in Ely is the neighborhood known as East Ely, along East Eleventh Street. East Ely developed as a second commercial center around the Nevada Northern Railway's maintenance yards and depot at the north end of Eleventh Street. The two-story sandstone Nevada Northern depot, built in 1907, was the main station and home office of the railroad, which operated between 1907 and 1981.

The handsome old depot is now the centerpiece of the Nevada Northern Railway Museum and Historic Railroad complex. The complex encompasses many of East Ely's historic buildings, as well as rolling train equipment and tracks. Adjacent to the depot is the Nevada Northern's former communications building, built in 1915, now used for museum and railroad offices. This utilitarian brick structure once housed the offices of the railroad's superintendent, trainmaster, chief clerk, and roadmaster. On the opposite side of the depot is the freight and express building, a wooden structure built in 1906, the oldest structure in the complex.

# US 50
# ELY–AUSTIN
### 147 MILES

## RUTH

Ruth is five miles west of Ely off US 50. The town's best claim to fame is that Thelma Catherine Ryan, a.k.a. Pat Nixon, may have been born there in 1912, although officially her birthplace is listed as Ely. Nixon herself made inconsistent claims regarding the place and circumstances of her birth. The former first lady's family moved to southern California a few years after she was born, and the reported site of her birth was swallowed up by an open-pit mine. In fact, in the late 1950s the Liberty Pit Mine devoured most of the original town site and Ruth had to be relocated.

Ruth traces its beginnings to 1903, when it was founded as a company town for workers employed at nearby copper mines. It was named for the daughter of one of the local mine owners. Within a year, Ruth had a post office, a hospital, and several boardinghouses—but no saloons because the mining company banned liquor in the town.

Originally, Ruth's mines were underground, but they were enlarged into open-pit operations after the introduction of steam shovels in 1907. By the time Pat Nixon was born, Ruth was already the site of one of the state's largest open-pit mines. In the late 1920s, the town had more than 2,000 residents.

Several companies had interests in Ruth's mining operations until the Kennecott Copper Corporation acquired and consolidated them in 1958. Immediately, the new owner began an aggressive expansion of the mines. That is when Ruth moved to its present location. The boom lasted until the early 1980s. Then Kennecott shut down operations due to dropping copper prices. In recent years, other mining companies have explored the area and some have begun reworking the mine pits.

## HAMILTON

The remains of Hamilton are forty-six miles west of Ely. To reach it take US 50 west from Ely for thirty-seven miles, then exit south at the sign on a dirt road and continue nine miles. Hamilton was once White Pine County's largest community, with more than 12,000 residents, twelve years before Cherry Creek made that claim. Prospectors discovered Hamilton's silver and gold resources in late 1867. The find sparked one of the most intense mining rushes in the state's history—newspapers called it "White Pine Fever"—and thousands of people poured into the area.

By May 1868 a town site had been platted at the base of Treasure Hill. Because there were many caves in the area, the town was named Cave City. As the place grew, it changed its name to Hamilton in honor of W. H. Hamilton, one of the town's founders. By the spring of 1869, an estimated 10,000 people lived in Hamilton. For the next few years, the community thrived as the commercial center of the White Pine Mining District, which included the nearby towns of Shermantown, Eberhardt, and Treasure City. Hamilton became the county seat in 1869.

*The brick ruins of Hamilton's J. B. Withington Hotel.*

In its heyday, Hamilton had more than a hundred saloons, sixty general stores, several stage lines, its own water company, and dozens of other businesses. But the town's prosperity was short-lived; the silver deposits were less extensive than originally believed. By 1871 the town was in rapid decline. Two years later, a local merchant tried to torch his business for the insurance money and caused damages of more than $500,000 to the business district. By 1875 the town's population had shrunk to less than 500. Ten years later another fire destroyed the courthouse and many other buildings. In 1887 the county seat was moved to more populous Ely. The post office managed to stay open until 1931.

Hamilton is no longer inhabited. Visitors can see the town's ruins, including what was once the two-story J. B. Withington Hotel, erected in 1869. Old photographs from as recently as the 1940s show that it was an impressive structure made of native sandstone, with arched doors and windows and several chimneys. The hotel was deserted in the late nineteenth century, however, and over the years the outer walls began to decay, then mostly collapsed during an earthquake in the 1950s. All that remains today is a mound of sandstone and red brick.

A few hundred yards from the hotel is the brick front wall of the Wells Fargo building. Scraps of wood and mortar somehow hold together this leaning monolith, indicating a high quality of workmanship. Among the scattered mounds of rubble and sagebrush are foundations, stone walls, and studs from other buildings. The ruins are spread across the entirety of the original town site. Surrounding the historic remains are reminders of more modern mining operations, including rusted trailers on a hillside, large metal storage buildings, assorted mining equipment, and the shallow pool of an abandoned leach pond.

Unfortunately, Hamilton's accessibility contributed to the loss of many of its artifacts. Residents of nearby communities tell of ghost-town souvenir hunters who nearly looted Hamilton out of existence during the 1950s.

## EUREKA

In 1864 five men, W. O. Arnold, W. R. Tannehill, G. J. Tannehill, I. W. Stotts, and Moses Wilson, staked promising silver claims in the vicinity of what would become Eureka, seventy-seven miles west of Ely on US 50. These prospectors soon sold their claims to a New York mining company, which gradually developed the district.

A high percentage of lead found in the silver ore created smelting problems and prevented significant mining until 1869, when the company built a draft furnace that could accommodate the silver-lead deposits. Within a short time a ragtag community of canvas tents, crude log cabins, and wooden shanties had appeared. By October 1869 about 100 people lived in the community, which was originally named Napias, from the Shoshone word for "silver." The name was changed shortly after to Eureka.

The community grew quickly during the 1870s, reaching a peak population of about 9,000 residents in 1878. At its height, the town had its own municipal water company, six newspapers, and more than a hundred saloons. The town also supported twenty-four smelters, which poured a near-constant stream of smoke into the air. As a result, Eureka earned the less-than-flattering nickname "Pittsburgh of the West."

In 1875 the Eureka & Palisade Railroad connected Eureka's mines with the Central Pacific Railroad line at Palisade, west of Carlin. The line ceased operations in 1900 but was revived in 1912 and renamed the Eureka-Nevada Railroad. The railroad managed to survive until 1938.

Haphazard construction made early Eureka vulnerable to fire, and the first occurred in 1872. Three years later another fire destroyed several major downtown buildings—despite the best efforts of a new steam-powered water pump the community had purchased. Eureka's worst fire took place in April 1879, when nearly half the town burned. Flash floods also tore through the town's flimsy structures in 1874, 1876, and 1878. Seventeen people died during the flood of 1874.

By the late 1870s, Eureka's residents had begun rebuilding their homes and businesses out of fire-resistant brick, with iron shutters and doors. The solid construction lessened the potential for fires and allowed the town to survive the ravages of time better than most mining towns. Well-preserved brick buildings, most of them still in use, line Eureka's main street today.

Eureka's mines began to fail in the mid-1880s, and the town gradually declined over the next twenty years. The mines reopened in 1905, and that revival lasted about five years. Because it has remained the county seat, Eureka was never completely deserted and supports a permanent population of about 200.

### The Charcoal Burners' War of 1879

In the late 1870s, Eureka's two dozen smelters consumed massive amounts of charcoal. Smelter furnaces had to reach extremely high temperatures to process ore. Hundreds of men, mostly from Italy, worked as woodcutters and charcoal burners. Known as *carbonari*, Italian for "charcoal-burner," the men cut juniper and pine in the surrounding mountains, then carried the wood to huge, beehive-shaped ovens or covered charcoal pits. The ovens' intense heat converted the wood to charcoal.

In 1879 the smelter owners conspired to pay the carbonari lower wages. The workers responded by organizing the Charcoal Burners' Association and boycotting Eureka's smelters. They also blocked attempts to bring wood into the city. Tensions escalated when the smelter owners telegraphed Governor John Kinkead to request that state militia be brought in. Kinkead declined to become involved, but meanwhile an overzealous local sheriff's posse rode out to a carbonari camp at Fish Creek, about thirty miles south of Eureka, and attacked the workers, killing five. Even though no one was ever charged with the murders, the two sides were able to negotiate a compromise.

*Historic Eureka*

Two of Eureka's most prominent historic buildings are the Eureka County Courthouse and the Eureka Opera House. The two-story brick courthouse, completed in 1880 and recently restored, is one of the state's most elegant halls of justice, with its elaborate white cornices. Like many of Eureka's buildings, the courthouse has iron shutters on its doors and windows as protection against fire. The Eureka Opera House, restored and reopened as a convention center in the mid-1990s, was also built in 1880. It has two-foot-thick masonry walls, a brick-and-iron facade, and a slate roof, making it completely fireproof.

Eureka also has many other noteworthy historic structures. The Tannehill log cabin, east of town on US 50, is Eureka's oldest existing building, built in either 1864 or 1865. It may have been the first house built in Eureka. The cabin later served as the town's first commercial store. St. Brendan's Catholic Church was built in 1874 of volcanic tuff, a local stone taken from a quarry on the west end of town. The church is still is use.

The Eureka Sentinel Museum, behind the courthouse, was built in 1879. The two-story brick building is easily recognized by its three distinctive arched

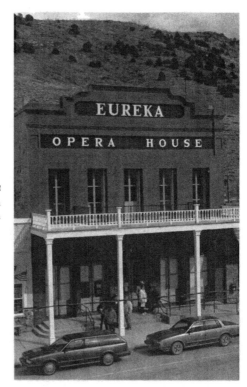

*The Eureka Opera House.* —Courtesy Nevada Commission on Tourism

doorways. The local newspaper was housed here for more than eighty years. The museum has an extensive collection of historic photographs as well as antique mining equipment and an 1872 printing press.

In addition to its dozens of historic buildings, Eureka has five large grave-yards on the western edge of the town—the city, county, Odd Fellows, Masonic, and Catholic cemeteries. In the 1880s locals called this part of town "Graveyard Flat" or "Death Valley." The Chinese and Jewish cemeteries that were also once here have mostly disappeared due to vandalism and neglect.

## HICKISON SUMMIT

Hickison Summit is about fifty miles west of Eureka, accessible by a marked dirt road off US 50. The Bureau of Land Management maintains a petroglyph site and picnic area there. An interpretive trail leads from the parking lot to the petroglyphs carved into the nearby cliffs.

*Petroglyphs at Hickison Summit.*

While archaeologists are uncertain about the meaning of these petroglyphs, the terrain at Hickison Summit supports the theory that they were somehow related to hunting and gathering food. In addition to the plentiful piñons, a source of pine nuts, the area's steep cliffs and narrow passes lent themselves to ambushing migrating deer. The Hickison Summit petroglyphs depict human stick figures as well as concentric circles and other designs.

## AUSTIN
Writer Oscar Lewis once called Austin "the town that died laughing." But to paraphrase Mark Twain—another writer who spent a little time in Nevada—reports of the town's demise are greatly exaggerated. It is true that Austin, like most nineteenth-century Nevada mining towns, has been in decline for years, but this community of about 600 has managed to survive.

Lewis, however, was half right: Austinites enjoy a good joke. The town, seventy miles west of Eureka on US 50, has been the site of some of the more outrageous hoaxes ever perpetrated in the Silver State. The instigator of some of this hilarity was the local newspaper, the *Reese River Reveille,* in publication since May 16, 1863. In the early 1870s the paper came under the guidance of editor Fred Hunt. In 1873 Hunt, always searching for ways to fill space, concocted a story about a social club dedicated to the fine art of prevarication, the Sazerac Lying Club.

In his initial story, Hunt simply announced the organization of the club and election of its officers—all of it, of course, fabricated. In the following months, he entertained readers by repeating the wild yarns and outrageous tales allegedly told by the club's members. Other western newspapers printed the stories, and eventually Austin's famed fibbing club was the subject of a short book, a collection of Hunt's columns called *The Sazerac Lying Club: A Nevada Book,* published in 1878.

The town's sensibility also found expression in the name of its 2.8-mile steam railroad, built in 1880. The narrow-gauge line replaced a mule-driven trolley that had struggled to haul freight up the town's steep main street. Hence the train's name, Mule's Relief.

Austin gained a measure of notoriety in the 1860s with an investment scandal involving a company called the Reese River Navigation Company. It sold stock in a steamboat freight service to East Coast investors. Unfortunately for those investors, the Reese River is little more than a sickly rivulet that would not float a canoe—there was no steamboat operation.

There is more to Austin's history than tall tales, scams, and legends. In May 1862 William H. Talcott, an ex–Pony Express rider, was gathering wood for the stage stop at Jacob's Station in central Nevada. Talcott wandered into nearby Pony Canyon, where he spotted an intriguing quartz ledge and took ore samples. Talcott sent the rocks to Virginia City, 170 miles west, for testing. The subsequent report told him that the samples were rich in silver—and Austin was born.

There are several different stories regarding the origin of Austin's name. The most widely held belief is that the town was named by one of its founders, David Buel, for his hometown in Texas. However in 1883 the *Mining and Scientific Press* claimed that Buel named the place after his partner, Alvah C. Austin. Yet another report, in the *De Lamar Lode* in 1903, stated that Austin was named for John Austin, a pioneer in the community.

In September 1863 Austin was made the seat of Lander County for Nevada Territory. Within two years, nearly 10,000 people had flocked to Austin, making it the second-largest city in the state, after Virginia City. During the next few decades, until the 1890s, Austin supported a thriving business district, three banks, six churches, a couple of newspapers, a dozen doctors, and its own stock exchange.

Austin's mines had produced more than $50 million in silver before the town began the slide from a thriving mining community to a sleepy roadside hamlet almost entirely dependent on ranching and pass-through traffic. Probably the town's most devastating setback of recent times was the loss of the county seat to Battle Mountain in 1979. Within a few years, the town's only bank had closed, which forced most Austinites to bank in Fallon, 110 miles away, and the venerable *Reese River Reveille*, the state's oldest continuously operated newspaper, folded.

Yet Austin has survived. The wooden buildings may lean a little and many of the stone and brick ones may be shuttered, but Austin has overcome challenges that bested most other mining towns.

### Austin's Rail Tale

Although silver was found in Pony Canyon in 1862, it was not until a decade later that serious efforts began to bring a railroad to the region. In 1875 the Nevada legislature authorized Lander County to grant $200,000 in bonds to subsidize the construction of a railroad to Austin. To expedite the project, legislators said the offer would expire if the tracks were not put in by midnight on February 9, 1880.

Unfortunately for Austin, during the next four years the railroad's supporters were unable to find an investor for the project. Finally, in late 1879 Austin mine owner Anson Phelps Stokes agreed to finance construction of a line connecting Austin to the Central Pacific Railroad at Battle Mountain. The new corporation, the Nevada Central Railway, had only five months to build ninety-three miles of track. No sooner had work begun when the railroad graders went on strike. Their demands were quickly settled, and by late October the first ten miles had been laid.

By mid-November, with winter settling in, the Nevada Central still had sixty-three miles of track to construct. The railroad began laying track as fast as it could, at times not even nailing the iron rails to the wooden ties. According to local legend, six hours before the midnight deadline the railroad was still about a mile and a half from Austin. At an emergency meeting, city officials agreed to enlarge the city limits by one mile to bring the town closer to the approaching railroad. While there are no records indicating that such a meeting took place, it is a fact that the railroad managed to reach Austin city limits only ten minutes before midnight on the day of the deadline. Volunteers from the town helped lay the last half mile of track—without wood ties.

### Reuel Gridley's Sack of Flour

Austin's most famous resident may have been shop owner and local politician Reuel Gridley, renowned for his legendary walk with a sack of flour. In 1864 Gridley lost an election bet and agreed to carry a fifty-pound sack of flour the length of the town, which was about a mile. After Gridley's trek, the sack of flour was auctioned, with the proceeds going to the Sanitary Fund, predecessor of the Red Cross.

During the auction, the flour was resold many times, each buyer returning it to be bid on again. By the end of the day, the sack had raised more than $6,000 for the fund. Other communities heard about Gridley's fundraising flour and invited him to conduct similar auctions throughout the West. Over the course of the next year, Gridley raised about $275,000 for the fund, which aided sick and wounded Civil War soldiers. Today the famous sack of flour is on display at the Nevada Historical Society in Reno.

East of downtown Austin is the restored Gridley Store, built in the early 1860s from native stone. Unfortunately, Gridley spent so much time traveling around the country conducting auctions with his flour that his store went bankrupt.

### Nevada's First Woman Sheriff

Austin was also the home of Nevada's first female sheriff. In 1919 Clara Dunham Crowell became sheriff of Lander County after her husband, George, died halfway through his term of office. The Lander County Commission asked Clara Crowell to replace her husband because it was widely known that she had assisted him with his duties, had a clear head, and knew how to use a gun. She had popular support too—a petition circulated calling on the commission to appoint her. The forty-two-year-old widow was the unanimous choice.

Crowell soon proved her law-enforcement mettle. She apprehended cattle rustlers, horse thieves, robbers, and the like. Once she went undercover as an old Indian woman and caught a man illegally selling liquor to Indians. One of her more dangerous escapades was when she rode into the mountains alone to snare a man suspected of fraud. The *Reese River Reveille* printed a front-page story: "Lady Sheriff Brings Back Her Prisoner." Crowell declined to run for reelection and instead took a job as administrator for the local hospital, a position she held until her death in 1942.

### Historic Austin

Despite its worn appearance, there is something special about Austin. Wandering its steep, narrow streets offers a chance to explore perhaps the best unreconstructed nineteenth-century mining town in Nevada. Main Street is lined with survivors from the town's early days. The Masonic–Odd Fellows Hall was built in 1867. The Lander County Courthouse, still in use, was completed in 1872.

Austin also has three magnificent churches. The oldest is St. Augustine's Catholic Church, built in 1866. Though it no longer holds regular services, local residents have restored parts of the church and now use it for special services and holidays. The Methodist church, also erected in 1866, was financed from donated mining stock and was later converted into a community center. St. George's Episcopal Church was built in 1878; it is the only one of Austin's historic houses of worship that is still in use. A single pass of the collection

*St. Augustine's is just one of Austin's magnificent churches.*

plate on Easter Sunday 1877 was said to have financed the church's construction. An interesting feature of the building is that in order to reach the rope that rings the church bell, one must stand atop a toilet.

Austin's other historic buildings include the International Hotel, still operating as a restaurant and saloon. Part of this building was constructed in 1859–60 in Virginia City, then dismantled in 1863 and moved to Austin. A block northeast of the International, at Water and Virginia Streets, is the former home of Emma Nevada, a famous nineteenth-century opera diva. Born Emma Wixom, she was the daughter of a pioneer Austin doctor and began her singing career in the local Methodist church choir. Emma Nevada gained her greatest fame in Europe, where she became a favorite of England's Queen Victoria and sang at the coronation of King George V. She died in Liverpool, England, in 1940, at the age of eighty-one.

A half mile west of Austin is the now empty Stokes Castle, an unusual stone tower built on the mountainside overlooking the Reese River Valley. Anson

*Stokes Castle in Austin.*

Phelps Stokes, a wealthy mine owner from the East Coast and builder of the Nevada Central Railway, built the three-story structure as a family summer home in 1897. Constructed with native granite slabs, it was made to resemble a villa that Stokes had seen outside of Rome.

## NV 376 AND 377
## US 50–BELMONT
**82 MILES**

### KINGSTON

Kingston, sixteen miles south of US 50 on NV 376, was created in 1864 after prospectors uncovered promising silver deposits at Bunker Hill, which overlooked the site of the future town. The founders chose a relatively level town site near water. By 1865 Kingston had 125 residents, a handful of businesses, and several mills, including the twenty-stamp Sterling Mill at the mouth of Kingston Canyon.

Kingston's prosperity was short-lived. In late 1867 the post office closed, and by 1870 all mining had ceased. The district remained closed until 1880, when new discoveries sparked a revival. The town, now called Morgan, re-opened the post office and erected a small schoolhouse. Six years later the

*The ruins of the Sterling Mill at Kingston.*

mines once again shut down, and the town began a two-decade-long slump. In 1906 the Kingston Mining Company began reworking the area's mines, with moderate success. The company constructed a sixty-ton mill in 1909 but closed it along with the mines two years later after exhausting the ore.

In the 1980s Kingston became the site of a small housing development with a dozen ranch-style homes, a general store, and a church. About a mile west of the new settlement, at the entrance to Kingston Canyon, are the remains of old Kingston, comprising the ruins of the Sterling Mill and a few scattered foundations and walls.

## ROUND MOUNTAIN AND HADLEY

The turnoff for Round Mountain and, slightly beyond that, the one for Hadley are about thirty-six miles south of Kingston on NV 376. Round Mountain is about three miles east of NV 376 on NV 378, Hadley about a mile west. While gold was first discovered at Round Mountain in 1905, it was not until February of the following year that active mining began. Soon after that, a small camp formed at the base of a round-topped hill—hence the community's name—on the east side of the Big Smoky Valley, adjacent to the Toquima Range.

At first the camp was called Gordon, after Louis Gordon, one of the mining district's founders. Within months it had grown to about 400 people. On March 4, 1907, the name was changed to Round Mountain. Later that year, Thomas Wilson of Manhattan, Nevada, discovered placer gold in the flats below the town. Wilson incorporated his claims as the Round Mountain Hydraulic Mining Company and built a five-mile pipeline to bring in water from nearby canyons for his extensive placer-mining operation.

Round Mountain's mines remained productive for nearly three decades, generating gold ore worth an estimated $3 million in the first ten years. The community had daily stage and freight service from Tonopah and local businesses ranging from general stores to brokerage houses. During the late 1920s, the Nevada Porphyry Gold Mines Company consolidated the mines in Round Mountain.

In 1935 underground mining ceased and the focus of the district's operations shifted to surface mining, which was moderately successful for the next two decades. In the late 1950s, Round Mountain's mines were closed and the community faced economic decline. Then, new mining techniques revived Round Mountain in the early 1970s, and the district has remained active since that time.

The new prosperity has come with a price, however. The massive open-pit mine will eventually wipe Round Mountain out of existence. As the mine grows larger, it swallows up more of the town. In the 1980s the mine's operator, Round Mountain Gold, built a new community a few miles west of the original town and named it Hadley. Most of Round Mountain's original buildings have been removed, and many more are threatened by future expansion of the mine.

## MANHATTAN

Nevada's Manhattan is no Big Apple. It does not have a Broadway or a Wall Street, and it has never seen a Rockette. But over the years, this Manhattan, eleven miles south of the Round Mountain turnoff on NV 376, then seven miles east on NV 377, has produced more than $10 million in gold and silver. George Nicholl made the initial discovery in 1866. Within a year the area, known as Manhattan Gulch, had fifty small mines. But these mines were quickly tapped out and most of the miners moved on to more lucrative diggings.

The district was dormant from 1869 until April 1905, when John C. Humphrey, a cowboy from a nearby ranch, noticed a promising ledge while herding cattle through the gulch. The samples he and several friends removed tested high in both silver and gold. This bonanza proved more sustained than the first, and within a short time a substantial town had emerged. Soon Manhattan had 4,000 residents and many businesses, including a telephone and telegraph service, three banks, and two newspapers.

Most of the financing for Nevada's mines was filtered through San Francisco banks and stock exchanges, so San Francisco's great earthquake in 1906 had a detrimental effect on Manhattan and many other Nevada mining camps. Following the earthquake, these traditional money sources dried up as investors diverted their funds to rebuild San Francisco. But Manhattan revived again after 1909 with the discovery of new gold deposits.

The community prospered into the 1920s, then began a gradual decline. In 1939 investors built a 3,000-ton gold dredge below the town. The operation's large pond was created with water piped in from nearby Peavine Creek. The dredge sustained the town for several years until it was no longer profitable,

*This old fire engine in Manhattan hasn't seen much use lately.*

and it was removed in 1946. In the late 1970s the Houston International Minerals Company began operating an open-pit mine on the site of the old mines. This mine still helps support Manhattan's economy.

Today's Manhattan has a number of old buildings and ruins from its glory days. The picturesque Manhattan Church sits prominently on a hillside overlooking the town. This simple one-room wooden building topped by a bullet-shaped cupola was built in 1874 in the nearby mining town of Belmont and moved to Manhattan in 1908. Local residents restored the church in the 1970s and still maintain it.

Manhattan's main street is lined with aging wooden headframes (mining hoists), stone ruins, and a few intact historic buildings, including two saloons—the only businesses still open in the town—and several small Victorian houses. The green-and-white cottage belonged to town founder John C. Humphrey, and his family still owns the house.

Of special note is the rusted fire truck parked adjacent to the roofless bank building. Its tires have rotted away, and a tongue-in-cheek sign perched atop the truck proclaims it the "Manhattan Volunteer Fire Dept."

Maybe they drag it to fires.

## BELMONT

The site of Belmont lies twelve miles east of Manhattan on NV 377. Prospectors discovered high-grade silver ore in Belmont in 1865. The district was originally called Silver Bend, then Philadelphia. It was finally named Belmont, a derivative of the French *beau mont*, meaning "beautiful mountain," because of its location at the base of the scenic Toiyabe Mountains.

In 1867 Belmont was designated the Nye County seat and became a regional center for trade, milling, and mining. In short order the community had several businesses, including two newspapers. By the next year the population of Belmont had risen to 2,000, but in 1869 its mines began to decline. The district revived in 1873, after a second major silver vein was uncovered, then began a permanent slide when the mines again began to fail in 1887. Its mills finally closed during World War I, and the town became a ghost.

Despite its abandonment almost a century ago, Belmont has remained relatively intact and is one of the state's best-preserved ghost towns. More than a dozen buildings poke through the sagebrush, including a partially restored, red brick courthouse. The shady cemetery at the town's western edge has several hand-carved wooden markers. North of the cemetery is the site of the Belmont-Monitor Mill, whose extensive brick ruins include a fifteen-foot smokestack.

East of the mill site is the center of town. A few newcomers have built homes around the ruins in recent years, so Belmont is a now a "living" ghost town. The Belmont Saloon, open in the summer, is one of Belmont's few active businesses. The antique bar was originally in the historic Cosmopolitan Saloon until the 1980s, when vandals destroyed that building by chaining its front pillars to a truck and pulling it down. No one was ever charged in the incident. The Cosmopolitan stood on Belmont's main street, and you can still see the flattened remains of the two-story wooden structure. Adjacent to the Belmont Saloon is a picturesque row of dilapidated brick-and-wood storefronts. It is a classic ghost-town scene, one of the most photographed in the state.

Just beyond the main drag, on a knoll overlooking the town, is the Belmont Courthouse. This impressive two-story building was constructed for $25,000 in 1876 from brick manufactured in Belmont's own kilns. The courthouse was used until 1905, when Belmont lost the county seat to Tonopah. It eventually fell into disrepair, but the Nevada Division of State Parks acquired it in the 1970s and partially restored it.

At the east end of the old mining camp, entrepreneurs have rebuilt one of the town's original stone houses and transformed it into a beautiful bed-and-

*The Belmont Courthouse is now a state historic park.*

breakfast. Directly south are the ruins of a once-substantial brick-manufacturing facility, with a twenty-foot smokestack rising from a large kiln. A quarter mile west of the brick plant is the site of the Highbridge Mill. The two-story building retains its brick facade and massive sidewalls.

## US 50
## AUSTIN–FALLON
### 110 MILES

## CLIFTON

Three-quarters of a mile west of Austin off US 50 are the remains of a former rival community, Clifton. After prospectors discovered silver in Pony Canyon, a tent city of about 500 miners popped on the flats at the mouth of the canyon. By mid-1863, Clifton had hotels, restaurants, saloons, shops, and a Wells Fargo office. But it soon had competition when later that year the town site of Austin was platted.

Initially, Clifton had the advantage of a flat location, while Austin was in a steep canyon. However, Austin's promoters offered free lots to businesses in exchange for help in developing a graded road from the Reese River Valley. Also, land in Clifton was expensive, and property owners there did nothing to try to attract new residents despite the challenge posed by Austin's free lots.

While Clifton was larger than Austin as of May 1863, it declined rapidly. By that fall, the town had lost its bid for the Lander County seat, and within months most of its residents had moved to Austin or other mining camps. The post office closed in February 1864 and only briefly reopened from 1867 to 1868.

In 1880 the Nevada Central Railway and the Austin City Railway built a terminus with a thirty-car train siding on the former site of Clifton. The site, called Austin Junction, housed a small engine house, turntable, and depot. Despite the railroad activity, area residents built no houses or businesses there.

In 1894 the Austin Silver Mining Company, owned by J. G. Phelps Stokes, son of tycoon Anson Stokes, constructed the forty-stamp Clifton Mill at the mouth of the 6,000-foot-long Austin Tunnel mine shaft, just above the Clifton site. Today the shell of the Clifton Mill remains, and adjacent to the structure are massive stone walls and foundations of other buildings once part of the mill operation.

## NEW PASS, COLD SPRINGS, AND ROCK CREEK

The Overland Stage and the Pony Express had an extensive network of stations across Nevada. While most have disappeared, a handful have been fenced and preserved along US 50 including Overland stations at New Pass and Rock Creek, and the Pony Express station at Cold Springs.

At New Pass, about twenty-five miles west of Austin on US 50, a wire fence protects substantial rock walls. The stone station's willow-twig roof is long gone, but the foundations and walls offer some idea of its size. A historical marker at the site notes that a nearby spring was inadequate for the station's needs, so water was brought from a ranch a mile away. There was also a small hotel and store that served local miners.

Rock Creek is about twenty-five miles west of New Pass and is the site of a stage stop that dates to about 1862. Drivers could find fresh horses, humble accommodations, a blacksmith shop, and wagon-repair services here. The site, now surrounded by a high fence, is little more than stone rubble. A half mile north are more stone walls, surrounded by a fence. These are the remains of a telegraph repeater and maintenance station that was built in the early 1860s as part of the Overland Telegraph–Pacific Telegraph Company's transcontinental line between Sacramento, California, and Omaha, Nebraska. The stone facility was abandoned in August 1869.

About a mile and half east of the Rock Creek site are the substantial rock ruins of the Cold Springs Pony Express station. These are among the best-preserved Pony Express station ruins in Nevada and can be reached only on foot. There are an information kiosk and a small parking lot near the trailhead.

*Dozens of shoes hang from the Old Shoe Tree, off US 50 near Middlegate.*
—Courtesy K. J. Evans

## THE OLD SHOE TREE

Travelers on US 50 encounter a strange sight about three miles east of the tiny roadside stop of Middlegate—a giant cottonwood tree filled with old shoes. The Old Shoe Tree holds dozens of pairs of boots, sneakers, loafers, and pumps. According to local legend, the tree began acquiring shoes in the late 1980s or early 1990s during a fight between a newlywed couple.

Apparently, the two were camping near the tree and had an argument. The wife threatened to walk home, so the husband tied her shoes together and threw them into the tree. He drove off, leaving his wife to cool her bare heels under the cottonwood, and stopped at the Middlegate Bar for a drink. After half an hour he returned to the camp. The two made up, but only after he agreed to throw his shoes into the tree, too. The tree now bears a wooden plaque inviting visitors to add to its collection of footwear.

## FAIRVIEW

The mangled remains of Fairview lay in the hills about nine miles west of Middlegate off US 50. Prospectors discovered rich silver deposits at the site in 1905. A full-scale mining boom kicked off a year later, when well-known Nevada mining investors George Wingfield and George Nixon purchased several claims in the district. By June 1906 a town site had been laid out and lots were being sold. Thousands of people drifted in and out of the town over the next year, and soon Fairview had two dozen saloons, several hotels and banks, and a newspaper.

*This old bank vault is one of the few reminders of Fairview.*

Because of its remoteness, basic commodities were expensive in Fairview. Ice was $4 per 100 pounds, water was $2.50 a barrel, and wood was $20 per cord. Several private stage companies transported supplies to Fairview from Fallon, about thirty-five miles west, where there was a railroad line from Hazen. Because of the high costs, by 1907 there was widespread talk of building a spur from the Nevada Central Railway, which ran from Battle Mountain to Austin.

Despite the early optimism and the development of a fairly large community, Fairview's mines began to decline in 1908. The newspaper folded, and many miners moved on to more lucrative districts. New discoveries in 1911 sparked a new, small boom. Much of the new development was clustered around the large Nevada Hills Mill, built south of the original town site. Mining continued until about 1917, but by the 1920s only a handful of folks remained in Fairview. Photographs from the 1950s show about a dozen dilapidated buildings still standing in the upper canyon.

Sadly, even those ruins no longer exist. In the early 1980s, pilots from the nearby Fallon Naval Air Station bombed the wooden structures, thinking they were practice targets. Only the concrete bank vault, standing alone on the flat ground of the original town site, now remains.

## FRENCHMAN

A few scruffy trees in a wide alkali flat northwest of the site of Fairview are the only remnants of Frenchman, a longtime roadside stop that the U.S. military removed in the 1980s when it expanded its restricted airspace into the Dixie Valley. From US 50 travelers can often observe military exercises in the surrounding desert. Another reminder of the military's presence are the many "Beware of Low Flying Aircraft" signs throughout the basin.

Frenchman goes back to 1906, when M. Bermond—a Frenchman—opened a saloon and stable here. The business served travelers heading to Fairview and the mining camp of Wonder, about twenty miles north. A post office operated from 1920 to 1926, using the name Bermond. Later, a gas station popped up. A 1924 Lincoln Highway guide notes that at M. Bermond's establishment, Frenchman's Station, he "has built and fitted up splendid rooms, and will serve a meal as you might expect on Fifth Ave. in New York." In 1983 the diner in Frenchman appeared in William Least Heat-Moon's bestseller *Blue Highways*.

## SAND MOUNTAIN AND THE
## SAND SPRINGS PONY EXPRESS STATION

Sand Mountain is a 300-foot-high dune formed from sandy deposits from prehistoric Lake Lahontan, the giant inland sea that covered much of Nevada until about 11,000 years ago. The dune was created when wind blew sand from the surrounding flats against nearby mountain walls. Sand Mountain lies thirty-two miles east of Fallon on US 50.

Just west of Sand Mountain are the well-preserved ruins of the Sand Spring Pony Express station. For many years the shifting sands of Sand Mountain covered the site. Several decades ago, the University of Nevada and the Bureau of Land Management excavated the site and listed it on the National Register of Historic Places.

*Ruins of the Pony Express station at Sand Springs.*
—Courtesy Nevada Commission on Tourism

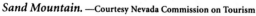
*Sand Mountain.* —Courtesy Nevada Commission on Tourism

The Sand Spring station was described in the diary of nineteenth-century explorer and author Sir Richard Burton, who traveled with Pony Express riders in the autumn of 1860:

> [Sand Spring] deserves its name. . . . The land is cumbered here and there with drifted ridges of the finest sand, sometimes 200-feet high and shifting before every gale. . . . The station house was no unfit object in such a scene, roofless and chairless, filthy and squalid, with a smoky fire in one corner and a table in the centre of an impure floor, the walls open to every wind and interior full of dust.

## GRIMES POINT AND HIDDEN CAVE

Some of central Nevada's best examples of petroglyphs (prehistoric Indian rock carvings) are at Grimes Point, about twelve miles east of Fallon on US 50. An interpretive trail winds about a mile through a small forest of engraved rocks and boulders. Some of these petroglyphs are more than 3,000 years old, and their styles vary according to their era.

Interpretative signs expound on various theories about the carvings and their possible meanings. Archaeologists believe that the simplest petroglyphs, a pit-and-groove pattern on several boulders, resembling pock marks, are the oldest. Later designs have more elaborate images of deer, lizards, and the sun.

*One of several caves near Grimes Point.*

While some archaeologists believe petroglyphs have religious significance, perhaps prayers for a good hunt or harvest, other experts say they are most likely prehistoric graffiti.

A mile north of Grimes Point along an interpretive trail is Hidden Cave, an archaeological site that offers a fascinating glimpse of Nevada's first inhabitants. The cave was discovered in the 1930s and first excavated in 1940, then further excavated in 1950 and 1979–80. Following the last excavation, a metal door was erected at the cave's entrance to protect it.

Migrating tribes once used Hidden Cave as a cache. Archaeologists have found prehistoric fishing nets, pots, tools, seeds, and food remains here. Part of the reason the cave remained relatively undisturbed over the centuries is that it once housed a large number of bats, which filled the inside of the cave with centuries of guano.

Hidden Cave is an ongoing dig site, and the chance to watch archaeologists at work is part of its appeal. The walls have small tags marking the various strata, or rock layers. One layer is clearly white, indicating where the cave was once covered in volcanic ash. The ash is believed to have come from a prehistoric eruption of Mount St. Helens, in Washington. The Churchill County Museum in Fallon offers guided tours of Hidden Cave twice a month.

## FALLON

Sixty miles east of Reno is Fallon. Fallon owes a lot to Teddy Roosevelt. If not for the twenty-sixth president, the Reclamation Act of 1902 would not have become law, and the Newlands Project (originally called the Truckee-Carson Project), the nation's first federal reclamation program, would not have been built. In the project's first phase, completed in 1905, engineers brought water from the Carson and Truckee Rivers to the desert lands southeast of Reno, and Fallon was born.

The Fallon area, however, had inhabitants long before the Newlands Project began. Archaeologists have found evidence of human life dating back more than 3,800 years, and the area was home to the Northern Paiute for centuries before the arrival of white settlers. In the 1840s and 1850s, Emigrant Trail pioneers passed through here on their way to California.

In 1861 the Nevada territorial government created Churchill County and named as its seat Bucklands Station, a Pony Express stop near Fort Churchill. But two years later, the county moved its base of operations to a small mining town called La Plata. When that town's fortunes waned in 1867, the county seat was moved again, to Stillwater, a farming town to the east of the future site of Fallon.

In 1896 rancher Mike Fallon and his wife settled on land between Stillwater and St. Clair, a stage station to the west. Their spread included a ranch house with a post office bearing Fallon's name and a small store operated by Jim

Richards. Nevada state senator Warren W. Williams, who planned to build a town at the spot where the new Newlands Project would deliver water, purchased the ranch just after the turn of the century.

Williams began selling lots in the community of Fallon and named streets after himself, his friends, and his home state—main street is called Maine Street. Using his political clout, he succeeded in getting the county seat moved to his new town in 1903. Fallon quickly blossomed. A distinctive two-story wooden courthouse, still in use today, was completed almost immediately, and homes and businesses soon appeared. The irrigation project was finished in 1905 and began delivering water to the surrounding ranches. By 1907 Fallon had its own telephone company—still the only county-owned and -maintained telephone company in the United States—and a branch line of the Southern Pacific Railroad.

As quickly as it was built, Fallon almost failed. The Bureau of Reclamation's engineers had thought the Newlands Project capable of supporting 400,000 acres of irrigated land, but they had vastly underestimated the amount of water needed to make the desert bloom. Attempts to find crops that would grow in the desert had mixed results. An ambitious sugar-beet program flopped,

*The Churchill County Courthouse in Fallon, built in 1903.*

but cantaloupe and alfalfa proved more successful. In 1911 work started on the Lahontan Dam on the Carson River to impound a reservoir for a steady source of water. The dam was completed in 1915, and within a few years Fallon had finally become the "Oasis of Nevada" its founders had envisioned.

Since then, Fallon has diversified. In 1942 the Fallon Naval Air Station opened, and it continues to be an important part of the town's economy. It is the county's largest employer and home of the Navy's famed "top gun" flight school. Since the 1980s the Fallon Air Show has attracted crowds averaging 50,000 each spring with spectacular aerial stunts, including a show by the Blue Angels, the USAF's precision aerial team. In addition, Fallon's thriving tourism industry includes casinos such as the Fallon Nugget, the Depot, and Stockman's. Fallon is also noted for its Hearts o' Gold cantaloupes, grown in the fields west of town. About 20,000 people annually attend the Hearts o' Gold Cantaloupe Festival held on Labor Day weekend.

### Historic Fallon

Fallon still has many reminders of the town's rich history. The whitewashed courthouse, with its picturesque pillars and cupola, is the only wooden courthouse still in use in Nevada. The brown brick Fallon City Hall, across US 50 from the courthouse, was built in 1930. Downtown, on South Maine Street, architectural styles range from the streamlined facade of the R. L. Douglass Bank building, built in the mid-1930s, to the boxy 1960s exterior of the Fallon Nugget casino.

The brick-and-stucco Overland Hotel, at 125 East Center Street, was added to Nevada's Register of Historic Places in 1999. A row of distinctive, wide Mission-style arches lines the front of this two-story 1907 hotel. Its rooms contain original appointments including steam radiators and porcelain hand sinks.

The Churchill County Museum, at 1050 South Maine Street, was founded in 1968. Exhibits illustrate significant places, events, and advancements of the Fallon area. One large display details the story of the Pony Express, which passed through the area. Another exhibit has a weather-worn wagon found in the nearby Forty Mile Desert, a barren stretch of alkali flats on the Emigrant Trail. Surrounding the wagon are dozens of rusted and sun-bleached items also picked up in the desert, such as barrels, shoes, and a pair of wooden roller skates. Outside the museum's main building is a large array of antique farming equipment. The Woodliff Novelty Store is an eighty-year-old, two-room wooden building that has been restored and stocked with vintage dry goods.

# NV 722
# OLD US 50 LOOP
**60 MILES**

While Nevada's US 50 has received plenty of attention for being "America's Loneliest Road," that honor more rightly belongs to NV 722, which was once part of US 50. The highway, also called Old US 50 or the Carroll Summit Road, is a fifty-eight-mile stretch of asphalt running parallel to present-day US 50 between Austin and Eastgate. The turnoff from US 50 is about two miles west of Austin.

State highway planners bypassed NV 722 several decades ago when they realized that a more-northern route would avoid the Desatoya Mountains. Since then, folks have not exactly been queueing up to travel NV 722. Nevada Department of Transportation records indicate that it is one of the least-traveled paved roads in the state, with only forty-five cars per day in either direction.

Heading west from Austin, NV 722 drifts south through the Reese River Valley and crosses the Reese River, which in a normal year barely deserves to be called a small creek. From the river, the road travels straight across the valley into the Shoshone Mountains. About twenty-seven miles down the road from Austin, the old highway climbs to 6,431 feet elevation, over Railroad Pass, then drops into the Smith Creek Valley. In most years this valley is a dry lakebed, or playa, but in some years it fills with water.

The route then heads west into the Desatoya Mountains. It passes a handful of ranches, including the former Carroll Station, an Overland Stage stop in the mid-nineteenth century. Several stone buildings with sod roofs still stand there. Near Carroll Summit, at elevation 7,452 feet, the highway passes a deserted house, groves of pine trees, and a small rest area. It joins US 50 again five miles past Eastgate.

## EASTGATE

About fifty miles west of Austin, NV 722 winds through narrow rock cliffs and passes a stone house, once part of an Overland Stage station called Eastgate. Eastgate was established in 1859 by explorer James H. Simpson, who named it for the local terrain: it formed a natural gateway into a valley to the west. The craggy rock cliffs there are littered with small caves. A historical marker here says that Eastgate is also the site of the Wagon Jack Shelter, where archaeologists have found prehistoric artifacts, some dating back more than 1,500 years. Today, only a few ranches can be found at Eastgate.

# US 50
## FALLON–CARSON CITY
### 61 MILES

### SODA LAKE

Five miles west of Fallon via US 50 and Lucas Road is Soda Lake, a collapsed volcanic crater filled with water. In the 1840s pioneers emerging from the Forty Mile Desert on the Emigrant Trail frequently stopped at the lake and the adjacent natural springs, the first fresh water they had found for miles. In the mid-1850s several claims were filed on the lake because of the presence of pure soda, used in processing ore. Commercial soda extraction on the lake commenced in 1875 with the construction of two major soda works, among the first in the West. Soda taken from the lakebed was of such high quality it won a gold medal at the 1876 Centennial Exposition in Philadelphia.

But the 1915 completion of the Newlands Project, which spurred agricultural development in the Lahontan Valley, precipitated the end of the local soda business. The massive aqueduct system's irrigation water percolated into the groundwater, diluting the soda quality and causing the lake to rise over fifty feet. Soon the soda factory was submerged under thirty-five feet of water. Its owners sued the federal government for damages. The case was ultimately decided in the government's favor, setting the legal precedent that the federal government could not be held responsible for unintended consequences.

Today the lake is popular with divers who like to explore the old soda plant. They can also view a "ghost forest," a grove of skeletal cottonwood trees, under the southeastern end of the lake. The lake has also become a sanctuary for a

*Soda Lake.*

wide variety of seagulls, terns, and ducks. Brine shrimp and a host of underwater plants are well adapted to the water's high alkali level.

## RAGTOWN

Eight miles west of Fallon once lay Ragtown, the first permanent settlement in the area, established in the early 1850s as a trading post to serve travelers on the Emigrant Trail. Upon arriving at the post, many of the emigrants immediately washed their dirty clothing in the nearby Carson River, then hung them to dry in the trees. Their clothing, having just undergone a trip through the harsh Forty Mile Desert, was often tattered and torn—thus Ragtown earned its name.

The trading post was also well situated for travelers crossing central Nevada on the trail blazed by James H. Simpson in 1859. In 1861 Ragtown became a stop on the Overland Stage route as well. After 1863 Ragtown further thrived as a station for miners heading to the Austin area on the east-west toll road. Within a few years, Ragtown had a post office and several small farms. But in 1880 the Central Pacific Railroad completed its line to the north, reducing travel through Ragtown. By the early twentieth century, the community had disappeared. Today, only a historical marker on US 50 notes its former location.

## LAHONTAN STATE RECREATION AREA

In 1902 Congress created the U.S. Bureau of Reclamation to develop large-scale irrigation projects in the western states. Among the agency's first undertakings was the Truckee-Carson Project, later known as the Newlands Project, named for U.S. congressman Francis G. Newlands of Nevada, author of the National Reclamation Act. The project was grand in scope, with 104 miles of canals and 335 miles of open ditches—all designed to move water from the Truckee and Carson Rivers to a planned oasis in the desert.

Work began in 1903 with the building of the Truckee Canal and the Derby Diversion Dam, which together divert water from the Truckee River at a point about thirty-two miles east of Reno and carry it to Fallon. Construction continued for nearly fifteen years and included the Carson River Diversion Dam (1905), the Lahontan power plant (1911), Lake Tahoe Dam's sluiceway (1913), and the Lahontan Dam, completed in 1914.

The Lahontan Dam, nine miles west of Fallon off US 50, is the project's most impressive structure. The earthen dam is 120 feet high and 1,300 feet wide. Curving concrete spillways, which look like giant steps, flank the dam, and a massive concrete outlet tower stands in front. The dam has many early-twentieth-century architectural touches, such as a row of elegant lampposts along its top and a molded-concrete archway and wrought-iron fence on the suspension footbridge leading to the tower.

*Gateway to the outlet tower at Lahontan Dam.*

Downstream from the dam is a small electrical power plant. The plant's three generators are still in use inside the substantial stone-and-concrete structure on the river's edge. The plant, completed before the dam, supplied hydroelectric power for the dam's construction. Behind the dam, the Lahontan Reservoir covers ten thousand acres. The seventeen-mile-long reservoir has sixty-nine miles of shore.

While the original supporters of the Newlands Project had been overly optimistic in their predictions about how much land the project would ultimately irrigate, the Lahontan Reservoir surpassed expections in terms of recreational use. It is now part of a Nevada state recreation area, popular with swimmers, boaters, and picnickers. The reservoir has more than two dozen beaches, fifty campsites, and several boat-launching facilities.

## THE SUTRO TUNNEL

The Sutro Tunnel is three miles northeast of Dayton, off US 50 on a marked dirt road. Adolph Sutro, a Prussian immigrant who arrived in Virginia City in 1860, designed the Sutro Tunnel, one of the engineering marvels of the nineteenth century. At only thirty years of age, Sutro had already operated a successful merchandising company in San Francisco before heading off to make his fortune, first in California's goldfields, then in Nevada.

*The entrance to the Sutro Tunnel.*

In the early 1860s one of the biggest problems facing Comstock mine operators was the abundance of scalding hot water released as they dug mine shafts deeper into the earth. Sutro proposed to drill a four-mile-long horizontal tunnel beneath Virginia City that would drain the water into the nearby Dayton Valley. The tunnel would also provide better ventilation for the miners working deep underground and an easy transport route for the ore.

When Sutro first pitched his idea to the mine owners, they dismissed him as a dreamer. But in 1865 he persuaded the Nevada legislature to grant him permission to drill a tunnel beneath the Comstock mines. Within a year of gaining approval, Sutro had signed up two dozen of the Comstock's largest mining companies to pay a fee for each ton of ore they transported through the tunnel once it was built. But Virginia City's powerful Bank Crowd opposed the project. They feared the tunnel would shift the balance of power away from them, since the ore would be processed in Dayton, about three miles west, rather than in their Virginia City mills. As a result, Sutro spent three years attempting to find financing for his project.

Finally, on October 19, 1869, work began on Sutro's tunnel. It took nine years to complete, stretched more than 20,000 feet, and cost $3.5 million. It opened on July 8, 1878. Unfortunately for its investors, the tunnel was completed just as the Comstock mines began to decline. Also, by the time the tunnel was completed, many mines had gone deeper than the tunnel's level, so it had limited usefulness as a drainage system. The tunnel never broke even.

Sutro, however, had quietly and cleverly unloaded his stock shortly after the tunnel's completion. He reportedly realized more than $1 million from his shares. He successfully reinvested it in San Francisco real estate and built the famous Sutro Baths and Cliff House there, overlooking the Pacific Ocean. He later served as mayor of San Francisco, from 1894 to 1896.

While his tunnel was under construction, Sutro had also developed a community at the tunnel's mouth and named it after himself. He hoped the town would eventually surpass Virginia City in importance, and by 1876 it had nearly 800 residents, a hospital, a church, a newspaper, and Sutro's gigantic Victorian mansion. Once the tunnel was completed, however, the town began to decline. Today, little remains of it besides the tunnel, a few wooden houses and barns, and mountains of dirt removed from the tunnel during its construction. Sutro's lavish residence burned in 1941.

## DAYTON

Dayton, eleven miles east of Carson City on US 50, is one of the state's oldest communities—perhaps even the oldest. Martin Griffith, a journalist and expert on the Emigrant Trail, uncovered emigrant diaries that describe a small mining camp of about 200 people thriving in Gold Canyon, now Dayton, in 1851. That is the same year John Reese, founder of Genoa—the place generally recognized as Nevada's first town—arrived in western Nevada. The Gold Canyon settlement, however, was probably a crude, transient camp, whereas Genoa, started a few months later, was a permanent community with substantial wooden and brick buildings. Because of the difficulties in defining what constitutes a settlement, both towns claim to be the first one in Nevada.

Regardless of whether it was first, Dayton certainly has an interesting history—and more than a few name changes. In addition to Gold Canyon, it was also named Ponderer's Rest, Spafford Hall's Station, and McMartin's Station—all in the 1850s. By 1857 a large number of Chinese had settled in the area to work on the ditch from the Carson River to the entrance of Gold Canyon, and people started calling it Chinatown. Finally, in 1861, county surveyor John Day platted a formal town site, and it was dubbed Dayton in his honor.

Comstock mining interests built several large mills near Dayton in the early 1860s. Then fires in 1866 and 1870 destroyed much of the original town. Yet some structures dating to the 1860s and 1870s still stand in Dayton's historic downtown. The two-story Union Hotel on Main Street was built in 1870, as was the red brick Odeon Hall on Pike Street, still operating as a popular restaurant. Half a block east of the Odeon Hall is the former jail and firehouse, also built in 1870, which housed the new fire engine purchased after the disastrous fire of 1870. Nearby, the former Dayton Public School, constructed of local stone in 1865, now houses the Dayton Historic Society Museum.

Half a mile west of downtown Dayton on Cemetery Road is the Dayton Cemetery, reportedly the oldest in the state. In addition to offering a beautiful

*Odeon Hall is one of a handful of historic buildings still in use in Dayton.*

view of the surrounding valley, the cemetery contains unusual porcelain markers on some of the graves of early Italian settlers. Among the more prominent names found in the cemetery is James "Old Virginny" Finney, the man who named Virginia City and one of the Comstock's first miners.

Dayton State Park, at the east end of town, is a picturesque spot on the banks of the Carson River. Tall cottonwoods shade the picnic areas and campsites. Adjacent to the park are the remains of the Rock Point Mill, built in 1861 by Charles C. Stevenson, Nevada's governor from 1887 to 1890. The mill cost $75,000 to build and had forty stamps to crush the ore, carried from Gold Hill by way of an aerial tram. At the peak of the Comstock mining boom, the mill was enlarged to include fifty-six stamps. One of three important ore-processing plants located in Dayton, the Rock Point Mill was instrumental in the development of the Comstock Mining District. In 1909 a fire destroyed the mill, but its owners immediately rebuilt it using galvanized iron. The second mill remained in use until about 1920, when it was dismantled.

## COMO

The site of the former mining town of Como is eleven miles south of Dayton on a signed dirt road, in the Pine Nut Mountains. Como had its roots in another community, Palmyra. Prospectors struck gold in Palmyra in about 1860. During the next two years, the mines supported a small camp of more than 400. In 1862, however, miners uncovered gold half a mile east. The new camp, named Como, soon eclipsed Palmyra and had a steam-powered mill, hotels, bars, and a weekly newspaper.

The mines, though, were soon tapped out, and by 1864 the town had begun to fade. The district experienced brief revivals in 1879–81 and 1902–5. In the 1930s a large mill was built but never used. Nothing remains of Como or the Como Mining District today except for a few foundations and assorted pieces of tanks, pipes, and other debris.

## EMPIRE CITY

By the early 1860s, stamp mills lined the banks the length of the Carson River between Dayton and Carson City. They operated almost continuously to process the large quantities of ore coming from Virginia City. At the western end of this industrial strip was the community of Empire City, the site of the first Carson River mill, erected in 1860. By the late 1860s, Empire City had several mills and nearly 700 residents. Ore was hauled to Empire City's mills first by wagon, then, after 1870, by the Virginia & Truckee Railroad.

Empire City had evolved from an 1850s emigrant way station and ranch. In addition to its mills, the community had several thriving logging companies transporting lumber from the Sierra Nevada. The wood was floated down the Carson River to the town, where it was cut and loaded on rail cars to Virginia City. Empire City's decline began in the late 1870s with the end of the Comstock boom.

Today at the site of Empire City, on the eastern edge of Carson City, a quarter mile south of US 50, nothing remains except a small cemetery with about three dozen graves, adjacent to a large cement plant. A dirt road follows the old Virginia & Truckee rail bed along the Carson River, which still has traces of mercury pollution from the mills. A few foundations and stone walls mark the mill sites.

**ALTERNATE US 95**
# US 50–YERINGTON
**32 MILES**

## FORT CHURCHILL HISTORIC STATE MONUMENT

The Fort Churchill Historic State Monument is just off Alternate US 95, eight miles south of that highway's turnoff from US 50 at Silver Springs. The U.S. Army built Fort Churchill in July 1860 to house a garrison of troops assigned to protect western Nevada settlers from Indian uprisings in the wake of the Pyramid Lake War. The fort was also a sanctuary for Pony Express riders, whom the Indians occasionally harassed. During the Civil War, the fort

*Adobe ruins at Fort Churchill Historic State Monument.*

became a western outpost for the Union Army. While the Fort Churchill garrison was never called into action during the war, the fort was an important training ground and supply depot for the Nevada Military District.

The military abandoned the fort in 1869 after deciding it was too expensive to operate. They dismantled many of its buildings and auctioned off the wooden roofs, supports, and porches. The adobe walls, left unprotected over the decades, gradually sank into the sand and sagebrush. In the 1930s the federal government sent in the Civilian Conservation Corps to stabilize and partially rebuild the ruins for posterity. The state of Nevada acquired the property in 1957 and created a state historic monument and park. Since then, Nevada has maintained the buildings in a state of "arrested decay."

A replica of an original fort building overlooking the site serves as the park's excellent visitor center. On view are a model of the fort as it appeared in the 1860s and a display of authentic 1860s U.S. Army uniforms and weapons. Adjacent to the visitor center is the Fort Churchill Cemetery. The army removed its dead when it left the fort in 1869, but visitors will still find a handful of wooden markers for the nonmilitary pioneers buried there.

While the park has developed trails in the area, it remains largely agricultural fields bordered by white fences, with mature trees providing shade and a pastoral view. In fall, the cottonwoods along the Carson River turn a beautiful shade of yellow, casting a warm, pleasant glow over the banks.

### Bucklands Station

The sound of a stagecoach creaking to a stop in front of Bucklands Station plays in the imagination on a visit to the site, directly east of the entrance to Fort Churchill on Alternate US 95. The large white clapboard building reminds us of an adventurous age when traveling west was an ordeal. Not only was the ride on rutted and rocky dirt roads uncomfortable, but there were also occasional encounters with robbers and hostile natives.

Rancher Samuel S. Buckland settled on this site near the Carson River in 1859. He soon established a tent hotel to accommodate the wagon trains crossing Nevada on the Emigrant Trail, along with a station for the Overland Stage. He may have also constructed the first bridge across the Carson River. By March 1860 Buckland had erected a large building to house a trading post, tavern, and hotel. It was also a stop for the Pony Express.

On May 11, 1860, Bucklands Station assumed a minor but important role in Nevada history. That day a citizen militia stayed overnight at Bucklands before heading north to participate in the first battle of the Pyramid Lake War. The men requisitioned Pony Express horses and headed north. Four days later, the survivors of the battle straggled back to Bucklands, having been soundly defeated by the Indians. By that summer, the U.S. government was building Fort Churchill a mile from the station.

In November 1861 the Nevada territorial government designated Bucklands Station the seat of Churchill County. The site retained this status until 1864,

*Bucklands Station.*

when Nevada became a state and more accurate county lines were drawn. At that point, Bucklands became part of Lyon County. In 1870 Samuel Buckland built the present two-story structure as a hotel with dance hall, dining room, and saloon, using wood from buildings at Fort Churchill; he had bought the wood from the army when it decommissioned the fort.

Bucklands Station ceased to be an important way stop as stage traffic waned in the late 1870s. The building was later converted into a private residence and was inhabited until about the 1950s. In the 1990s the Nevada Division of State Parks acquired the station, renovated the building, and incorporated it into the Fort Churchill Historic State Monument.

## THOMPSON

About a dozen tall, thick, rectangular concrete blocks—once the foundation for a complex of smelters—silently stand watch over what was once the town of Thompson, off Alternate US 95 seventeen miles south of US 50. If not for them, there would probably be little to indicate the location of this former mining camp, which in its heyday had more than 350 residents. Now, only lizards and field mice call it home.

Between 1910 and 1914 the Mason Valley Mines Company built two 500-ton smelters here to process ore from the large copper mines west of Yerington. By 1914 a small town, named for William B. Thompson, one of the mining company's original owners, had formed in the valley below the smelters. The

*Concrete ruins of the Thompson smelter.*

mines shipped ore to Thompson on a branch line of the Nevada Copper Belt Railroad.

While the treated ore was reasonably pure, the smelters were only marginally profitable and the company shut them down in late 1914. Operations resumed for a short time from 1917 to 1919, then again from 1926 to 1928. The smelters were finally dismantled in the late 1920s; by then the town had all but disappeared.

Today, on the flat desert below the smelter site are the crumbling remains of once-substantial buildings. Walls, foundations, and assorted brick and rock fragments lie scattered in various stages of decay along with rusting cars, ovens, and other detritus. But it is the ruins of the smelters that dominate the terrain. These giant hunks of concrete follow the contours of the land, rising up from the hillside like a Nevada Stonehenge.

## WABUSKA

Wabuska (wuh-BUS-kuh), on Alternate US 95 twenty miles south of US 50, was once an important junction for the Carson & Colorado Railroad, which later became part of the Southern Pacific. The community began in the early 1870s as a small settlement and freight station at the northern end of the Mason Valley. In 1874 a post office opened in the tiny hamlet, which took its name from the Washo word for "white grass," since there was plenty in the area. The town experienced a brief expansion in 1881 when the Carson & Colorado Railroad arrived.

The railroad agent who built the station at Wabuska was Edward Lovejoy, the only son of one of nineteenth century's most famous abolitionists, Elijah P. Lovejoy. Edward Lovejoy was a close friend of Sam Davis, editor of the *Carson Appeal*. To tease his friend, Davis concocted an imaginary newspaper, the *Wabuska Mangler*, and claimed that Lovejoy was its editor. From 1889 until Lovejoy's death in 1891, Davis frequently cited nonexistent stories and editorials from the *Mangler*.

Wabuska's acme came after 1900, when the Southern Pacific Railroad absorbed the Carson & Colorado and the town became an essential junction for the lines serving the central and southern Nevada mining camps. In 1911 the Nevada Copper Belt Railroad connected the line at Wabuska to several copper mines near Yerington and to the smelters in Thompson. For the next few years, Wabuska thrived.

But when the copper industry slumped in the early 1920s, Wabuska began to shrink. By the 1950s the town had only half a dozen houses, a grocery store, and a bar. In the 1980s the Nevada State Railroad Museum moved Wabuska's depot to its grounds in Carson City. Today the train still passes through Wabuska, but it does not stop. Only a small bar and restaurant remains open.

## WEED HEIGHTS

Weed Heights, two miles west of Yerington on Alternate US 95, has one of the most accessible of Nevada's "glory holes" (mining slang for open-pit mines). The owner of this huge copper mine, the Anaconda Copper Company, built Weed Heights in the early 1950s, on the hillside adjacent to the mine, to accommodate workers and their families. The town was named for Clyde E. Weed, the company's vice president.

The town is not much more than an assemblage of several dozen boxy little houses overlooking the pit. The mine closed in the late 1970s, and many of the homes were abandoned. In recent years, a developer has been renovating them for resale. Nearby, an enclosed overlook offers a panoramic view of the mine. Bright bluish green water—seepage from groundwater—fills much of the glory hole.

## YERINGTON

Yerington is fifteen miles south of Wabuska on Alternate US 95. Until it collapsed a few years ago in a windstorm, there was a billboard at the north end of Yerington that said, "Welcome to Yerington, Cattle Kingdom in the Copper Hills." With its brightly colored, 1930s-postcard design and its cornball slogan, the sign was perfect for Yerington, a place that truly embodies Main Street USA.

The most prominent buildings on Yerington's Main Street are the Lyon County Courthouse, surrounded by a beautiful shady park, and the brick post office, painted with an authentic WPA art-deco mural. There are also half a dozen churches, a VFW hall, and a National Guard armory. The local paper, the *Mason Valley News*, has the most bracing slogan in the state: "The only newspaper in the world that gives a damn about Yerington."

The first settler in the Yerington area was Hock Mason, who was herding cattle through the valley in 1857 on his way to California. Impressed by the fertile fields here, he returned a year later and built a small ranch on the East Walker River. The Mason Valley, as the area became known, soon attracted other ranchers and settlers. By the 1870s a saloon and a handful of other businesses had sprung up in the valley.

Local legend has it that Yerington was originally called the Switch, after the town's main landmark, a crude saloon built of willow branches. Locals called the whiskey served there "poison," pronounced "pizen," and the town's name mutated into Pizen Switch, a moniker that stuck until 1879. Then the town was called Greenfield, a name that better reflected its pastoral setting. Finally, in 1894 the town changed its name to honor Henry Marvin Yerington, a prominent official with the Virginia & Truckee and Carson & Colorado Railroads.

In 1909 prospectors discovered significant copper reserves in the Singatse Range, west of Yerington. For most of the next sixty-nine years, Yerington benefited from the vast copper operations in the nearby mountains. Soon after

*This sign once welcomed visitors to Yerington, self-proclaimed "Cattle Kingdom in the Copper Hills."*

mining began, the town had electric and telephone service and a short-line railroad. In 1911 Yerington took the county seat from Dayton.

Since Yerington's copper mines closed in 1978, the local economy has depended on agriculture—the Mason Valley is among the premier garlic-growing regions in the country—and tourism. Among Yerington's attractions are the old Yerington School, a two-story brick structure built in 1912 and restored as an arts center, and the Lyon County Museum, housed in an old church. The museum has a large selection of photographs, antiques, and artifacts. On the museum grounds are a blacksmith shop, a one-room schoolhouse, and other historic Yerington buildings.

### Wovoka and the Ghost Dance

The Paiute shaman named Wovoka, a.k.a. Jack Wilson, was born near Yerington in 1858. In 1890 he gained national attention by leading the Ghost Dance movement, a ritualistic cult that promised followers a return to happier times. Wovoka's inspiration for the movement came on New Year's Day 1889, when, he claimed, he had a revelation from God. In this vision he learned a ritual dance and was told that those who performed it would be rewarded with everlasting life. Wovoka's message appealed to many Indians, whose way of life had been destroyed.

Wovoka's teachings, which were essentially peaceful, spread across the country, particularly among the Plains tribes. As followers performed the Ghost Dance with increasing fervor, whites began to fear that it would lead to an

*Wovoka, founder of the Ghost Dance movement.* —Courtesy Nevada Historical Society

Indian uprising. The United States government attempted to suppress the movement through military force. Tensions finally culminated in 1890 at the tragic Battle of Wounded Knee in South Dakota. In a confrontation with several hundred Sioux men, women, and children, federal troops opened fire on the group, killing about 150 (some estimates put the death count closer to 300).

The Wounded Knee massacre, the last major conflict between whites and Indians in North America, ended the Ghost Dance movement. A small group of followers continued to revere Wovoka for the rest of his life. He died near Yerington in 1932.

*The Garden of Eden*

On August 17, 1924, the *San Francisco Examiner* announced to its readers that the Garden of Eden had been found in Nevada. The front-page story said that the biblical birthplace of mankind lay on a hilltop thirty miles south of Yerington, by the East Walker River. For the next week, the newspaper printed a series of articles about how an amateur archaeologist, Alan Le Baron, had uncovered proof of the incredible claim, including rock art that appeared to be related to—and was possibly older than—Egyptian hieroglyphics.

The articles dramatically called the site the "Hill of a Thousand Tombs," and they included photographs of petroglyphs depicting sheep, snakes, birds, and various shapes and designs. In classic purple prose, the reporter proclaimed the discovery of "tremendous importance," telling how Le Baron found bones of elephants, lions, and camels mingled with the petrified remnants of lush forests.

While the articles sold newspapers and generated quite a buzz about Yerington and its environs, later experts discounted Le Baron's findings. Archaeologists who studied the site concluded that the rock art was noteworthy only because it was a good example of prehistoric Indian petroglyphs. Visitors can find Le Baron's Garden of Eden via NV 208 and Pine Grove Road. The petroglyphs are carved on a series of natural rock enclosures near the top of a hill overlooking the river.

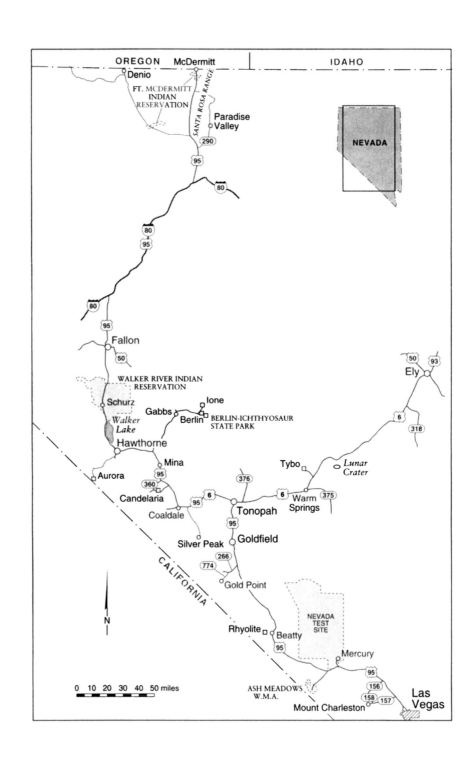

# 4

# US 95 AND US 6: THE SILVER TRAILS

*Off the beaten track, at the end of those unmarked dirt roads that are forever branching off from the main highways, a hundred ghost towns dot the Nevada landscape. A collapsing hulk of a stone building, a scattering of brown-board shacks defeated by time and abandonment, the barely discernible remnant of a wide main street, a nearby hillside riddled with the black apertures of mine tunnels and littered with mounds of discarded rock, and the moaning of the desert wind in the encompassing silence are all that remain of the boom-and-bust towns that flourished and died in the wreckage of broken dreams.*

— Robert Laxalt, *Nevada: A History*

A journey on Nevada's Silver Trails—US 95 and US 6—is a chance to see the boom-and-bust nature of the mining business up close. The routes follow the early-twentieth-century wagon roads and railroad lines that served as links between a string of second-wave mining towns and camps. The first wave included the discoveries in Virginia City, Austin, and Eureka and lasted from about 1860 to 1880. Then came a twenty-year statewide economic slump. But at about the turn of the twentieth century, silver deposits were uncovered in Tonopah, Goldfield, Rhyolite, Tybo, and other places. This second wave revived Nevada's economy and prospects.

US 95 is Nevada's longest road, running 665 miles from McDermitt, on the Nevada-Oregon border, to the California border fifty-five miles south of Las Vegas. In the 1930s the road was sometimes called the "Bonanza Highway," reflecting the mining wealth along the route. Part of US 95 skirts the western edge of the Nellis Air Force Bombing and Gunnery Range and the Nevada Test Site, a huge chunk of south-central Nevada real estate that is off-limits to civilians. US 6 runs almost the full width of Nevada. From the Utah border it enters Nevada near Great Basin National Park; it exits on the California side just north of Boundary Peak, Nevada's highest point at 13,143 feet.

# US 95
# MCDERMITT–WINNEMUCCA
**73 MILES**

### MCDERMITT
McDermitt grew up west of the Fort McDermitt Indian Reservation on US 95 on the Nevada-Oregon line. The town was named after the late-nineteenth-century army camp that later became the reservation. For many years, mercury mining kept the local economy thriving. More recently the town has enjoyed modest success as a gaming destination for Oregon residents.

### FORT MCDERMITT INDIAN RESERVATION
The main part of the Fort McDermitt Indian Reservation straddles the Oregon-Nevada border, north and east of the town of McDermitt; the rest lies off NV 140 about halfway between the US 95 junction and Denio. The reservation began as a military camp in early 1865. The camp, originally called Quinn River Camp Number 33, housed troops assigned to deter Indian uprisings and to protect travelers on the stage route and wagon road from Virginia City to Boise, Idaho.

In August 1865, Lieutenant Colonel Charles McDermit, commander of the Military District of Nevada, was ambushed and killed by Indians while traveling to the camp. A week after his death, the post's name was changed to Camp McDermit, then later to Fort McDermit. The post office added an extra *t* when it was established in 1879. In 1889, after white-Indian hostilities ceased, the fort was converted into an Indian reservation.

### THE SANTA ROSA RANGE
The Santa Rosa mountain range, encompassing the Humboldt National Forest, rises along the east side of US 95 between McDermitt and Winnemucca. This fifty-mile-long range is among the state's least-visited mountains, though the scenery is spectacular. The highest elevation is 9,732 feet at the summit of Granite Peak, and there are miles of trails leading to alpine lakes surrounded by dramatic peaks and flower-filled meadows.

The easiest access into the Santa Rosas is NV 290, the Paradise Valley Road, to Hinckey Summit (7,840 feet). This road passes through the heart of the range, offering a memorable drive through rugged wilderness. About forty miles north of the town of Paradise Valley, the road drops down from the mountains and reconnects with US 95.

# PARADISE VALLEY

The tiny town of Paradise Valley is twenty-two miles northeast of US 95 on NV 290; the turnoff is fifty-one miles south of McDermitt. Paradise Valley has been appreciated for its rich and fertile soil since it was settled in 1864. While there has been some mining in the surrounding mountains, this has always been ranch and farm country. The town is encircled by vast, grassy fields where cattle graze. Walk its shady lanes and it is difficult not to be impressed by the town's serenity. No traffic. Just a few residents. A cowboy rides across a golden field just west of town. It is not a ghost town, yet Paradise Valley has that same sense of a place out of time.

## Edna Purviance

Paradise Valley should be famous as the birthplace of actress Edna Purviance, except few people remember her—or recall that she appeared in more than thirty films with Charlie Chaplin. Purviance was born here on October 21, 1896, and attended school in Lovelock. In 1913 she graduated from high school and moved to San Francisco, where she met Chaplin, who cast her in his 1915 film *A Night Out*.

In addition to being his leading lady for much of the next decade, Purviance was Chaplin's lover and close friend. By the mid-1920s, however, she had grown too mature for Chaplin's ingenue roles. She starred in *A Woman of Paris* in 1923, but critics ignored her performance. She retired shortly after, at the age of thirty, and lived in Los Angeles until her death on January 13, 1958.

*Abandoned buildings line the main street of Paradise Valley.*

# NV 140
# US 95–OREGON BORDER
**110 MILES**

### THE VIRGIN VALLEY

For nearly a century, miners have known about the black fire-opals of the Virgin Creek valley, about 15 miles west of Denio Junction off NV 140, near the Oregon border. These magnificent dark gems sparkle with rainbow hues when seen in sunlight. Geologists trace the origins of these unique opals to Nevada's volcanic period, about 20 million years ago. Several area mines allow rockhounds to hunt for opals on their property for a fee.

One of the largest opals was discovered in 1917 by Colonel W. A. Robeling, a civil engineer who had helped design the Brooklyn Bridge. Robeling later donated his one-and-a-half-pound stone to the Smithsonian Institution. It is on display in the Smithsonian's Gem Hall, along with a handful of smaller but equally beautiful black opals from Virgin Valley.

# US 95
# FALLON–TONOPAH
**176 MILES**

### SCHURZ

Schurz is at the junction of Alternate US 95 and US 95 on the Walker River Indian Reservation. The town was established in 1881 when the Carson & Colorado Railroad built a depot here. Later, the federal government set up a Bureau of Indian Affairs day school and administrative offices in the community. The town was named for Carl Schurz, secretary of the Interior Department and administrator of Indian Affairs from 1877 to 1881. The town remains the tribal headquarters for the reservation, which is home to about 500 Paiute. In addition to administrative offices, the headquarters building houses a small gallery of Paiute arts, crafts, and artifacts.

### WALKER LAKE

South of Fallon on US 95, past the Walker River Indian Reservation, is Walker Lake. Walker Lake is one of Nevada's largest natural lakes, fourteen miles long and nearly five miles wide. Like Pyramid Lake to the north, it is a remnant of prehistoric Lake Lahontan.

Ever since people first appeared in Nevada, Walker Lake has played an important role in their survival. Trout from this lake were an essential part of the early Nevadans' diet. In fact, the Paiute people inhabiting the area were known

*Sportsman's Beach at Walker Lake.* —Courtesy Nevada Commission on Tourism

as the *Agai Ticutta*, which translates as Trout Eaters, and the lake was known as *Agai Pah*, or Trout Lake. The lake gained its present name in the 1840s, after explorer John C. Frémont named it for his scout Joseph Walker.

In the 1850s and 1860s, as miners and other emigrants rapidly settled Nevada, they sometimes had conflicts with the native people. So the federal government segregated the region's Indians on reservations, as it had done throughout the West and elsewhere. The Walker River Indian Reservation originally included all of Walker Lake. In 1906, however, the boundaries were reduced so that only a tiny portion of the lake remained with the tribe.

In the late 1870s a ferry service began running between Walker Lake's north and south shores. Prospectors had discovered silver in the mountains south of the lake, and the mining activity generated considerable freight traffic between the camps and the northern railroad lines. Because it was faster and easier to travel by water than to navigate wagons along the steep cliffs of the lake's west side or the soft and sandy beaches of its east side, the ferry was a success at first. But in 1881, after completion of the Carson & Colorado Railroad, the ferry went out of business.

Some of the best fish stories about Walker Lake are not about record-size trout, but about the giant sea serpents said to live there. Paiute legend tells of two sea monsters, a male and a female, who reside in the lake's depths. In 1883 a local newspaper reported a story told by a group of Paiute who had been camping on the lakeshore. The Indians told the newspaper that loud screeching had awakened them, and they watched two monstrous sea serpents fighting in the lake. After one of the creatures was severely wounded in the battle, the Paiute killed it and sold the carcass to a white man. Before the body disappeared with the white man, however, the Indians measured it. The paper reported that the creature had been seventy-nine feet, seven and a quarter inches long.

For most of the twentieth century, farmers upstream have intercepted most of the water from the Walker River, which feeds the lake. As a result, the lake's water level has dropped more than 100 feet since the 1920s, and saline levels have increased. Native trout species were nearly gone by the late 1940s. In the 1950s wildlife officials introduced trout bred to survive the lake's salty waters, and those trout interbred with the remaining native fish, preserving Walker Lake's trout population. Today the lake is a popular recreation spot, with fishing, boating, and swimming. The Nevada Division of State Parks maintains a picnic area and boat launch on the west shore, accessible from US 95.

## HAWTHORNE

Hawthorne is seventy-two miles south of Fallon on US 95. The Carson & Colorado Railroad established it in 1881 as a commercial hub for the region. Ore from nearby Candelaria and Aurora flowed through Hawthorne, and the town became the region's commercial center. In 1883 Hawthorne took the Esmeralda County seat away from Aurora. In 1907, however, the booming community of Goldfield snatched the county seat from Hawthorne. Then state lawmakers created Mineral County out of the northern portion of Esmeralda County in 1911—and named Hawthorne seat of the new county.

During the next several decades, Hawthorne's fortunes fluctuated with those of the local mining industry. Then, in the 1930s the U.S. government selected Hawthorne as the site of a new navy ammunition dump. During World War II the town ballooned to more than 13,000 residents. Following the war, the population began to decline again, but the military has remained a presence in the area over the years. In fact, one of the most scenic parts of Hawthorne is the military base, which has tree-lined streets and sturdy brick buildings, most built in the 1930s. The base also has one of the best-groomed public golf courses in rural Nevada.

The Mineral County Museum, at Tenth and D Streets, is one of the state's finest rural museums. One interesting display is of seventeen tarnished copper bells of varying sizes. The bells are engraved with dates from the early 1800s. One bell is engraved "Mexico" and another "Mejico." According to the museum, the bells were found buried in the desert about fifteen miles south of Hawthorne. While no one is certain how they came to Nevada, they may have been left behind by an early-nineteenth-century Spanish expedition from

Mexico that local historians claim predates any known exploration of that part of Nevada.

Hawthorne also has historical artifacts less formally arranged on the walls of Joe's Tavern, one of the state's best watering holes. There are old firearms, mining tools, antique signs—and each has a story that any of the bartenders will be happy to share.

## RAWHIDE

The site of Rawhide is thirty-seven miles northeast of Hawthorne by way of NV 839 (Ryan Canyon Road), portions of which are paved. The place had what ghost-town historian Stanley W. Paher described as "a spectacular two-year career." Miners discovered gold in Rawhide late in 1906, and within a few months a boomtown had appeared in the desert. By October 1907 Rawhide had a post office—which replaced an old tobacco-can mailbox nailed to a pole—as well as a newspaper, the *Rawhide Rustler*. The paper was the town's biggest booster, often printing stories that claimed Rawhide was the greatest gold camp in the world.

The hyperbole worked for a while, and by 1908 Rawhide had nearly 8,000 residents. Its thriving business district included more than three dozen saloons—the famous Tex Rickard, who later built New York's Madison Square Garden, owned one—and more than a hundred brokerage firms handling mining stocks. The latter illustrates the disproportionate influence that mining promoters and speculators had on the local economy. The future seemed so promising that the city installed expensive municipal telephone and water systems. Work even began on a railroad to link the camp to the outside world.

*Citizens of Rawhide line up to collect their mail, early 1900s.*
—Courtesy Nevada Historical Society

However, in September 1908 a fire swept through the community, causing more than $1 million in damages. While residents rebuilt some of the businesses and homes, the fire caused many investors to take stock of the region's potential—and many noticed that behind all the hype was the inescapable fact that Rawhide's mines had earned less than $1.5 million.

In subsequent months the railroad construction was abandoned, and most residents began to drift to other camps. Though three mills went up in 1909, they operated for only a few months before being dismantled. In the end, gold production at Rawhide—"the greatest gold camp in the world"—amounted to less than $2 million. Today, nothing remains of the town except for a few foundations.

## AURORA

The ransacked remains of Aurora are twenty-three miles southwest of Hawthorne off NV 359, on Lucky Boy Pass Road, passable only with four-wheel drive. This is one of Nevada's most abused historic sites—in a sense a victim of its own attempts at stability. You see, Aurora was constructed mostly of brick, and after the town's demise, droves of salvagers came in and destroyed the vacant buildings for the bricks.

Shortly after prospectors discovered gold and silver in Gregory Flats in August 1860, hundreds of miners began streaming into the region from other camps. A small camp formed, named Esmeralda. A couple of months later, the town of Aurora—named for the goddess of the dawn by some poetically inclined miner—was platted to the west of the Esmeralda camp.

By 1861 the new town had a large stamp mill, stagecoach service to Carson City, assorted other businesses, and more than 2,000 inhabitants. Aurora's success did not escape the notice of state officials in California and Nevada, who coveted its resources. The boundary between the two states was not clear at that time, so both states claimed Aurora. In the spring of 1861, California created Mono County and named Aurora as the seat. Nevada responded a few months later by designating Aurora the seat of Esmeralda County. Each state appointed its own set of judges and county officials. The states waged a legal battle for nearly two years. Finally, in October 1863 both states agreed to have the border properly surveyed. In the end, the survey proved that Aurora was four miles from the California border.

Aurora continued to prosper over the next few years; by the middle of 1863 it had grown to a city of nearly 10,000 people. As with many mining towns, however, much of the wealth was illusory. Overbuilding of mills and overly optimistic mining-stock speculation created a boom that could not be sustained. In 1865 the mines began to fade, and Aurora lost almost half its population and businesses.

A second, smaller boom occurred in the late 1870s, but it was also short-lived. By 1883 the population had fallen so dramatically that Hawthorne took the county seat. But Aurora was not quite ready for an obituary. At the turn of the twentieth century, several of Aurora's mines reopened, and by 1906 several hundred people were again living in Aurora. But this prosperity, too, ended when Aurora's mines closed in 1919.

In the late 1940s scavengers leveled the town's remaining buildings to reuse the bricks. In his book *The Complete Nevada Traveler*, David W. Toll wrote that as a ten-year-old boy in the late 1940s, he once visited Aurora with his eighty-eight-year-old great-grandfather. The two wandered the empty town, which included a fully stocked but abandoned hardware store:

> I remember the awe I felt, listening to the old man's voice and feeling the emptiness of the brick city in the summer afternoon.... Aurora's gone now, torn down for the bricks not long after the old man and I made our pilgrimage. The buildings are now a row of factory chimneys in California.

Today, if you search, you can still find a few wooden shacks, a cement wall or two, the remains of an old stamp, and a few foundations in Aurora. The town's large cemetery is the best surviving testament to the town's former importance.

*Little remains of Aurora besides its cemetery.*

## MINA

The tiny town of Mina, thirty-four miles southeast of Hawthorne on US 95, was named for the colorful Ferminia "Mina" Sarras, also known as the Copper Queen. The Carson & Colorado Railroad (later called the Nevada & California Railway), owned by the Southern Pacific Railroad, established Mina in 1905 with a ten-stall engine house, depot, and other facilities. By 1907 Mina had nearly 400 residents and a weekly paper, the *Western Nevada Miner*. Around 1910 the two-story, sixty-room Hotel Mina opened.

For about twenty years Mina thrived as a shipping point for area mines and as a link between the Southern Pacific and the Tonopah & Goldfield Railroads. However by the early 1930s most of the mines had closed and Mina began to lose population. In the 1980s the rail line was abandoned and the tracks removed. Today Mina is a quiet community with a gas station and convenience store, two motels, and an RV park.

### Ferminia Sarras

Ferminia "Mina" Sarras was one of early Nevada's true free spirits. As a miner and a hell-raiser, her behavior was quite unconventional for a woman in the nineteenth century. Sarras was born in Nicaragua in 1840 and arrived in Nevada in the 1870s. After several years doing menial jobs, such as taking in laundry, she began to mine in a central Nevada camp called Belleville. With the help of more-experienced miners, she accumulated a small fortune in Belleville, but she quickly lost it speculating in mining stocks and other ventures.

Then, in 1899 Sarras, who had by now become an adept prospector, began mining in the mountains near Soda Spring Valley, south of Hawthorne. Within a few years, she had sold two dozen copper claims at a handsome profit. Following the example of many of her male counterparts—who were not known for their thrift—Sarras celebrated by spending the money. She headed for San Francisco and Los Angeles, where she took rooms at the most expensive hotels, purchased the most elegant gowns, and hired herself an escort. She wined, dined, and pampered herself until the money was all gone, then she returned to Nevada to prospect some more so she could do it all over again.

Her love life was equally scandalous. She is believed to have had from three to six husbands and countless lovers, most much younger than she. Despite—or perhaps because of—her notoriety, in 1905 the Carson & Colorado Railroad established a small depot near her former claims and named it Mina in her honor. By the time Sarras died in 1915, she had made and lost several fortunes—and broken at least a few hearts.

## MARIETTA

To reach the former site of Marietta, now part of the Marietta Wild Burro Range, take US 95 fifty-six miles southeast of Hawthorne, then turn west on NV 360 to the sign on a maintained dirt road. Marietta, established in the late

*A dilapidated post office in Marietta.*

1870s, was not a typical central-Nevada mining camp. Its fortunes were based not on gold and silver, but on borax and salt. The salt mine was first developed in 1867 at Teels Marsh, one of several salt marshes in the area. The salt was transported by camel to Virginia City, where it was used in processing ore. The borax was discovered a few years later. Marietta grew up out of the Teels Marsh borax operation in 1877, and within a year it had several businesses and more than 150 residents.

Francis M. Smith, who would soon achieve renown as "Borax" Smith, was working in the Columbus Salt Marsh, about twenty miles southeast, when he learned about Teels Marsh in 1872. He took a sample from a dry lakebed there, and it proved to be rich in borax, or colmanite. Smith immediately staked a claim on much of the area. Full-scale borax mining began within months of the discovery. Smith and other miners constructed borax-processing facilities at the southeastern end of the marsh. Wagon trains hauled the borax to the train depot at Wadsworth, about 115 miles north.

The success of the operation led Smith to create the Teels Marsh Borax Company, precursor of the Pacific Borax Salt & Soda Company, which eventually controlled the world borax market. Smith's genius was in recognizing that the mineral could be profitable if marketed correctly. Prior to his efforts, borax was used primarily in pharmaceuticals. Since he was sitting on such large reserves, Smith began promoting the substance as an effective cleanser. He created an immense market for his product, and in the process became one of the era's most successful industrialists. Smith eventually moved farther west to larger borax deposits in Death Valley and became famed for his twenty-mule teams that carried the borax out. His naming the product Twenty Mule Team Pure Borax was another example of Smith's marketing acumen.

Smith's departure after the borax discoveries in Death Valley meant the eventual end of Marietta. By the 1890s Smith's company had ceased mining there, and the town began its slide into oblivion. Today the most prominent ruins are the stone walls of Smith's company store. East of the store is the foundation of the stamp mill and, buried in the sagebrush, a handful of dirt mounds where the town cemetery was.

In the 1990s the federal government created the Marietta Wild Burro Range at Teels Marsh, the nation's first wild-burro refuge, setting aside 68,000 acres as rangeland for about eighty-five burros. Visitors can see the burros from designated viewing areas above the marsh.

## CANDELARIA

The remains of Candelaria lie six miles southwest of US 95 on Candelaria Road, the turnoff for which is fifteen miles south of Mina. In the early 1860s Spanish prospectors discovered silver in Candelaria. The name is believed to be either a derivation of the Roman Catholic holiday Candlemass—perhaps the day the mine was claimed—or a family surname.

Sustained mining did not begin in the district until the mid-1870s with development of the Northern Belle mine. Soon investors erected large stamp mills at Belleville, eight miles northwest, and Candelaria's silver began to attract attention. By 1876 Candelaria had many thriving businesses. As with many central-Nevada mining towns, water was a scarce commodity—a gallon of drinking water cost $1, and it cost $2 to take a bath.

By the early 1880s Candelaria's mines were producing more than $1 million in ore a year. In 1882 a pipeline was built to bring in water, and the price of that commodity dipped to five cents per gallon. That same year, Candelaria's population reached 1,500, making it the largest city in Mineral County. By then the town had a bank, a telegraph office, a newspaper, and two breweries, but despite its (perhaps) Christian-based name, it never had a church. Also in 1882, a spur of the Carson & Colorado Railroad connected Candelaria to shipping points at Mina and Keeler, a town near Owens Lake, California.

A fire destroyed part of the community in 1883, and the next year its miners went on strike. Unfortunately, those events coincided with the beginning of the mines' decline. The town perked up again at the turn of the century with new mining discoveries, but the revival did not last. In 1932 the railroad, which had operated sporadically during the previous three decades, abandoned its spur to Candelaria and removed the tracks. In the 1980s an open-pit mine opened adjacent to the town site, which by then, due to neglect, had become little more than a scattering of ruins.

## SILVER PEAK

Silver Peak (sometimes spelled as one word) is about halfway between Hawthorne and Tonopah via US 95 and NV 265. The town goes back to 1863, when miners from the Austin area found gold and silver here. Within two years they had erected a ten-stamp mill. They built a larger, twenty-stamp mill in 1867, and a small camp developed. The mill, however, shut down in 1870, and over the next thirty years the mines were only sporadically worked.

In 1906 the Pittsburgh Silver Peak Gold Mining Company reopened the mines and built the Silver Peak Railroad to carry ore from a large mill at Blair, a mining camp about three miles north, to the Tonopah & Goldfield Railroad, about twenty miles north. But Silver Peak's fortunes fell farther than they rose, and by 1913 the population had dropped so much the town lost its post office. Then came another mining boom in the mid-1920s, during which Silver Peak produced more than $8.5 million in gold.

A fire destroyed much of the town in 1948. The present community of Silver Peak dates to the 1960s, when large-scale lithium mining began in nearby Clayton Valley. Today Silver Peak has a permanent population of about a hundred. Visitors can still find a few ruins mixed in among the newer buildings.

## BLAIR

Of the hundreds of flash-in-the-pan mining camps in Nevada, few were as short-lived as Blair. This company town, two miles northwest of Silver Peak, was established between 1906 and 1907 and was gone by 1918.

Because land in Silver Peak was expensive, the Pittsburgh Silver Peak Gold Mining Company created Blair nearby as a site for its mill. The company named the town for John I. Blair, an eastern banker who had developed the Silver Peak Mining District. The 100-stamp mill at Blair was the largest in the state at the time. The Silver Peak Railroad, a 14,000-foot aerial tramway, carried ore from the Silver Peak mines to the mill. By 1907 Blair had a few dozen homes and a handful of businesses. Blair's residents were resourceful when it came to financing public works: to raise money for fire hydrants, they put on a minstrel show.

Silver Peak's mines played out within a few years, and by 1915 Blair's mill had closed. The company dismantled the facility and sold it to another mine, and the railroad was torn up in 1918. Today it is easy to overlook the site of Blair. Perched on a slope overlooking the road, the town has almost blended back into the surrounding sagebrush-covered hills.

## TONOPAH

Legend has it that Tonopah (tuh-NO-puh), at the junction of US 6 and US 95, owes its founding to a jackass. In May 1900 a local rancher named Jim Butler was traveling with two burros through central Nevada. He had just completed a term as the Nye County district attorney and was heading home to his

*Jim Butler.* —Courtesy
Nevada Historical Society

ranch in the Monitor Valley. It was getting late, so he set up camp near a rock outcropping at Sawtooth Pass.

When he awoke the next morning, Butler discovered that one of his burros had wandered up a hillside. Picking up a loose rock, he prepared to toss it at the errant animal, but stopped when he noticed the rock's heaviness. He collected a bag full of samples, gathered his burros, and continued home.

Most historians agree on what happened next. Butler believed the rocks looked promising but had no money to have them assayed, nor could he interest anyone in testing them in exchange for a share in his claim. One day Butler's friend Tasker Oddie, a lawyer who later became a governor of Nevada and a U.S. senator, stopped in to visit Butler, and Butler showed him the samples. Oddie offered to have the rocks assayed after Butler promised him a quarter of the claim if they amounted to anything. Oddie took the ore to Walter Gayheart, a teacher and amateur assayer in Austin. For a small share in the action, Gayheart ran the samples. They tested rich in silver—Grayheart estimated some of them to be worth as much as $600 per ton.

In late August Butler and his wife, Belle, returned to the site and staked several claims: the Desert Queen, the Burro, and the Mizpah. Belle Butler staked the last, which proved to be the richest. Shortly after establishing their claims, the Butlers began leasing mining rights to the properties for one-year terms. The arrangement spurred the development of the town of Butler, later known as Tonopah. A year later, Butler and his partners sold their interests to the Tonopah Mining Company, which began to fully develop the mines. Between 1902 and 1948 the mines produced ore worth more than $48 million.

Butler's discovery helped to end Nevada's twenty-year economic depression. Within a year of the find, Tonopah (from the Paiute word for "brush water," or spring) had several thousand residents. By the end of 1901 miners had extracted nearly $4 million in silver. In 1905 Tonopah was sufficiently prosperous to take the county seat from the declining town of Belmont.

By 1907 Tonopah had a population of more than 10,000, and the community had become, in the words of mining historian Shawn Hall, "a regular city," with it own electric and water companies and hundreds of businesses. Tonopah's most prominent building, the recently closed Mizpah Hotel, opened in 1908 with hot and cold running water, an electric elevator, and the finest furniture and fixtures. The three-story stone structure cost more than $200,000 to build.

Tonopah remained a productive mining town until the Great Depression. By the 1940s only a handful of mines remained in operation. In 1947 the Tonopah & Goldfield Railroad ceased operations and removed its rails. Despite these losses, Tonopah did not completely fade away like many other Nevada mining communities. It benefited from being the Nye County seat and from its diverse other industries, including ranching and tourism. In addition, the U.S. military operation at the nearby Nevada Test Site has been an important source of jobs for the community.

*An overview of Tonopah, one of central Nevada's most historically interesting communities.* —Courtesy K. J. Evans

### Famous Temporary Tonopahans

Among Tonopah's early citizens was legendary lawman Wyatt Earp, who lived in the town for about eight months in 1902. After hearing about the Tonopah silver strike, Earp and his wife, Josie, moved to Tonopah in January 1902. Earp told the local newspaper that he came to open a saloon. Within weeks of their arrival, the Northern, partly owned by Earp, opened for business.

In April, Earp began working as a teamster for the Tonopah Mining Company. Driving freight wagons was lucrative work. Drivers were paid to haul ore to the closest railroad depot but could make even more money bringing merchandise and goods back to the community. In August or September 1902 the Earps departed Tonopah for California. During the next three years they returned to Nevada on periodic prospecting trips, but they never settled in the state.

Another famous temporary Tonopah resident was Jack Dempsey, the heavyweight boxing champion of the world from 1919 to 1926. Dempsey lived in Tonopah from about 1915 to 1916, working as a laborer in the silver mines and as a bartender and bouncer at the Mizpah Hotel. It is also said that he participated in a few informal back-alley boxing matches.

### The Central Nevada Museum

The grounds of Tonopah's Central Nevada Museum, on Logan Field Road, are an outdoor warehouse of antique mining equipment, historic buildings,

*The Northern Saloon in Tonopah, 1902.* —Courtesy Nevada Historical Society

and other artifacts preserved from camps and ghost towns throughout the region. There is even a full-size headframe hoist from the mining camp of Manhattan. Inside the museum are old photographs of Tonopah and other camps as well as Native American baskets and arrowheads.

# NV 361 AND NV 844
# US 95–IONE
### 57 MILES

## GABBS

Gabbs, fifty-six miles northeast of Hawthorne via US 95 and NV 361, is Nevada's smallest incorporated city, with about 600 residents. The community began in the early 1940s, when the federal government opened a magnesite and brucite mine in the area during World War II. Both minerals contain magnesium, a metal vital to the manufacture of airplanes and bombs. Ore from the Gabbs mine was shipped 300 miles to the massive Basic Magnesium plant, which the federal government had built in Henderson, then known as Basic, south of Las Vegas. The mine is still active today.

A post office was established in 1942 under the name Toiyabe, then it changed to Gabbs about six months later. The name comes from the surrounding Gabbs Valley; its namesake was William M. Gabb, a paleontologist who surveyed and mapped California in the 1860s.

### Melvin and Howard

Perhaps the most famous person to come from Gabbs was Melvin Dummar, a one-time milkman and gas-station operator who in the 1970s claimed that several years earlier he had found billionaire Howard Hughes lying semiconcious by the side of the highway and had given him a ride. Dummar's story was popularized in the 1980 film *Melvin and Howard.*

According to Dummar, in late 1967 he was driving on US 95 south of Beatty when he spotted a long-haired, bearded man facedown on the side of the road. Dummar revived the old man, who was somewhat delirious, and agreed to take him to Las Vegas. Once the old man warmed up in the car, he became more coherent and began talking to Dummar about the aircraft industry. When Dummar remarked that he would like to get a job in an aircraft plant, the old man said he would see what he could do, since he owned Hughes Aircraft. Dummar, however, dismissed the old man's promise as the ramblings of an old drunk who had spent a little too much time in the desert. Once in Las Vegas, the old man told Dummar to drive him to the Sands Hotel—where Howard Hughes lived at the time.

In April 1976, following Hughes's death, a handwritten version of Hughes's will turned up at the offices of the Church of Jesus Christ of Latter-day Saints in Salt Lake City, Utah. The document, which became known as the "Mormon Will," named Dummar as a one-sixteenth beneficiary of the Hughes estate (his share would be roughly $156 million). Dummar claimed he didn't know that the old man he'd picked up in the desert was Howard Hughes until his name appeared in the will. The Mormon Will, however, had never been formally filed, so its authenticity was immediately questioned. Following a lengthy trial, the will was ruled a fake and Dummar received nothing.

## BERLIN-ICHTHYOSAUR STATE PARK

Berlin-Ichthyosaur State Park, sixteen miles east of Gabbs on NV 844, combines both the preserved mining ghost town of Berlin and an archaeological site. The park sits within the boundaries of Toiyabe National Forest, on the southeastern edge of the Shoshone Mountains, overlooking the Ione Valley.

Berlin was founded in 1897 near the site of a gold discovery, and within a few years the town had nearly 900 residents, a thirty-stamp mill, a company store, an auto-repair shop, an assay office, and various other businesses. In 1907 however, the mill and the mine closed during a labor dispute. The mine reopened in 1909 when investors constructed a cyanide plant to leach gold from the low-grade ore, but by 1918 mining activity had again ceased.

The Goldfield Blue Bell Mining Company purchased the deserted town's mining claims in the 1920s and did periodic exploratory work. The company paid mine superintendent Daniel Johnson to live in the town for the next several decades and act as a caretaker, keeping vandals and souvenir hunters

*Berlin-Ichthyosaur State Park.*

away from company property. His presence saved Berlin from the fate of most ghost towns, which are often ransacked. In 1947 the company dismantled the milling equipment and sold the metal for scrap.

In the 1970s Berlin became part of a state park. The park service stabilized the dozen buildings still standing and put up interpretive signs, and it offers guided tours in summer. A small cemetery southeast of the town has only a few graves; most families took their dead with them when they left Berlin.

About a mile south of Berlin is an enclosed archaeological dig site where scientists have found the remains of thirty-seven ichthyosaurs. Ichthyosaurs were among the largest creatures to swim in the Mesozoic oceans of more than 200 million years ago. These massive dinosaurs were fifty to sixty feet long and weighed forty to fifty tons. The park has not only the largest ichthyosaur skeleton ever uncovered—nearly sixty feet long—but also the world's greatest concentration of ichthyosaur remains.

Two hundred million years ago, most of Nevada was underwater. Mud and sand thousands of feet deep covered the skeletons, ultimately hardening into rock. Later, the geologic uplifting that created the Shoshone Mountains also exposed the fossils. Exactly how these "fish lizards" died remains a mystery, though several theories have emerged.

Miners first stumbled upon the ichthyosaur fossils at the turn of the twentieth century. Not certain of the bones' origins, the miners often kept them as souvenirs, sometimes even using the large, round vertebrae as dinner plates! In the early 1950s, Charles L. Camp, director of the Paleontological Museum in Berkeley, heard about the bones and decided to conduct a formal excavation at the site. Working with a colleague, Samuel P. Wells, and students, Camp conducted digs from 1954 to 1957 and from 1963 to 1965. His efforts yielded thirty-seven adult ichthyosaurs, which lived during the Triassic period of the Mesozoic era.

Camp found that the Berlin ichthyosaurs had several distinctive features and assigned them to a new branch of the family, which he named *Shonisaurus*, after the surrounding Shoshone Mountains. Camp's research also hinted at possible reasons for the creatures' demise. He noticed that the majority of the skeletons were found lying in a north-south direction and that all were adults. There were no complete skeletons, and many bones appeared crushed or damaged. Camp concluded that the ichthyosaurs had become beached in a mud flat when the tide receded, as happens to modern-day whales. The bones had become scattered by scavengers and the force of crashing waves. In the 1980s, however, other paleontologists concluded that the massive creatures may have died of food poisoning from consuming toxic shellfish.

Camp's pioneering work persuaded the Nevada legislature to create the Ichthyosaur State Monument in 1955. The government constructed a large A-frame shelter over one of the largest quarries to protect the bones and provide a place for public observation. The site was combined with the Berlin ghost town and became Berlin-Ichthyosaur State Park in 1970. Nevada designated ichthyosaur the official state fossil in 1977.

## IONE

Ione (EYE-own), six miles north of Berlin-Ichthyosaur State Park, is one of the oldest surviving former mining towns in the state. In 1863 prospectors found silver in the Ione Valley, and a small camp known as Ione City quickly developed. Miner P. A. Haven named the district in honor of a place he knew in California. By 1864 the camp had a population of 600 and had been designated the first seat of Nye County. The prosperity, however, was short-lived. A year later, word of significant discoveries at Belmont, about fifty miles southeast, attracted many of Ione's prospectors, and in 1867 Belmont succeeded in snatching away the county seat.

Modest silver discoveries in 1868 might have expanded Ione's success, but White Pine's mining boom of the same year garnered considerably more attention. Still, those finds kept the town fairly flush until 1880. After that, the town managed to struggle along, never completely abandoned, due to occasional mining activity, including mercury mining in the 1920s and 1930s.

The town's most recent revival occurred in 1983, with Marshall Earth Resources' development of a large gold-mining operation. This boom eventually ebbed as well, though, and the town lapsed into a quasi slumber. But not before Marshall, which owns most of the town, restored several of Ione's historic buildings. The company converted the schoolhouse into a general store and renovated the post office for company offices, furnishing them with antiques.

Ione's quaint town park is also worth a visit. It has a Victorian charm, encircled by a white picket fence and graced with turn-of-the-century street lamps. The large shade trees make it a pleasant place for a picnic or to simply enjoy Ione's tranquil ambiance. North of the park lie other remains from the original Ione, such as a dilapidated barn that some believe was the original Nye County courthouse and several half-buried sod homes.

# US 6
# TONOPAH–ELY
**167** MILES

## WARM SPRINGS

Warm Springs, at the junction of US 6 and NV 375, has a long history as a rest stop for travelers. As its name suggests, the site has several natural hot springs. The first structure to appear here was a small stone house, built in 1866. Freight wagons and stages stopped there, and eventually someone set up a small store and inn.

The settlement never had more than a few dozen residents, and in the 1980s the last business in Warm Springs, a small roadside diner and gas station, closed. Today, visitors will find stone ruins, boarded-up buildings, and an empty swimming pool.

## TYBO

About ten miles north of Warm Springs via US 6 and a marked dirt road is the ghost town of Tybo. The name is derived from *tai-vu*, the Western Shoshone word for "white man." Prospectors discovered silver in the Tybo Canyon area in 1866. Large-scale mining began about six years later with the construction of a smelter.

While known as a fairly peaceful camp in its early years, by the mid-1870s Tybo had evolved into three distinct districts divided by ethnicity—Irish, Cornish, and central European—and had experienced some cultural tensions. One of the few times the three groups banded together was, ironically, to repel Chinese woodcutters who tried to settle in the area.

By 1876 Tybo had 1,000 residents, a small commercial district, and a newspaper, the *Tybo Sun*. The mines experienced a slump beginning in 1879; some of the mines closed, the smelter shut down, the newspaper folded, and the population dropped below 100. During the next fifty years, Tybo's fortunes rose and fell with those of the local mines. Revivals occurred in 1901, 1905, 1917, and 1925. The last was fairly significant: a 350-ton mill and a new smelter went up, sustaining the town for the next twelve years.

*The brick schoolhouse in Tybo.*

In the years since the end of that boom, Tybo has supported small mining operations. The town was never completely deserted, although only one home has been inhabited since the late 1990s. Though occupied, Tybo is considered a ghost town, with ruins open to visitors.

In the center of town is the stone shell of the Trowbridge Store, built in the late nineteenth century. It began as a cash-and-credit store, then became a recreation hall for miners. It is in remarkably good condition, with most of its roof intact and glass still in the front windows. Opposite the store are the remains of more-recent mining operations, including a large metal headframe and assorted scraps of wood, metal, and wire. A series of wooden structures up the canyon appear to date from the 1930s revival. One is a large bunkhouse. On the hillside is a sod-roof house built of railroad ties.

About half a mile from the town center are the brick walls of the old schoolhouse, built in 1880. At the mouth of Tybo Canyon, about a mile from town, is a small cemetery with a few stone and wood headstones dating to the late nineteenth century. Heading out of Tybo, an extremely rocky and steep road leads to three well-preserved charcoal kilns, four miles northwest of town. These thirty-foot high, beehive-shaped structures were built in 1874 of native stone.

## LUNAR CRATER

Despite its name, Lunar Crater owes its existence to geological rather than extraterrestrial forces. It is actually the remnants of an exploded volcanic cinder cone. The crater is about eighty-three miles northeast of Tonopah via US 6 and a signed dirt road.

Part of Lunar Crater's attraction is its tremendous size—three-quarters of a mile wide and 420 feet deep. It is so massive that it seems to generate its own weather, including fierce winds that whip up its steep walls and blast anyone admiring the view. There are several of these extinct volcanic cones as well as lava flows in the area, known as the Lunar Crater Volcanic Field.

Lunar Crater formed about a thousand years ago when a thin layer of lava clogged one of the cones. Pressure began to build under the rock lid and it exploded, leaving a deep conical hole. Early Nye County miners and ranchers considered Lunar Crater an interesting novelty. In 1939, Nevada state park officials erected a sign on the highway guiding visitors to the site. Later, it became an official Bureau of Land Management attraction. Interestingly, the site does have an outer-space connection. In the mid-1960s, Apollo astronauts trained in the 140,000-acre faux moonscape to prepare for their lunar landing.

The Lunar Crater Volcanic Field has many other, equally interesting geological formations. Easy Chair Crater, another collapsed cinder cone, looks like a giant overstuffed chair. The Black Rock Lava Flow spreads over 1,900 acres. The dark basalt contains specks of green, red, and black glass that formed when the lava quickly cooled.

*Stretching three-quarters of a mile across, Lunar Crater is one of central Nevada's most intriguing geological formations.*

# US 95
# TONOPAH–LAS VEGAS
### 207 MILES

## GOLDFIELD

The once glorious Goldfield is now a tiny town on US 95, twenty-six miles south of Tonopah. In 1902, two years after Tonopah's rich silver deposits were discovered, a Shoshone man named Tom Fisherman found gold in the mountains south of Tonopah. He led two miners, Harry Stimler and William Marsh, to his find, and within months a small mining camp had developed at the base of Columbia Mountain. The site was originally called Grandpa, allegedly because Marsh declared it was going to be the granddaddy of all mining camps. Interest in the camp was lukewarm until 1903, when miners made larger gold strikes here. The following year, the town was platted and named Goldfield.

Goldfield's growth was explosive. At its peak in 1907, Goldfield was the largest community in Nevada, with 15,000 to 20,000 residents. That same year, it wrested the Esmeralda County seat from less populated Hawthorne and erected a magnificent castlelike courthouse. Goldfield became the center of commerce and political might in Nevada. It created the mining millionaires and power brokers who would control the state for the next several decades.

*This stone arch, which served as the entrance to the Montezuma Club, survived the 1923 fire that destroyed more than 200 buildings in Goldfield. In the background is the Goldfield Hotel.*

Goldfield's fall was nearly as spectacular as its rise. By 1908 most of its mines had come under the control of one company, the Goldfield Consolidated Mines Company, owned by George Wingfield with George Nixon. Wingfield controlled most of Goldfield's mines and was one of the most influential political and business forces in Nevada during the first quarter of the twentieth century. But many miners working in Goldfield were "wildcat" lessors who preferred not to work for a large corporation, so they moved on. The U.S. census of 1910 reported that the town's population had dropped to 4,838.

By 1911 gold was becoming harder to find in Goldfield. The ore was high in gold content, but the deposits did not go deep. The town continued its rapid tailspin. In September 1913 a flash flood washed away several blocks of homes, and they were not rebuilt. While the town had experienced earlier fires (most notably in 1905 and 1906), it suffered perhaps its greatest conflagration in 1923; that fire destroyed more than 200 structures. Another fire in 1924 burned a one-block area of the downtown, including the *Goldfield News* building and the Elks Club.

Goldfield today has a permanent population of about 400. It remains one of the most vivid reminders of Nevada's early-twentieth-century cycle of boom and bust.

### The Gans-Nelson Fight

In September 1906 Goldfield hosted the world lightweight boxing championship between Joe Gans and Oscar Matthew "Battlin'" Nelson. The fight attracted national press attention for the town, in part because of promoter Tex Rickard. The *Goldfield News* puffed, "The name of Goldfield is now on the lips of men who never before knew of its existence."

George Lewis "Tex" Rickard, the man who built New York's Madison Square Garden in 1924 to stage prizefights, got his start in boxing promotion with the Gans-Nelson fight. After a successful tour as a professional gambler in Alaska during the Klondike gold rush of the 1890s, Rickard arrived in Goldfield in 1904. He opened the Northern Saloon and purchased a stake in several gold mines. He built the elegant Victorian brick home on the corner of Crook and Franklin Streets in 1906, the same year he embarked on his career as a promoter. In an early demonstration of his instincts for publicity, he displayed the entire $33,500 fight purse—in $10 and $20 gold coins—in the window of his saloon.

The fight lasted forty-two rounds, with Gans finally winning on a foul when Nelson struck a low blow. Though he was the winner, Gans collected a purse of only $11,000, while Nelson received $22,500, simply on the basis of race. Following the success of the Gans-Nelson fight, Rickard promoted other bouts in Nevada, such as the 1910 Jack Johnson–Jim Jefferies heavyweight championship in Reno. He moved up to bigger fights, including several with Jack Dempsey. Rickard died in 1929 of appendicitis.

### Labor Unrest in Goldfield

With so much gold being produced in Goldfield, it should have been no surprise that some miners wanted not only their fair share, but a little extra. "High-grading"—stealing valuable ore by hiding it in clothing—became widespread. In 1907 the mine owners installed changing rooms at the mines and insisted that all mine workers had to change from their work clothes to their street clothes in the presence of company inspectors.

The rule incensed many miners, particularly those who belonged to the more radical mining unions, including the Industrial Workers of the World (IWW, or Wobblies) and the Western Federation of Miners. The unions decided to challenge the mining companies and threatened a strike. Following a tense standoff, the sides agreed that the changing rooms could stay but that union members would serve as inspectors.

But the labor situation worsened later that year when Goldfield Consolidated Mines Company experienced a slump and tried to pay workers with scrip rather than cash. Flexing their muscle, the unions called a general strike. In an attempt to break the unions, owner George Wingfield claimed that the miners were threatening violence and persuaded Governor John Sparks to ask President Theodore Roosevelt to send federal troops to keep the peace.

Roosevelt complied, and soon Goldfield was under military control. But the president quickly realized that the company was using the troops to bust the unions, and he withdrew them. Governor Sparks, however, remained convinced that violence was likely and called a special session of the Nevada legislature to create a state militia, who then replaced the departing federal soldiers. Consequently, Wingfield successfully broke the unions.

A sidebar to Goldfield's labor unrest was the murder trial and conviction of two union members, Morrie R. Preston and Joseph W. Smith. In March 1907 Preston shot and killed John Silva, a Goldfield restaurant owner. The IWW was boycotting Silva's restaurant because Silva had refused to pay a waitress, who was a union member, after she left work without notice. Smith was the IWW labor leader who ordered the boycott, so he was indicted as an accessory to the murder.

According to reliable witnesses, Silva grew angry after watching Preston dissuade several potential customers from coming into his restaurant. He grabbed a pistol and rushed out to confront Preston, who was also armed. After inflammatory words, Preston thought that Silva was advancing toward him with the intention of firing his gun, so he shot first. The restaurant owner clutched his stomach and fell to the ground.

The subsequent trial attracted national attention, largely because of how Smith—who was not present at the shooting—and Preston were railroaded by prosecutors, who were loyal to Wingfield. The prosecution relied greatly on witnesses of questionable credibility such as "Diamondfield" Jack Davis, a union-busting gunfighter who worked for Wingfield. Despite evidence that Preston shot Silva in self-defense, and that Smith had nothing to do with the shooting, the two were convicted and sent to prison. Wingfield saw the trial as an opportunity to discredit the union and had used his considerable influence and resources to obtain the convictions. Preston and Smith were eventually paroled, but it was not until nearly seventy-five years later, long after both were dead, that the court cleared their names during a formal reconsideration of the case.

### Historic Goldfield

In spite of disasters, neglect, and decay, more than 100 historic structures have survived in Goldfield. The West Crook Street School, built in 1908, is now the county library. The Santa Fe Saloon, which opened in 1905, is the oldest business in Goldfield. The Santa Fe has retained much of its mining-camp atmosphere, with its huge nineteenth-century oak backbar and uneven wooden floors.

One of the most obvious symbols of Goldfield's prosperity at the time was the Goldfield Hotel, completed in 1908. The four-story brick structure was the most luxurious hotel in the state. It had an elevator, crystal chandeliers, and an elegant mahogany-trimmed lobby with black leather upholstery and gilded

*The Santa Fe Saloon in Goldfield.*

columns. One of Goldfield's largest mining consortiums, the Hayes-Monette Syndicate, financed the hotel at a cost of nearly $350,000. Shortly after the building's completion, Hayes-Monette sold it to George Wingfield. The hotel managed to stay open until the 1940s, but it has not operated since. In the mid-1980s a San Francisco developer partially restored the building, but he ran out of money before the work was completed.

## GOLD POINT

The barely inhabited town of Gold Point is thirty miles southwest of Goldfield via US 95, NV 266, and NV 774. At first it was called Lime Point, because of lime deposits discovered there in 1868. The area was occasionally mined for lime until the early 1880s, when prospectors uncovered silver. The high cost of transportation at that time, however, made silver mining unfeasible, and the deposits sat unexploited for a couple of decades.

In 1905 the Great Western silver mine opened, and the discovery of high-grade ore in 1908 sparked a boom. Lime Point became Hornsilver, after the type of ore found there—silver chloride, or horn silver. Over the next few years, more than 200 buildings went up in the community, including a newspaper office for the *Hornsilver Herald*. In 1932 the town's name was changed to Gold Point, as by then gold had become the primary mineral in production. The area's mines were closed for good in 1942, during World War II, and by the 1950s Gold Point was nearly deserted. In recent years private owners have restored several of the town's buildings.

*A row of miner's cottages in Gold Point.*

## BEATTY

Beatty is sixty-seven miles south of Goldfield on US 95. Its first settler was a man named Landers, who arrived about 1870. All that seems to be known about Landers is that he built a small stone cabin adjacent to a bubbling spring. In 1896 the future town's namesake, Montillus Murray Beatty, acquired the Landers ranch and moved into the stone cabin. Beatty was born in Iowa and later moved west, married a Paiute woman, and began ranching.

Beatty soon planted trees on his ranch and cultivated a variety of crops. When prospectors struck gold in the nearby Bullfrog Mining District, the rancher benefited from selling goods to the miners. Since his ranch had plenty of good water from the Amargosa River, which runs underground in the area, he was able to sell that, too, to thirsty miners.

Miners established the town of Beatty, south of the ranch, in 1904. It soon became an important supply point for Bullfrog and Rhyolite. Montillus Beatty sold his ranch in 1906 and moved into the town bearing his name. He died two years later at the age of seventy-three, after suffering an injury while hauling wood. In 1906 a rail line linked Beatty to Las Vegas, and the following year, another railroad connected Beatty to Goldfield.

Most of the Bullfrog and Rhyolite mines closed in 1909, and Beatty experienced a significant drop in population. But after the highways replaced the railroads, Beatty survived by catering to automobile travelers, as it does today.

## GOLD CENTER

Despite its glittery name, the former community of Gold Center, which was two miles south of Beatty, never produced any gold. The town was established in 1904 to supply water to nearby mines and mining camps. When the Las Vegas & Tonopah Railroad was built two years later, it selected Gold Center for a depot. Unfortunately for Gold Center, that was the high point of its existence. A year later the railroad connected directly with Rhyolite, making Gold Center's depot superfluous.

Nonetheless, a large brewery and ice plant were built here in 1907, in addition to a number of homes and businesses. Investors built a large mill on the hillside above the town to process ore, and a mining company even sank several shafts in adjacent hills to test the area for mineral potential but found nothing. Gold Center faded away when the Bullfrog and Rhyolite mines went bust.

## RHYOLITE AND BULLFROG

The sibling mining camps of Rhyolite and Bullfrog sprang to life in the Amargosa Desert at about the same time and for the same reasons. And, as with many siblings, there was some rivalry involved. The site of Rhyolite is four miles west of Beatty off NV 374, and that of Bullfrog is about half a mile north of Rhyolite, off an unmarked dirt road. Both are now ghost towns.

Bullfrog had perhaps the most colorful name of all of Nevada's mining camps; it took its moniker from the nearby Bullfrog gold mine, so called for its greenish ore. Bullfrog was the first community to be settled here. In August 1904 novice prospector Eddie Cross and his more experienced partner, the liquor-loving Frank "Shorty" Harris, discovered gold in the hills around the Amargosa River. The young Cross made the initial discovery and showed it to Harris, who immediately recognized its worth. Later in Goldfield, seventy-five miles north, Cross sold his share for $25,000; an inebriated Harris sold his half for $500 and a mule.

Word of the claim spread, and within a few months tents and wooden shacks had sprung up throughout the district. A tent city near the Bullfrog Mine was named Amargosa City. In early 1905 residents moved Amargosa City to a flatter area and renamed it Bullfrog. The camp soon had more than 1,000 people as well as a newspaper, a water system, and a small commercial district.

Around the same time, Rhyolite also assembled, and for a brief time the two communities competed for residents and businesses. Rhyolite's promoters were the more aggressive. A man named Pete Busch envisioned Rhyolite as a desert metropolis and began promoting the virtues of the community to eastern investors. Some, who had missed out on the Tonopah and Goldfield booms, began pouring funds into developing Rhyolite. By the end of 1907 the town had between 8,000 and 12,000 residents, as well as dozens of substantial stone and concrete buildings.

*Ruins of the Porter Store in Rhyolite.*

As Rhyolite thrived, Bullfrog faltered. Many Bullfrog businesses saw greater opportunity in the larger city and relocated to Rhyolite. On May 4, 1906, the *Rhyolite Herald* printed the headline "Verily, the Bullfrog Croaketh" and noted with some satisfaction that Bullfrog's last remaining business had closed. Little did they know that in just a few years they would be reporting on their own demise.

At its peak in 1907, Rhyolite had a two-story school that could accommodate nearly 250 students, an electric-power company, forty-five saloons, three newspapers, a stock exchange, and 400 streetlights. Three regional rail lines, the Las Vegas & Tonopah, the Tonopah & Goldfield, and the Bullfrog-Goldfield Railroads, extended their tracks to the community.

A national financial panic in 1907 triggered Rhyolite's downfall, and the descent was remarkably rapid. The town's eastern investors withdrew their backing, which forced the mines to close. By the spring of 1908, people were streaming out of Rhyolite. The 1910 census reported only 675 residents. That year, the power company was forced to turn off the streetlights.

Rhyolite's businesses began selling off their assets: the Porter Store liquidated its entire stock on May 7, 1910; the Commercial Hotel was sold on May 28 and physically moved to Las Vegas; and the J. S. Cook Bank sold everything from vault doors to desks on December 31. The *Rhyolite Herald* struggled until 1911, then folded. Two of the railroads consolidated in 1914, then finally ended service to Rhyolite in 1918. The 1920 census counted only fourteen people in the town.

Today Rhyolite's downtown looks familiar to anyone who has read about Nevada ghost towns. The evocative shadows of the J. S. Cook Bank building and the elegant Mission-style train depot have appeared in hundreds of photographs by some of the West's best-known photographers. You can also see the walls of the former school and the famous Rhyolite Bottle House, an actual residence that was built out of some 15,000 beer bottles. In recent years, the Bureau of Land Management has erected fences around the remains to protect them from vandalism.

## CARRARA

The ruins of Carrara are nine miles south of Beatty, just off US 95. Carrara was the only Nevada mining town where marble was king. Significant marble deposits, said to contain as many as twenty colors, were uncovered in Carrara's hills in 1904. With great optimism—and a bit of hyperbole—the area was called Carrara, after the Italian city that is the source of the world's most famous marble. Investors opened a small quarry, but they quickly dropped the effort when the marble proved too fractured to be commercially viable.

In 1912, however, more-massive deposits were uncovered, and the American Carrara Marble Company formed. The company platted a town and in 1914 completed a three-mile short-line railroad to connect the quarry to the Las Vegas & Tonopah line, which ran through the valley past the town. Soon American Carrara Marble was shipping large blocks of marble from Carrara to Los Angeles. By 1915 Carrara had nearly forty buildings and a weekly newspaper, the *Carrara Obelisk*. The company also constructed a large outdoor fountain with multicolored lights. A pipeline from Gold Center supplied water for the fountain and the town.

In the end, however, the marble operation was not profitable, and the quarry closed in 1917. Within a few weeks the paper had folded, the short line had stopped running, and people had begun to drift off. Carrara briefly revived in the 1920s, when the quarry reopened. In 1927 the Tonopah & Tidewater Railroad built a spur to the quarry to transport the marble. By the early 1930s, however, the revival was over. The quarry closed, the railroad pulled out, and Carrara began to disappear into the sagebrush.

A short time later, Filipino investors built a cement plant a mile north of the former site of Carrara, but they abandoned it in 1936 before production had even started. Today you can see the extensive, graffiti-covered ruins of the cement plant from US 95. Little remains of Carrara itself except for a few foundations and chimneys.

## ASH MEADOWS NATIONAL WILDLIFE REFUGE

Nevada's wide open, seemingly empty expanses are actually a biological wonderland filled with unique plants, fish, and animals. One of the best places to discover Nevada's often overlooked flora and fauna is the Ash

Meadows National Wildlife Refuge, about forty-five miles southeast of Beatty on US 95 and NV 373. The 24,000-acre refuge has the greatest concentration of endemic species in the country; an estimated twenty-seven are listed as rare and endangered.

The refuge was initially created in the late 1980s because of the Devil's Hole pupfish. This inch-long, almost transparent fish lives only in a deep, narrow, spring-fed opening in the ground known as Devil's Hole. Ninety percent of the pupfish live just above a rock ledge near the surface of the water, where they spawn and sun themselves. Because the pupfish is endangered, water use in the surrounding Amargosa Valley is regulated to ensure that water levels in Devil's Hole do not drop. Scientists believe that the springs in the Amargosa Valley have a common source, and activities that can change the area's water table, such as excessive pumping, can affect pupfish habitat.

In addition to Devil's Hole, Ash Meadows has about half a dozen other warm spring-fed pools, each with its own species of pupfish. The Ash Meadows Amargosa pupfish lives in Crystal Springs, while the Warm Springs pupfish can be found only in Warm Springs. The pools are believed to have once been part of a larger body of water that receded into separate smaller ponds, where each subspecies of pupfish evolved.

## MERCURY AND THE NEVADA TEST SITE

The military camp of Mercury is five miles north of US 95 on a closed military road, about fifty-four miles southeast of Beatty. It marks the entrance to the Nevada Test Site, originally known as the Nevada Proving Grounds. Since 1951 the test site has been the location of hundreds of aboveground and underground atomic-weapons tests. The federal government selected southern Nevada as the nation's atomic-testing laboratory because it was far from any population centers—the entire state had only 160,000 residents in 1950—and, in the government's view, not much was out there.

The government established the original 350-square-mile site in December 1950. Six weeks later, on January 27, 1951, the first atomic bomb exploded above Frenchman Flat, a section of desert about sixty-five miles north of Las Vegas. The site was soon expanded to 640 square miles, and by the 1990s had grown to 1,350 square miles. Between that first atomic test, in 1951, and 1962, when the first nuclear-test-ban treaty was signed, scientists detonated 126 atmospheric tests of atomic devices at the test site. All were exploded above the earth or on metal platforms, and they produced spectacular mushroom-shaped clouds that could be seen in Las Vegas.

During that time—long before the public became aware of the dangers of nuclear radiation—many enterprising Las Vegas businesses promoted the tests as a tourist attraction, marketing "atomic cocktails," mushroom hairdos, and even a Miss Atomic Blast pageant. The grand opening of the Desert Inn in 1950 was scheduled to coincide with the date of a detonation. A famous 1951

*A crater at the Nevada Test Site.* —Courtesy Nevada Historical Society

publicity photo from the Las Vegas News Bureau depicted a clutter of Las Vegas casino rooftops in the foreground with a mushroom cloud behind, hovering high in the sky.

Sadly, few understood the dangers associated with nuclear radiation, particularly the consequences of aboveground testing. In some instances the military stationed soldiers close to the detonation site following a test, to determine the effects of radiation. The clouds from the blasts sometimes drifted southeast over Utah, Arizona, and New Mexico, where the fallout rained down on unsuspecting people and livestock. Despite dozens of lawsuits brought by people who claim to have been adversely affected by the tests—former test-site employees, people living downwind, and soldiers stationed at the site—the federal government has never acknowledged a connection between their ailments and the tests.

In 1952 the federal government established Camp Mercury to provide housing and services for test-site workers. Since its inception, Mercury and the entire Nevada Test Site has remained closed to the general public for security reasons.

## FLOYD LAMB STATE PARK (TULE SPRINGS)

At Floyd Lamb State Park, also known as Tule Springs, archaeologists discovered evidence of humans in the area from 11,000 to 14,000 years ago,

*Excavations at Tule Springs have yielded the earliest evidence of humans in Nevada.*

making it one of the oldest known sites of human habitation in the United States. The 700-acre park is ten miles northwest of Las Vegas, via US 95 and Durango Drive.

In 1933 an archaeologist uncovered bones of animals and humans at Tule Springs, and his carbon-dates of the bones showed ages of more than 10,000 years. This discovery was the first proof of the existence of humans in North America in Pleistocene time, thousands of years earlier than previously believed. Additional evidence indicated that the Tule Springs area once consisted of several springs and that it was covered with sagebrush and bordered by ponderosa pine forests. The presence of water made the area a center of activity for big game animals and the humans who hunted them. Fossils found at the springs included the skeletons of prehistoric ground sloths, mammoths, horses, camels, and a giant condor.

The artifacts also indicated that early humans were more advanced than scientists had thought. Archaeologists uncovered evidence of established households, such as prehistoric hearths, hide scrapers, and charred animal bones, as well as weapons like fluted arrows and spear points. Other artifacts, from about 7,000 years ago, show that at that time the region was populated by small groups of Desert Culture people, who survived on native vegetation and small game.

In the early twentieth century, Tule Springs became the site of a horse-changing station, servicing horse-drawn wagons and freight trains traveling between Las Vegas and the mining camps to the north. Later the station was converted into a dude ranch, of the type popular during Nevada's "divorce capital" era of the 1920s and 1930s. The whitewashed, green-trimmed ranch buildings from that time are still there. Tule Springs became a state park in 1977.

# NV 156 AND NV 157
# MOUNT CHARLESTON LOOP
### 38 MILES

Charleston Peak, southern Nevada's tallest point, is fifteen miles west of US 95 on NV 157, twenty-nine miles north of Las Vegas in the Mount Charleston Wilderness Area. The 11,918-foot-tall mountain is named after Charleston, South Carolina, hometown of several members of an army survey team that mapped the area in 1869. Charleston Peak is part of the Spring Mountains, which have the steepest vertical rise of any Nevada Range, climbing nearly 10,000 feet.

The road from Las Vegas to Charleston Peak rises from the flats of the Mojave Desert to barren, rocky heights, where only bristlecone pine thrives. The plant life shifts gradually from creosote and Joshua trees to piñon and juniper woodlands, where sagebrush is the dominant shrub. A few miles higher, the terrain becomes thick with ponderosa pine, fir, and aspen. Craggy cliffs peek out from the pine forests, which in winter at this elevation are heavy with snow. Charleston Peak has an average annual snowfall of 100 inches and offers the only skiing in southern Nevada. The Las Vegas Ski and Snowboard Resort in Lee Canyon, near the base of the mountain, has a full range of services and a dozen runs of varying difficulty.

The village of Mount Charleston is home of a U.S. Forest Service district office and a handful of residences. The Mount Charleston area has several picnic areas and over 140 campsites.

*Snow on the rocky cliffs of Mount Charleston.*

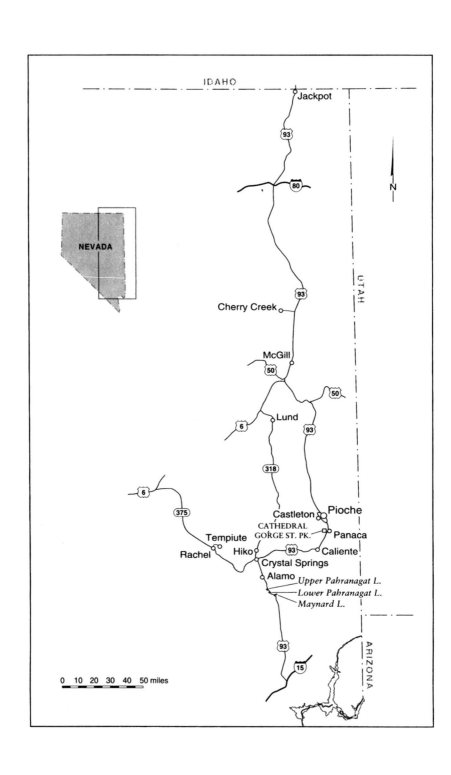

# 5

# US 93: THE MORMON TRAIL

*It has a spectacular beauty—great, jagged mountains of banded limestone rising high above desert valleys; vast basins sparsely dotted with the green of the creosote bush and the silvery tint of the burrobush on the gray, desert soil; dry stream beds; Joshua trees; dunes of white sand; and endless, sunbright space. To some it is austere and frightening; to others it has a lonely grandeur, which is friendly and comforting.*

—Sessions S. Wheeler, *The Nevada Desert*

Eastern Nevada is the least populated, most wide-open part of a state that has more elbow room than almost any other. Eastern Nevada's main artery is US 93, a two-lane highway that covers more than 500 miles of the state, from Jackpot, on the Idaho border, to Hoover Dam, at the Arizona border. When the 1940 Works Progress Administration guide to Nevada described the state as "the great unknown," it may well have been referring to eastern Nevada.

Southeastern Nevada has shared much history with neighboring Utah. In the late 1850s Brigham Young, president of the Church of Jesus Christ of Latter-day Saints—the Mormon Church—directed his missionaries to explore and colonize the far-off corners of Utah Territory, which at that time included Nevada. Young had led the "Saints" to the valley of the Great Salt Lake in 1847, following years of religious persecution in New York, Ohio, Missouri, and Illinois. He established Salt Lake City and hoped to claim the land covering most of modern Utah, Nevada, and Arizona and parts of Wyoming, Idaho, California, Colorado, and New Mexico as the state of Deseret.

The early Mormon Church, however, held religious views that were controversial, including a belief in polygamy. In 1857 the federal government decided to challenge Young's authority and impose national law on Utah Territory. In the conflict, known as the Utah War or the Mormon War, President James Buchanan ordered 2,500 troops to march on Salt Lake City to squelch an alleged rebellion. In response, Young recalled his followers to Salt Lake to

*Cows along a lonely road in eastern Nevada.*

help defend the city. Fortunately, the issues were resolved before any blood was shed.

During the height of the tensions, Young sent scouts to several remote areas to identify potential sites where church leaders might hide in case of an invasion by federal troops. One such place was Meadow Valley, about 100 miles south of Ely in eastern Nevada. Here Mormons dug irrigation ditches and laid out fields for a possible refuge. When the crisis ended, they abandoned the colony.

A few years later, Mormon settlers returned to eastern Nevada to establish a string of communities linking Salt Lake City to Los Angeles along the Mormon Trail. In 1864 William Hamblin, a Mormon missionary, learned from local Paiute about silver-bearing ore in Meadow Valley. Hamblin shared the information with prospectors, who placed several claims in the area. In March of that year, the Meadow Valley Mining District was established and subsequently the town of Pioche. In May 1864 a group of Mormon colonists, led by Francis Lee, founded the agricultural community of Panaca a few miles south of Pioche. Panaca became an important trade center for the miners. Other Mormon settlements followed, south of Panaca, at Callville, St. Thomas, Moapa, and Overton.

South of Ely, US 93 is an official Nevada State Scenic Byway and one of the least-traveled federal highways in the state—far lonelier than US 50, the purported "Loneliest Road in America." While you won't see much traffic, you will see plenty of spectacular high-desert scenery. Between Majors Place and Pioche the road parallels the western slope of the Snake Range for eighty-one miles, passing by Wheeler Peak and Great Basin National Park. This is range country, dotted with hundreds of free-range cattle. Occasionally you can see cowboys on horseback running cattle beside the highway. Be advised that sometimes auto traffic must stop so that a buckaroo can usher a few loose steers across the road.

# US 93
# JACKPOT–WELLS
### 68 MILES

## JACKPOT
As its name implies, the community of Jackpot has but one main industry—gambling. Like many Nevada border towns—this one is on the Idaho line—Jackpot's reason for being is to cater to out-of-state gamers.

From 1973 until his death in 1992, Carl Hayden, the publicist for Cactus Petes Casino in Jackpot, brought the town national attention. Hayden, a former *Salt Lake City Tribune* newsman who counted writer Ernest Hemingway among his friends, was known for his quirky, pun-filled press releases. He had a gift for creating attention-getting special events, including a Fourth of July hollering competition, jackrabbit races, and a golf-club-throwing contest. His writing inspired a popular fiction-writing contest, still sponsored each year by Cactus Petes.

According to Hayden, Jackpot was founded in 1954 after Idaho lawmakers decided to outlaw slot machines. In the January-February 1988 issue of *Nevada Magazine*, he recalled:

> So gamer Don French scratched his noggin. What could he do for those slot-craving residents of Idaho? What he did was establish a town by erecting a slot-machine emporium in the lonely spaces of mesa country. So came into being the Horseshu Casino, notched into Nevada a dice throw from Idaho's southern Border.

## JARBIDGE
Going to Jarbidge is actually a long side trip from Jackpot, not on the way to Wells. Eighty miles west of Jackpot by car, Jarbidge is one of the most remote towns in Nevada. To get there, take US 93 to Rogerson, Idaho, and head west on Rogerson–Three Creek Highway for sixty-two miles. The final eighteen miles of the road are gravel.

Jarbidge had grown to 1,500 residents within the first six months of its founding in 1909, as settlers were drawn by exaggerated reports of the area's mining potential. For the next decade, the camp rode a cycle of booms and busts before its permanent decline. Today the town has a dozen residents and a handful of stone buildings and ruins within the boundaries of the 113,327-acre Jarbidge Wilderness, Nevada's first federally designated wilderness area.

Jarbidge's name is an adaptation of the western Shoshone word *Tswawbitts*, the name of a horrible, human-eating evil spirit said to live in the Jarbidge Canyon according to Native American legend. Tswawbitts was so huge he could step over mountains. He was said to carry a basket on his back that he stuffed with the people that he captured.

Jarbidge is the site of the last stagecoach robbery in the American West. In December 1916, a robber stopped an Idaho stage and killed the driver. He escaped with more than $3,000 in cash, but he was captured because he had smeared his hands with the driver's blood and left fingerprints on the envelopes that had contained the money. This case was one of the first in the nation in which fingerprints were used to convict a criminal.

# US 93
# WELLS–ELY
**139 MILES**

## CHERRY CREEK

About ninety-two miles south of Wells on US 93 is the turnoff for NV 489 to Cherry Creek, which lies nine miles west of the highway. This tiny town has a long and colorful history. Miners found gold and silver near the town in September 1872. Within a year, more than 400 people had moved into the boomtown, and by the middle of the following year the town had a number of businesses, including an astounding twenty saloons. The town entered a slump after 1875 but revived with new discoveries in 1880. By 1882 Cherry Creek was the largest community in White Pine County, with an estimated population in excess of 7,500. Two years later, the town made an unsuccessful attempt to wrest the county seat from the mining camp of Hamilton, fifty miles south, which was then in decline.

In 1884 Cherry Creek's mines closed because of poor management and the national financial crash of 1883, which dried up investments in the community. Fires in 1884, 1888, 1901, and 1904 added to the town's misfortunes. By the mid-1890s mining had virtually ceased in the Cherry Creek area and the town had only a few hundred residents.

In 1905, however, the town had another revival. Several mines reopened, and in 1906 the Nevada Northern Railway extended its line through Cherry

*Remnants of the past in Cherry Creek.*

Creek. This revival lasted only three years, though, and by 1910 the town was in another tailspin. The town became active again in the 1930s and 1940s as investors sought to rework the old mines. But those operations closed during World War II, when materials were scarce. In recent decades, Cherry Creek has seen only small-scale mining by individual leaseholders.

You can see remnants of Cherry Creek's old commercial district in the center of the town. The only surviving business from mining days is the charmingly rustic Cherry Creek Barrel Saloon. Nearby are the remains of several stone buildings. The Cherry Creek schoolhouse, still in good shape, is now a museum, open in the summer. On display are antique bicycles, mining tools, and furniture. South of town, with a beautiful view of the surrounding Steptoe Valley, is a large cemetery with many wooden markers.

## EGAN CANYON

Take a dirt road five miles south of Cherry Creek to find the ruins of the former mining town of Egan Canyon. Like Schellbourne, Egan Canyon was the site of a Pony Express station. Earlier, it had been part of George Chorpenning's "Jackass Mail" service.

Also like Schellbourne, Egan Canyon was plagued by Indian attacks, which culminated in July 1860 with the Battle of Egan Canyon. An estimated eighty renegade Indians rode up to the station demanding flour, bacon, and sugar. The stationmaster and his staff complied, then barricaded themselves in the building. In the meantime, a Pony Express rider arrived at the station, quickly assessed the situation, and rode to a nearby military fort. A company of soldiers immediately set out for Egan Canyon; there they engaged the Indians, killing eighteen. Despite the victory, attacks on the station continued, and in October, Indians burned the station. It was revived a short time later as an Overland Stage station and experienced no further difficulties with Indians.

In 1863 prospectors struck gold in Egan Canyon, and by 1866 it had grown into a small community. The town experienced sporadic, modest success for fifty-odd years, with a two-year mine closure in 1870 and another slowdown later that decade. The mines closed for good in the 1920s. Today, little remains of the community except for scattered wood, a few foundations, and a small cemetery.

## SCHELLBOURNE

The turnoff from US 93 for Schellbourne is six miles south of the one for Cherry Creek. The town site is three miles east of the highway via a marked dirt road. Schellbourne goes back to 1860, when the Pony Express built a station and corral here. Due to its remoteness, Schellbourne (originally Schell Creek Station) was frequently attacked by local Indians. On July 16, 1860, the stationmaster and two assistants were killed. In response, the U.S. Army built Fort Schellbourne at the site to house a small detachment of soldiers. The soldiers remained until the summer of 1862, when relations with the Indians improved. Following the demise of the Pony Express in October 1861, the Overland Stage used the station as a supply point.

In the spring of 1871, prospectors found gold and silver at Schellbourne. Within a year, more than 400 fortune seekers had arrived and several quartz mills were in operation. Then in 1872, promising silver discoveries in nearby Cherry Creek lured many prospectors away from Schellbourne—and some took their buildings with them. Schellbourne rapidly declined, and by 1884 only twenty-five people remained. The post office finally closed in 1925, but Schellbourne was never completely abandoned. Today a small ranch operates at the former town site, which still has a number of photogenic stone and wood ruins.

## MCGILL

One of the best-preserved and longest-lived of Nevada's mining company towns is McGill, twelve miles north of Ely on US 93. Founded in 1906, McGill was initially a tent city on the flats by the Steptoe Valley Mining Company's massive smelter. Within a year, the company had erected more substantial houses for company officials, and a small business district formed. The company also built modest wooden homes for the workers—hence the cookie-cutter appearance of many of the houses in McGill.

In 1908 the Nevada Northern Railway was extended through McGill on its way to Cobre, a transfer point on the Southern Pacific Railroad about 140 miles north of Ely. By the 1920s McGill rivaled nearby Ely as the largest town in White Pine County. Even a disastrous fire in 1922, which destroyed a large part of the smelting complex, did not slow McGill's progress. The town peaked in 1930, when its population exceeded 3,000 residents.

The unusually long life of this area's copper mines enabled McGill to maintain a relatively steady population of about 2,000 people, most working at the smelter, from the 1930s to the 1980s. Because the mining company aggressively recruited new immigrants to America, particularly in the 1920s and 1930s, McGill's population was also one of Nevada's most ethnically diverse. A large number of Greeks, Irish, Slavs, and other immigrants came to work in McGill.

But, as with all mining towns, when the mines shut down, most of the jobs disappeared. McGill's day of reckoning arrived in 1979, when Kennecott Corporation closed its eastern Nevada operations, including the venerable smelter, and the town's population began to drift away. Construction of a maximum-security state prison in the late 1980s, however, staunched the flow and brought in new people.

New residents have renovated many of the worker houses, but McGill has not fully recovered from the loss of the smelter, and the downtown business district is still partially shuttered. Recalling better days is the McGill Drug Store Museum, a unique time capsule that is open for tours. The store closed in the early 1980s after operating for several decades, and its shelves remain stocked with vintage goods.

The McGill Club, a local bar and social club, is a throwback to the days when neighborhood saloons had personality—and no ferns. It still has its century-old, smoky ambience. Note the wall near the entrance covered in dozens of yellowing black-and-white photographs of local young men who served in the military and, in some cases, lost their lives.

## US 93
## ELY–CRYSTAL SPRINGS
### 170 MILES

### BRISTOL AND BRISTOL WELL

The turnoff from US 93 for the sites of the former mining camps of Bristol and Bristol Well is fourteen miles northwest of Pioche. Bristol Well is seven miles west of the highway on a graded dirt road, and Bristol is four miles southeast of Bristol Well on a road that branches off the first one. In 1870 Mormon missionaries discovered silver on the western flank of the Bristol Range (for which both towns were later named). Within a year the Mormons had established a small mining camp at the site, originally known as National City. They built a smelter there, but it operated for only a short time due to the lack of high-quality ore. A few years later, however, new discoveries revived the smelter and the community, which was renamed Bristol.

At its peak in the early 1880s, Bristol had more than 700 residents, half a dozen stores, eight saloons, several hotels, and a brewery. But the town began to decline in the mid-1880s, and by the early twentieth century it had largely been abandoned. Little remains of the town today.

The silver strike at Bristol also led to Bristol Well's founding in 1872. Investors build a furnace here to treat ore from the mines at Bristol, then called National City; a few years later they added a five-stamp mill and a smelter, then three large beehive-shaped charcoal kilns built of native stone. These ovens converted local juniper into charcoal, used in the smelter and by local blacksmiths. Bristol Well reached its peak about 1890, with nearly 400 residents, after Bristol had already begun to wither. Despite several brief mining revivals in the early twentieth century, Bristol Well, too, faded away. All that remains are the three charcoal kilns.

## PIOCHE

Pioche (PEE-oach, as in poach) is about 108 miles south of Ely on US 93. Miners established Pioche in 1864 after hearing about silver at Panacker Ledge, on the northeast side of Ely Mountain, from Mormon missionary William Hamblin. The camp was first called Ely, after John H. Ely, owner of one of the earliest stamp mills (not to be confused with Smith Ely, namesake of today's Ely at the US 93, US 50, and US 6 interchange). In 1869 San Francisco financier Francois L. A. Pioche purchased most of the area's mining claims and platted a town.

Pioche prospered, and by 1871 it had 7,000 residents and had swiped the Lincoln County seat from the smaller mining camp of Hiko, to the west. The town was notorious for its lawlessness, which was encouraged by its remoteness. According to Myron Angel's *History of Nevada*, originally published by Thompson & West in 1881, there were 402 homicides in Pioche between 1864 and 1881. The town was so violent that seventy-two men were buried in the Pioche cemetery before anyone died of natural causes.

Pioche was also without peer in Nevada when it came to official corruption. In 1871 the community authorized the construction of a courthouse and jail at a cost of $26,400. However, by the time the building was completed the following year, the tab had grown to more than $88,000 from cost overruns, mismanagement, skimming, and kickbacks to contractors. Unfortunately for Pioche, the courthouse's completion coincided with a regionwide mining slump, which forced county officials to refinance the project.

*Pioche's Million Dollar Courthouse.*

For the next few decades, the county was unable to make regular payments on the loans and had to refinance the bonds several times—each time adding more interest payments and penalties. By the 1880s the debt on the courthouse was $180,000, and by the end of the nineteenth century it was a staggering $670,000. By the time the courthouse debt was finally retired in 1937—four years after the building had been condemned—the total cost of the simple, two-story building was nearly a million dollars. Today the building, which has been restored as a museum, is known as the Million Dollar Courthouse.

### The Lost Paintings of Robert Schofield

Robert G. Schofield, an Englishman who arrived in Pioche in 1870, was an eclectic individual who over the years worked as a gunsmith, a mine superintendent, and a jeweler. He also had an artistic side. He wrote poetry and essays, and he enjoyed painting watercolors. He painted detailed renditions of the places he lived, and since he moved around a lot during the more than forty years he spent in Nevada, his work includes scenes of the mining towns of Eureka, Cherry Creek, Osceola, Taylor, and Pioche. These were painted at a time when cameras were rare, so they are valuable records of those faded or vanished communities. Schofield died in 1915 and was buried in Pioche.

In 1950 Vern and Mary Smith moved into an old house in Pioche. While cleaning out the basement, the couple discovered two dozen watercolor paintings of early Nevada mining camps, including Pioche, stored in a trunk. The paintings were signed R. G. Schofield and were dated from 1878 to 1912. They were previously unknown works.

While Schofield was a gifted amateur painter, his work is valued not so much as art but as historical records. Today the paintings hang in the Francois L. A. Pioche Art Gallery on Main Street.

### Historic Pioche

Present-day Pioche has dozens of historic homes and buildings—many still in use. Adjacent to the Million Dollar Courthouse is the Mountain View Hotel, built in 1895 by Ely Valley Mines to house its guests. The three-story wooden structure combines several architectural styles including the early-1900s "classic box." Nearby is the restored St. John Masonic Lodge. Built in 1873, it is one of the state's oldest fraternal chapter houses.

*This mining tram, unused since the 1930s, still straddles the hills above Pioche.*

Across the street from the lodge are the Pioche Livery Stable and the Tin Fabrication Building, both from the early 1870s, as well as the Pioche Fire House and the Amsden Building, both built in 1865. Behind the firehouse, on Main Street, is the Brown-Thompson Opera House, erected in 1873. This is one of the oldest mining-town opera houses remaining in the state and is badly in need of restoration.

Pioche's commercial district lies south of the opera house on Main Street. The historic Stockham House, built in 1866, still stands here. Originally a boardinghouse, it is now the Francois L. A. Pioche Art Gallery. Also on Main Street, the Lincoln County Museum is housed in the A. S. Thompson Building, built in 1900. The museum has an extensive archive of historic photos and an eclectic collection of Pioche artifacts, including pianos, pipe organs, mining equipment, and nineteenth-century mortician's tools.

## CASELTON

Six miles west of Pioche on NV 320 is the tiny community of Caselton. Combined Metals Reduction Company established Caselton as a mining town in the 1920s on the south slope of Mount Ely. The camp was named for J. A. Caselton, a mining official. The area's silver and lead mines were productive for several decades; most of the buildings standing today, including a flotation mill, were built in the early 1940s. Combined Metals erected a lime kiln in the mid-1950s. Dozens of historic wooden structures remain standing, but none are open to the public.

### Gue Gim Wah

For more than fifty years, Gue Gim Wah operated a small boardinghouse and cafe in Caselton and became locally famous for her cooking. She arrived here from China in the 1920s as a mail-order bride, an arrangement made by her family. She was only sixteen years old at the time and spoke no English, and her new husband was twice her age. In 1933 her Chinese American husband, Tom Wah, died, and she was left to run by herself the boardinghouse they had operated together for many years. One of her regular customers was former president Herbert Hoover, who frequently visited the region because he owned shares in a Caselton mine.

During World War II, the government considered Caselton's mines important to the war effort, so military personnel operated them. Soldiers stayed in Wah's boardinghouse and ate at her cafe. After the war, her authentic Chinese cooking had fans not only in Lincoln County but also among travelers passing through eastern Nevada. As she grew older, however, Wah decided she wanted to cook only for friends or referrals from friends—who were required to call at least three days in advance. There was no menu—visitors ate whatever she was in the mood to cook.

In nearby Pioche, her restaurant was good-naturedly known as the "Not Open Cafe." However, those who were fortunate enough to partake of one of her feasts found it worth the inconvenience. Wah took great care in preparing the food, often spending two days to make a single meal. She used only fresh ingredients, some grown in her own garden. Wah continued to cook until her death in 1988.

## BULLIONVILLE

The remains of Bullionville are ten miles south of Pioche off US 93, the turnoff just south of Cathedral Gorge State Park. The town was established in 1870, after the five-stamp Raymond & Ely Mill at Pioche moved there because the site had more water. At first the small camp was called Ely City. In 1873 the narrow-gauge Pioche & Bullionville Railroad linked Bullionville's mills to Pioche's silver mines.

By1875 the thriving town had a population of more than 500 people, and it had five mills with a combined 110 stamps. Bullionville's decline began when Pioche finally built a waterworks. By 1877 most of Bullionville's mills were gone and the population had drifted away. Six years later, the railroad was sold and dismantled. Today, all that remains of Bullionville is a small cemetery and a few stone foundations.

## CATHEDRAL GORGE STATE PARK

Ten miles south of Pioche, just north and west of Panaca, is Cathedral Gorge State Park. Established in 1935, it is one of Nevada's oldest state parks. The park's unusual clay formations, many of them resembling church spires, fascinated early Nevadans. In the early twentieth century the site was the backdrop for local passion plays. It was originally known as Panaca Gulch, then at the turn of the twentieth century it was renamed Cathedral Gulch, later changed to Cathedral Gorge.

More than a million years ago, this area was mostly underwater. Streams emptied into a large lake that covered the entire valley. These rivulets eventually filled the lake with silt and clay. A few hundred thousand years ago, after the lake had dried up, water and wind eroded the clay sediment of the lakebed into cathedral-like spires, pillars, towers, and walls.

A visitor center at the entrance to the park—adjacent to US 93, a mile north of Panaca—shows informational videos about eastern Nevada in a small amphitheater. A display of artifacts found in the gorge includes a rusted gun and an ancient bison skull. The latter was discovered in 1975 by a family visiting the park. Unaware that the skull was prehistoric, they took it home. In 1993 a family member contacted the Nevada State Museum to return it. The museum carbon-dated the skull to about 1,200 A.D.

*Clay formations at Cathedral Gorge State Park.*

## PANACA

The small Mormon community of Panaca (puh-NAK-uh), sits near the juncture of US 93 and NV 319. In May 1864 a group of Mormon settlers arrived in the Meadow Valley Wash to establish an agricultural community. The settlement was named Panaca, from the Southern Paiute word for metal, *pa-na-ka*, though it was not a mining camp. Panaca began life with orderly, uniform blocks and lots. The settlers laid out fields, constructed homes, and established a school.

The mining booms in the region were a boon to Panaca, as Pioche, Bullionville, and other camps made ready markets for Panaca's agricultural products. Consistent with the communal nature of early Mormon settlements, a community store was among the first places of business. The Panaca branch of the Zion Cooperative Mercantile sold food, crafts, firewood, lumber, grain, and other items produced by the people of Panaca. At first its customers were from nearby mining camps, then after those mines faltered, from camps farther south, including Delamar.

Panaca has not changed much in the past 135 years. It remains a peaceful farming-and-ranching community. Many of the town's original buildings remain in use. The still-operating Panaca Mercantile is partially housed in its original 1868 adobe structure. Another adobe building, the Wadsworth Store, built in the 1880s, has been used as a school as well as a store. Many of Panaca's homes have sheltered several generations of direct descendents of the original settlers.

## CALIENTE

Caliente (cal-ee-EN-tay), fourteen miles south of Panaca on US 93, was built as a railroad town but began as ranch land. In the early 1860s two escaped slaves, Ike and Dow Barton, started ranching in the Meadow Valley and Clover Washes of eastern Nevada. After a few years, the brothers sold their holdings to Charles and William Culverwell, who began a cattle ranch that supplied beef to the nearby mining camps of Pioche and Delamar.

In the late 1890s each of two rival railroad companies began constructing a Salt Lake City–to–Los Angeles line. E. H. Harriman was president of one railroad, the Union Pacific, and Senator William A. Clark of Montana owned the other line, the San Pedro, Los Angeles & Salt Lake Railroad Company. In the race to finish first, each company's construction crew tried to sabotage its competitor's efforts.

The fight soon moved from the tracks to the courtroom, with each side filing claims and counterclaims against the other. At one point, the two railroads were constructing parallel grades on either side of the Meadow Valley Wash. The dispute was finally resolved in 1903 when Charles Culverwell refused to permit more than one railroad grade to be built through his land. The two factions reached a compromise that included joint ownership, and the line was finally completed.

While regular service did not begin until 1905, the San Pedro, Los Angeles & Salt Lake Railroad established Caliente in 1901 as a division point and supply hub for the workers. The company built an engine terminal and side tracks in the town and supported Caliente's economy with long-term employment for its residents. The name Caliente, Spanish for "hot," came from the nearby natural hot springs.

Caliente today still reflects its railroad roots. The massive Union Pacific depot sits in the center of the town. The Union Pacific, which acquired the San Pedro, Los Angeles & Salt Lake in 1921, constructed this two-story Mission-style building in 1923 to house not only the train station but also a hotel, a restaurant, and a telegraph office. Over the years, the depot has been used as an art gallery, a library, and a community center, and it now serves as city hall and offices.

In the 1920s, the pioneering Culverwell family built the former Train Service Store across the street from the depot to serve passengers. East of the depot, on Clover Street, is Caliente's business district, with many buildings dating to the late 1920s and some even earlier. Gottfredson's Store is one of the oldest commercial structures; Charles Culverwell built it in 1907 as a bank and hotel.

*The two-story Union Pacific Depot in Caliente reflects the community's beginnings as a railroad town.*

The San Pedro, Los Angeles & Salt Lake built Company Row, eighteen near-identical wooden homes adjacent to the tracks, for its workers in 1905. North of the tracks is the Cornelius-Scott Hotel, a three-story stucco structure built in 1928. The hotel has hosted many dignitaries, including President Herbert Hoover.

Fires in the early 1920s destroyed most of the town's earliest buildings. However, the J. C. Crawford Stone House, believed to have been built in the 1860s by the Barton brothers, still stands on Spring Street. This crude rectangular structure with a metal roof is no longer in use, but it had served as a food pantry and storage facility.

## RAINBOW CANYON

Directly south of Caliente is the Meadow Valley Wash, which includes beautiful Rainbow Canyon, named for its towering multicolored walls. NV 317 intersects the canyon. Rainbow Canyon was formed and colored in the aftermath of intense volcanic activity more than 34 million years ago. Active volcanoes deposited layers of ash over millions of years; each layer of hot ash settled and welded into rock called tuff. The tuff layers cracked as they cooled, and mineral-rich hot water flowed up into the fractures, depositing gold, iron, copper, manganese, and other metals. These mineral deposits stained the tuff, creating what was to become the canyon's palette: red and yellow came from

*Prehistoric petroglyphs, such as this one depicting
bighorn sheep, are prevalent in Rainbow Canyon.*

iron, while copper caused the blue and green hues. The white layers are nearly
pure deposits of volcanic ash.

About a million years ago, a volcanic chamber under much of what is eastern Nevada collapsed, leaving an enormous depression that eventually filled
with water. Faults in the earth at the southern end of this lake allowed the
water to escape, and the force of that water carved Rainbow Canyon.

A creek adjacent to NV 317 still runs in Rainbow Canyon, and that water
attracted Nevada's earliest residents. Tools and weapons found in the area indicate that humans have been here for nearly 5,000 years. Large boulders on
the canyon's slopes are decorated with many petroglyphs. Etna Cave, in a wash
off NV 317 about five miles south of Caliente, was first excavated in the 1930s.
Archaeologists discovered a large number of prehistoric Native American
artifacts in the cave, and some are thousands of years old. The cliff walls surrounding the cave are also covered with petroglyphs and pictographs.

## KERSHAW-RYAN STATE PARK

Two miles south of Caliente off NV 317 is the entrance to Kershaw-Ryan
State Park. Flash floods in the summer of 1984 severely damaged this small
park and it was closed for years. It reopened in 1997 after facilities were

rebuilt. This 240-acre park, tucked in a box canyon, is one of the most beautiful in the state park system. Groves of ash and cottonwood shade its hiking trails and picnic areas. The high cliffs encircling the park are thick with wild grapevines and scrub oak, and in the spring are damp with seasonal streams.

## DELAMAR

Delamar's brief life story began in the early 1890s with the discovery of gold. Miners from Pioche flocked to the district to stake their claims. The area was originally called the Ferguson Mining District, but became known as Delamar after Captain John De Lamar of Montana purchased its principal mines in 1893. To reach the site, take US 93 about sixteen miles west from Caliente, then go fifteen miles south on a gravel and dirt road.

De Lamar pumped considerable resources into the district, and by 1897 Delamar had a fifty-ton mill, a good-size business district, a hospital, a stage line, and nearly 3,000 residents. The town also gained a macabre nickname—"the Widow Maker." Water was scarce, and the dry-drilling technique used to extract gold from ore created a fine dust that, when inhaled, caused silicosis, a fatal lung disease.

Despite its deadly reputation, the town thrived because local mine owners paid exceptionally high wages for the time, $3 per day. And miners were very eager for the work: by the late 1890s the rest of Nevada was in the midst of a twenty-year mining slump. Eventually, a pipeline brought water in from the Meadow Valley Wash, twelve miles north. This improved working conditions, but not soon enough for those already afflicted with silicosis.

A fire destroyed about half of Delamar in 1900. The residents rebuilt the town, but two years later Captain De Lamar sensed that the boom had crested and sold his interests in the mines. The new owners continued operations until 1909. In the fifteen years its mines operated, Delamar had generated more than $13 million in gold; it had been the leading gold producer in the state during the 1890s.

Without the mines, Delamar deteriorated almost immediately. The people left and the buildings soon followed. Residents of other Lincoln County communities removed stone, brick, and wood for new construction. In the 1950s and 1960s, souvenir hunters discovered Delamar and hauled out anything that could be removed, even headstones in the Delamar Cemetery, north of the town.

Accordingly, not much remains of Delamar. A few stone foundations and walls are nearly hidden by sagebrush. Thick wooden beams, once part of the stamp mill, lie scattered below the town site. Tailing mounds litter the surrounding hills, and a large depression, perhaps once the site of considerable mining activity, sits near the top of the mountain overlooking the town.

## CRYSTAL SPRINGS

Except for thickets of overgrown bushes, clusters of trees, and a few natural springs gurgling into small ponds, there is not much to Crystal Springs now. But in 1866 a small settlement on this spot, at the junction of US 93 and NV 318, was sufficiently prosperous to merit appointment as the provisional seat of Lincoln County.

The springs had supported a small Native American village for several generations. After prospectors discovered silver here and built a town, it became a popular rest stop for travelers. When the silver was gone, the community, which probably never numbered more than a few dozen people, quickly faded away.

# NV 318
# US 6–CRYSTAL SPRINGS
### 122 MILES

## LUND

Lund is thirty-one miles south of Ely by way of US 6 and NV 318. Mormons founded the town in 1898 and named it for church leader Anthony C. Lund. Today the tiny ranching-and-farming community is home of the White River Valley Pioneer Museum, a repository of local artifacts such as mining-stock certificates, typewriters, furniture, and the first piano in the region. An old log cabin in the back of the museum is the setting for a collection of cream separators and farming equipment.

## HIKO

Hiko (HY-ko), five miles north of Crystal Springs on NV 318, was established in 1865 after a local silver discovery. The area experienced a small boom early in 1866, and by that spring it had a population of several hundred. Mining investor William Raymond purchased most of the region's claims later that year, constructed a mill, and platted a town. In March 1867 a post office opened in the community under the name Pah Ranagat, which was changed to Hiko in June. The name Hiko is believed to have been derived from the Southern Paiute word for "white man's city," or simply "white man."

Hiko's high point came in 1867, when it became the seat of Lincoln County, taking the title from tiny Crystal Springs. Two years later, however, Raymond decided that he had little to show for his considerable investment in the community and closed his operations. He relocated his mill to Pioche, which in 1871 also took the county seat. Within a few years, Hiko had faded away. Today Hiko consists of several small ranches, a graveyard, and a few stone ruins.

## NV 375 (THE EXTRATERRESTRIAL HIGHWAY)
## CRYSTAL SPRINGS–WARM SPRINGS
### 98 MILES

### RACHEL

Tiny Rachel, thirty-six miles west of Crystal Springs on NV 375, is said to be accustomed to visitors from far away. Very far away. Some Rachelites claim to have had close encounters with aliens from other planets. In recent years, the area has become a magnet for folks who believe in the existence of unidentified flying objects (UFOs), including those who are convinced that the United States government maintains a supersecret facility nearby—called Area 51—where it stores extraterrestrial aircraft.

Many books have been written about this hypothesis and other secrets of this remote desert. The stories have become so widespread that NV 375 was officially designated the "Extraterrestrial Highway" in 1996. Road signs with that name appear along the route.

Most folks in Rachel, however, take all the fuss with a wink and a half smile. The town's main business is the Little A' Le Inn, a motel-restaurant-bar that has capitalized on the area's popularity with the UFO crowd. They serve Alien Burgers with Secretions (cheese) and something called a Beam Me Up Scotty, a concoction made with a generous amount of whiskey. Drink two and you are just about guaranteed to be talking to aliens. Owners Joe and Pat Travis count themselves among the believers and maintain a small library of UFO-

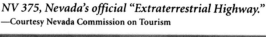

*NV 375, Nevada's official "Extraterrestrial Highway."*
—Courtesy Nevada Commission on Tourism

related books and a gallery of grainy black-and-white photographs depicting alien spacecraft.

Perhaps its sparse population—the town has fewer than 100 residents— and its remoteness make it easier to believe there might be something out there in those vast night skies. Are those the blinking lights of a passing airplane, or something more? Is that a shiny weather balloon, or something else? Some Rachelites recall one believer who arrived in a huge truck filled with exotic high-tech satellite equipment and listening devices. He stayed in town for several months in the hope that he might make contact with Rachel's aliens, but he left disappointed. Perhaps they were just shy.

There is a legitimate environment of secrecy in this region, however. The Air Force maintains an off-limits base at Groom Lake, about fifty miles from Rachel, that in the 1980s housed a squadron of the once-secret Stealth fighter planes. And at the Nevada Test Site, just southwest of Rachel, the military tries out all kinds of secret weapons.

## TEMPIUTE

The site of Tempiute (TEM-pie-oot) is eight miles east of Rachel on a marked dirt road. Prospectors found silver here in 1865, in the shadow of Grants Peak in the Timpahute Range. The town's name is an alternate spelling of the range's name, which comes from a Southern Paiute word meaning "rock, water, people." More miners staked claims in 1868, but because the area was so remote, only a few worked the mines here during the next forty years.

In 1916 miners discovered extensive tungsten deposits, but it was not until the 1940s that investors built a mill and began large-scale mining. By the mid-1950s Tempiute had 700 residents. But the mine closed in 1957 and the people soon moved away. Today, not much remains.

# US 93
# CRYSTAL SPRINGS–I-15

**85 MILES**

## THE PAHRANAGAT VALLEY

It's fitting that the name of this long narrow valley, which begins roughly at Crystal Springs and runs south along the lower White River to around the Pahranagat Lakes, means "land of many waters" in Paiute. The lakes are part of the Pahranagat National Wildlife Refuge, home to several species of ducks, geese, quails, pelicans, owls, hawks, and herons. Upper Pahranagat is the larger of the two lakes, spreading over 450 acres. Lower Pahranagat Lake covers 275 acres. There are several other small lakes, including Nesbit Lake and Maynard Lake, also nearby.

*Pahranagat Lakes.*

### Governor Henry Blasdel's Big Adventure

In March 1866 Nevada's first governor, Henry Blasdel, decided to travel to eastern Nevada to organize local settlers for the creation of a new county. The governor had received promising reports about the mining potential in the Pahranagat Valley, and he was interested in seeing the region, which was then still part of Utah Territory but had been proposed for inclusion into Nevada. Additionally, Blasdel sought to establish a direct route to the area from western Nevada.

Blasdel's proposed new route to the valley proved arduous, with scarce water being the biggest challenge. Traveling on horseback, the governor's party headed south from Carson City to Silver Peak, near Tonopah, and continued south into Death Valley, apparently in an attempt to avoid crossing the central-Nevada desert. After the group entered Death Valley, the newspaper reporter riding with them stopped sending stories to Carson City. No one heard from Blasdel or his party for more than a month. The *Sacramento Bee* reported that the expedition had failed and its members had most likely perished.

In late May news reached Carson City that the group had straggled into the Pahranagat Valley. The reporter traveling with the governor later wrote that the only thing the members of the expedition had found to eat had been a few doves and lizards that had wandered into their camp. He added, however, that cooked lizards were "equal to any frogs that were ever roasted."

After returning to Carson City by way of an established, but longer, northern route that passed through Austin, Blasdel acknowledged that his plan would not work because there was not a large enough population in the Pahranagat Valley to form a county. He also said that he would not recommend the shortcut through Death Valley.

In 1866 the Pahranagat Valley became part of the new Lincoln County, and Crystal Springs was named the county seat. A year later the seat went to Hiko, five miles north of Crystal Springs, and in 1871 to Pioche.

## ALAMO

Twelve miles south of Crystal Springs on US 93 is Alamo. With about 900 residents, it is the largest community in the lush Pahranagat Valley. Mormon settlers established Alamo in the late 1800s, though they did not lay out a formal town site until 1900. The name Alamo is from the Spanish word for "poplar," in reference to the many poplars, or cottonwoods, in the area. For most of its life, the town has been a sleepy farm-and-ranch community, with a few businesses catering to highway travelers. Descendents of the town's founders still occupy homes and other buildings from the 1920s.

# 6

# THE LAS VEGAS AREA

*There may be some who feel that Vegas is an abomination
and should be destroyed. They would then have to argue, with
me at least, that the oil companies are straight, the stock market is not a flimflam, and that our South American foreign
policy is not insane. They would even have to argue that the
Democratic Party and the Republican Party are more honest
than the Mafia.*

—Mario Puzo, *Inside Las Vegas*

"An idiot Disneyland of architectural parabolas, overloaded utility poles, ce-
lestial hamburger stands and gimcrackery fairy palaces," is how John Gregory
Dunne described Las Vegas. Everyone has an opinion about this city. It repels
some, compels others, and fascinates nearly all. Like a traffic accident, it is
hard not to look.

Mormon missionaries first settled the place that today many call "Sin City."
In the spring of 1855 Brigham Young, leader of the Church of Jesus Christ of
Latter-day Saints, instructed thirty men to establish a colony in the Las Vegas
Valley. Young's intention was threefold: to convert the area's Native Americans, whom he called Lamanites; to extend the church's sphere of influence
south along the Old Spanish Trail; and to provide a supply station for Mormons traveling between Salt Lake City and the colony in San Bernadino, California. The Las Vegas colony, however, did not succeed. Both farming and mining proved difficult there, and the colonists disbanded in 1858 after failing to
develop local lead deposits.

Various owners ran a trading post at the colony site until 1865, when local
politican Octavius Decatur Gass and his partners bought the land, then known
as the Las Vegas Ranch. After buying out his partners, Gass ran the Las Vegas
Ranch as a traveler's rest for a decade or so, but got into financial trouble in the
1870s by assuming too much debt to finance expansion of the ranch. In 1880

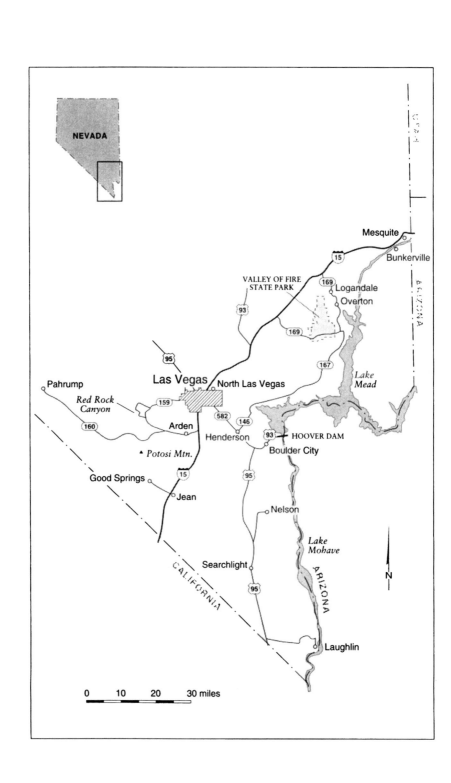

*The lights of Fremont Street in downtown Las Vegas in the 1940s.*
—Courtesy Nevada Historical Society

he turned the ranch over to his debtor, Archie Stewart, and soon moved to California.

In 1884, after Stewart was killed during a feud with his neighbors, his wife, Helen, assumed control of the ranch. Helen Stewart stayed in business until 1902, when she sold the property to the San Pedro, Los Angeles & Salt Lake Railroad. The railroad established a town at the site of the ranch in 1905, and modern Las Vegas was born.

The building of Hoover Dam from 1930 to 1935 attracted hundreds of workers to the area, creating a new economy for Las Vegas based on legal gambling and brothels to service them. After the dam was completed in 1935, many of the workers, attracted by the area's wide open spaces and attitudes, chose to stay.

In the late 1930s and early 1940s, Las Vegas was a burgeoning resort community, and it grew even more after World War II. Between 1940 and 1960, Las Vegas's population increased more than 500 percent. By the 1960s, many Las Vegas hotel-casinos—including Caesars Palace, the Sands, the Dunes, the Tropicana, the Desert Inn, and the venerable Flamingo—had become known around the world.

Today Las Vegas is more popular than ever, and bigger and more elaborate hotel-casinos go up every year. The Strip is no longer merely glitzy, but eye-popping, with special effects rivaling those of a Hollywood blockbuster.

# I-15
# MESQUITE–GOODSPRINGS
**106** MILES

## MESQUITE AND BUNKERVILLE

Mesquite lies just off US 15 near the Arizona border, and Bunkerville is three miles south on NV 170. Mesquite was on the route of the Old Spanish Trail, the first major trade route in Nevada, in use from 1829 to 1850. The trail crossed 130 miles of Clark County on its way from Santa Fe, New Mexico, to Los Angeles.

Mesquite and Bunkerville lie in the Virgin River Valley, an area originally settled by Mormons, briefly, in 1880. The unpredictable Virgin River dried up in the summer and flooded at other times, making irrigation nearly impossible, so the Mormons gave up on the colony after a few months. In 1882 another Mormon, Dudley Leavitt, moved his five wives and fifty-one children to Mesquite Flats, as the area was then known. He rebuilt the colony's abandoned irrigation ditches and also tried farming the area. But a flood soon destroyed his operation, and he too was forced to move on.

The Virgin Valley's first sustained settlement, Mesquite, took hold in 1894 with the arrival of yet more determined Mormon families. This time nature proved more cooperative, and the farmers were able to tame the river by rebuilding and fortifying the old dam and canals. Mesquite gradually grew over the next seventy-five years, then boomed in the early 1980s with the arrival of several hotel-casinos, which catered to visitors from neighboring Arizona and Utah. While Mormons, who do not gamble themselves, are still the mainstay of Mesquite, they have adopted a live-and-let-live philosophy regarding the presence of casinos in their community.

Mesquite's Desert Valley Museum, the former National Youth Administration building, has an extensive collection of historic photographs of the town, from its early farm days to its current incarnation as a gaming mecca. Vintage clothing and the town's first telephone switchboard are also on display.

Mormon farmers also established Bunkerville, just across the river from Mesquite. These farmers were followers of the United Order of Enoch, an offshoot of the main Mormon Church that practiced a communal lifestyle. The town's founder and namesake, Edward Bunker, settled on this site, on the south bank of the Virgin River, with twenty-seven relatives and friends in January 1877. The community immediately set out to dam the river and build an irrigation canal. They planted alfalfa, corn, cotton, grapes, and vegetables. A flash flood destroyed the dam in August 1877, but the settlers rebuilt it in time to save that year's crops.

Life in early Bunkerville was difficult. The river refused to stay within its banks, the soil was alkaline, the water quality was awful, and there was dissension

*One of several historic homes still found in the
Mormon farming community of Bunkerville.*

among the colony members over the division of labor and crops. By 1881 the
colonists had agreed to abandon the practices of the United Order, and they
parceled land to individual families. Farming proved viable despite the hardships, and the area developed into a reasonably productive agricultural
district, as it remains to this day.

Bunkerville's founders faced more than agricultural challenges. Because they
were polygamists, which was illegal in the United States, they were frequently
forced to hide from federal marshals, who periodically raided the town looking for offenders. The raids ended after 1890, when Mormon leader Wilford
Woodruff officially banned polygamy.

Over the years, residents have built some substantial homes in Bunkerville,
and many are still standing. Perhaps the most impressive is Edward Bunker's
two-story red brick house, with two large porches and a pair of fireplaces. A
pioneer cemetery at the edge of town has the graves of Bunker and other town
founders.

## NORTH LAS VEGAS

North Las Vegas, directly north of Las Vegas on I-15, began as the Kiel Ranch,
established in the 1860s by Conrad Kiel. For nearly three decades, the Kiel (or
Kyle) Ranch was second only to the Las Vegas Ranch, several miles to the south,

in providing fresh produce and meat to travelers on the Old Spanish Trail and to the region's mining camps.

In the early twentieth century, pioneer Las Vegas banker John S. Park bought the Kiel Ranch. But it was not until 1919 that an actual community was established north of Las Vegas. That year, Thomas L. Williams purchased 160 acres of land about a mile north of present-day downtown Las Vegas. He built a house for his wife and three sons, extended power lines to his property, dug a well, graded roads, and subdivided 100 of his acres. He began selling lots at $10 down, and to sweeten the pot, he offered free land to any church willing to locate at his town site.

Williams was a fervent libertarian. While he readily accepted the moral authority of God, hence his offer to the churches, he disliked government. So he established his community as a regulation-free zone. Residents did not have to worry about zoning rules, restrictions on livestock, or even law enforcement. Williams did have one rule: an avowed racist, he banned people of color.

Williams's "anything goes" philosophy did not, however, anticipate Prohibition. Bootleggers fled Las Vegas, where liquor laws were enforced, for the liberal-minded town to the north. One of the most popular legends about North Las Vegas is that bootleggers bought thirty-one of the first eighty lots Williams sold. Soon speakeasies cropped up throughout the community. The saloons built an elaborate network of underground tunnels where they could easily move their illegal liquor whenever threatened by a raid from federal agents.

During the Great Depression, North Las Vegas was the site of a large "Hooverville," or squatters' camp of homeless men, many of whom had come to the area hoping to be hired to work on the construction of Boulder (Hoover) Dam. The town's economy picked up during World War II, when the federal government established the Nellis Air Force Base nearby.

To fend off an incorporation attempt by Las Vegas, North Las Vegas formally incorporated on May 1, 1946. Eight years later, North Las Vegas became the first city in Nevada to elect a female mayor. Dorothy Parker, a retired Ziegfeld Follies dancer, was elected in 1953 on a pledge to make the town a more decent place for families. As the owner of a small motel, she had fought against brothel owners who tried to force her to sell her business to them. In the early 1950s the state and federal government had closed the brothels in Las Vegas, so many had simply moved to North Las Vegas. During her two years in office, Parker managed to straighten out the city's finances and initiated work on paved and lighted streets, a city water system, playgrounds, and a new city hall and post office.

### The Moulin Rouge

In spite of North Las Vegas's racist heritage, by the 1950s—after Thomas Williams's death in 1939—the town's entrenched libertarianism had expanded into a broader liberalism. In 1955 the Moulin Rouge, Nevada's first integrated nightclub, hotel, and casino, opened in North Las Vegas. Its owners were New York restauranteur Louis Rubin—inventor of the Reuben sandwich—and a group of investors that included former heavyweight boxing champion Joe Louis.

Prior to 1960, African Americans were not allowed to gamble or stay at Las Vegas's major hotel-casinos. So it was not surprising that the Moulin Rouge attracted some of the most famous black entertainers of the era. During the club's first weeks, the featured attraction was the Tropi-can-can floor show, with the young dance team of Maurice and Gregory Hines and jazz musician Benny Carter and his band. Often joining them onstage were other visiting entertainers, including Lionel Hampton, Dinah Washington, and Les Brown. White and black celebrities often packed the Moulin Rouge. On any given night, the crowd might include Jack Benny, Nat King Cole, Sammy Davis Jr., or Kay Starr.

The Moulin Rouge, however, did not make money. Because of mismanagement, undercapitalization, or, as some historians have speculated, threats from Las Vegas casinos that did not want an integrated competitor, the club closed after less than five months. In an interesting twist, five years later, in 1960, what used to be the Moulin Rouge coffee shop was the site of a meeting between civil-rights leaders and public officials that ultimately ended segregation at Las Vegas hotels.

## LAS VEGAS

The Las Vegas area was initially visited by either Antonio Armijo, a merchant leading a trading expedition from New Mexico to California in 1829–30, or more likely Rafael Rivera, Armijo's scout, who may have camped in the Las Vegas Valley prior to leading the party into the region. The Armijo party blazed the route that became known as the Old Spanish Trail.

The first significant exploration of the valley was in 1844, when John C. Frémont camped at a place the Spanish traders he had encountered called *Las Vegas*, Spanish for "meadows." Frémont described the area in a formal report and map he produced in 1845. More than 20,000 copies of the report were printed, and it became a guide for thousands of future travelers to Nevada.

The first Mormon settlers, under the leadership of William Bringhurst, built a small adobe fort in the valley near the Las Vegas springs in 1855. The men were allocated small plots for farming and ranching. The post's isolation and the hostile, hot desert climate—the missionaries arrived in Las Vegas in July—made life difficult during the first few months. Yet despite the hardships, the Mormons stayed through the winter and began planning to bring their families to the valley.

While the missionaries generally maintained friendly relations with the local Indians, there were occasional misunderstandings because the Southern

Paiute had no concept of individual property and often took what they wanted from the orchards and croplands. On the other hand, the settlers had taken a prime spot at the Paiute's traditional watering hole.

A year after the Mormons arrived, they found lead deposits in the nearby mountains. The church's leaders, eager to have industrial minerals, sent Nathaniel V. Jones with five men to help mine the ore. Bringhurst, who did not want to divert men from the colony's farming efforts, clashed with Jones over the directive. Brigham Young relieved Bringhurst of his command of the post, and Bringhurst left for California.

Despite the colonists' efforts, the ore proved difficult to process, and the mining attempt was unsuccessful. In February 1857 Young allowed most of the Las Vegas missionaries to return to Salt Lake City. The few remaining colonists, under the leadership of Benjamin R. Hulse, finally departed at the end of the summer of 1858. The mission site remained deserted until about 1860, after which a variety of owners operated a small trading post there.

In 1865 the property—then known as the Las Vegas Ranch—was acquired by Octavius Decatur Gass and his partners Nathaniel Lewis and Lewis Cole. They rebuilt many of the old fort structures, replanted crops in the fields, and erected a ranch house. Gass, an entrepreneur and occasional miner, later bought his partners out, and in the 1870s he expanded his holdings to include the nearby Spring Mountain Ranch, also known as the Wilson Ranch, and substantial portions of the valley. The ranch eventually reached 960 acres in size and had a workforce of more than thirty.

In the late 1860s and 1870s the Las Vegas Ranch was a haven for travelers on the Old Spanish Trail, who often stopped for several days to make repairs on their wagons, replenish their supplies, and regain their strength before pressing on to their destinations. In 1880, after several years of borrowing money to keep the ranch operating, Gass defaulted on a $5,000 loan from Pioche rancher Archibald Stewart. Gass and his family left in 1881 for California. Stewart moved in with his wife, Helen, and their daughter the following year.

The Stewarts attempted to make the ranch into a profitable operation. It continued to cater to travelers and even produced a commercial wine. In 1884, however, Archie Stewart was killed during a disagreement with several members of the Kiel family, who owned a nearby ranch. The dispute occurred after Stewart's ranch hand, Schyler Henry, abruptly quit his job and demanded his wages. At the time, Stewart was away from the ranch, delivering supplies to miners working in Eldorado Canyon, about sixty-five miles south of Las Vegas. Henry confronted Helen Stewart, who refused to pay him because she was not sure how much he was owed.

While no one is certain what was said, Henry apparently hurled such invectives at Helen that when her husband returned and was told about the episode, he grabbed his rifle and rode off to the Kiel Ranch, where he believed Henry was staying. Upon reaching the ranch, Stewart dismounted and walked

*The Helen Stewart Ranch, early twentieth century.*
—Courtesy Nevada Historical Society

toward the house, rifle in hand. What happened next has long been the subject of controversy. Stewart is believed to have fired first but was immediately cut down by several shots from those in the house.

When the gun battle was over, Stewart was dead from several bullets to the chest while Henry had two flesh wounds. The killing itself was ascribed to an outlaw named Hank Parrish, who was staying with the Kiels. Although Parrish was never charged with the crime, he was later hanged for other crimes. For the rest of her life, Helen Stewart believed the Kiels were part of a conspiracy to murder her husband.

Though she had originally agreed to move to Las Vegas only because her husband had promised her it would be temporary, Helen Stewart stayed on after Archie's death. Over the next twenty years, she continued to operate the guest ranch and laid the foundation for the future community of Las Vegas. In June 1893 she became postmistress of "Los Vegas," a spelling that U.S. postal authorities insisted on so the town would not be confused with Las Vegas, New Mexico. Stewart eventually became known as "the First Lady of Las Vegas."

In 1902 Stewart sold her ranch to the San Pedro, Los Angeles & Salt Lake Railroad for $55,000. The railroad built a line through the Las Vegas Valley, establishing a division point and town on the site of the Stewart ranch. In May 1905 the railroad auctioned off 1,200 lots; these became the core of downtown Las Vegas. Within a decade, the town had more than 3,000 residents and became the seat of newly created Clark County.

*Downtown Las Vegas, 1906.* —Courtesy Nevada Historical Society

Las Vegas was a quiet railroad town until 1930, when President Herbert Hoover signed legislation authorizing the initial funding for the construction of the Boulder Canyon Project, later known as Hoover Dam. The dam project was massive; it would cost nearly $50 million, stand more than 700 feet high, and take nearly five years to complete. And it put Las Vegas on the map.

During construction of the dam, thirty miles southeast of Las Vegas, more than 5,000 workers—all men—lived in the area, most in Boulder City, a planned community the federal government built for them. Since the government banned alcoholic beverages and most other diversions in Boulder City, nearby Las Vegas beckoned with its saloons, legal brothels, and legal gambling (as of 1931). By the time the dam was completed in 1935, Las Vegas's popularity was well established. In the early 1940s, the Nevada Biltmore and El Cortez Hotels were built downtown, and the El Rancho Vegas and Last Frontier Hotels sprang up on US 91, the Los Angeles Highway, a few miles south of town. These last two marked the beginning of the famed Las Vegas Strip.

World War II ushered in a new era of prosperity for Las Vegas. In the spring of 1941, the U.S. Army began developing an airfield complex nine miles north of town. Within a short time, several thousand personnel were stationed at the base, which was used to train crews for B-17s and B-29s. Also in 1941, the federal government built a giant industrial complex south of Las Vegas to process magnesium, a mineral used in airplanes and incendiary bombs. The $150-million Basic Magnesium plant was another boost to the southern Nevada economy.

By the end of World War II, Americans were growing comfortable with auto travel, and Las Vegas's temperate weather, legal gambling, and proximity to booming southern California made it an ideal resort destination for California motorists. In 1947 gangster Benjamin "Bugsy" Siegel, who recognized the area's potential, completed the Flamingo Hotel on the Las Vegas Strip. The $6-million, three-story hotel was the first major resort in Las Vegas that combined the luxury and glamour of a Miami-style hotel with a casino.

Siegel was later assassinated in Beverly Hills, allegedly either for skimming some of the mob money he used to fund the hotel or for spending too much money to build it. But his Flamingo was a success and soon led to the development of other resorts on the Strip, including Wilbur Clark's Desert Inn, the Thunderbird Hotel, and the Sahara.

By 1950, Las Vegas's population had swelled to 24,624—doubling in just ten years—and by 1960 the population was 64,405. Las Vegas had leapfrogged over Reno not only in population but also as a gambling destination and in terms of political muscle. As celebrities like Frank Sinatra, Dean Martin, and Sammy Davis Jr.—the so-called Rat Pack—frequently clowned around on Las Vegas stages, the city's popularity continued to grow in the 1960s.

Today's Las Vegas began to take shape in the late 1980s, when the city discovered that bigger really can be better. Starting with the opening of the 3,000-room Mirage Hotel in 1989, Las Vegas entered the era of the mega-resort. Within

*Bugsy Siegel's Flamingo Hotel, 1950.* —Courtesy Nevada Historical Society

a decade, more than two dozen major hotel-casinos, with a combined 38,600 rooms, had opened in the city, including the 1,149-foot Stratosphere Tower and Hotel, the tallest structure in Nevada, in 1996. Many of these new resorts incorporated elaborate fantasy themes far beyond anything previously imagined, from the pyramid-shaped Luxor to the magnificent Tuscan-style Bellagio.

Bugsy wouldn't even recognize the place.

### Senator William Clark

Contrary to what some believe, Clark County, of which Las Vegas is the seat, was named not after Wilbur Clark, the first owner of the Desert Inn Hotel, but after Senator William A. Clark of Montana. Senator Clark owned the San Pedro, Los Angeles & Salt Lake Railroad, the company that founded Las Vegas. Though he never lived in Nevada, Clark cast a large shadow here.

Clark was born in Pennsylvania in 1839. In the 1860s he began to build a mining fortune in Colorado and Montana. In spite of a scandal over his attempt to buy the votes of state electors, Clark was later elected to the U.S. Senate by the people of Montana in 1901.

In 1900 Clark and his younger brother, J. Ross Clark, began construction on the San Pedro, Los Angeles & Salt Lake Railroad between Salt Lake City and southern California. Previous attempts to build such a line, including two by the Union Pacific Railroad, had proven too costly to finish. The Clark brothers' project had been under way several months when the Union Pacific filed a lawsuit claiming exclusive building rights to the route. At one point during the dispute, rival construction crews from each railroad attempted to build parallel lines through Lincoln County, Nevada. Finally the two sides compromised and became partners in the line in 1902. It was completed on January 30, 1905, ending about four miles from the modern community of Jean, Nevada, near the California border.

The Clarks' railroad company established many communities along the line, including Las Vegas. The brothers saw potential in the desert town and tried to diversify its economy. They prospected for gypsum and other minerals, and they helped found the Home Building & Loan Association in 1905, and later the First State Bank. The Clarks also recognized the mineral potential of central Nevada and partnered with Francis E. "Borax" Smith, who had extensive borax-mining operations in Death Valley. The partners planned to put in a rail spur from Las Vegas to the mining camps at Rhyolite, Tonopah, and Goldfield. After eventually squeezing Smith out, the Clarks built the Las Vegas & Tonopah Railroad in 1906.

In 1921 the Clarks sold their railroad interests to the Union Pacific. While J. Ross Clark continued to be involved in various Las Vegas business ventures until his death in 1927, William Clark abandoned his Nevada enterprises and settled in New York. His opulent 100-room mansion on Fifth Avenue was a testimonial to excess—Clark had bought several quarries and a bronze foundry specifically to provide the materials for its construction. By the time of his death in 1925, Clark had amassed a fortune estimated at more than $200 million.

### Divorce, Las Vegas Style

In the early twentieth century, Reno was the undisputed divorce capital of America. Actress Mary Pickford was among the many celebrities who had trekked there to "take the cure." But Reno gained a competitor in 1939, when Ria Gable, wife of actor Clark Gable, traveled to Las Vegas to seek a divorce. Clark Gable was one of the biggest stars in Hollywood, and he had made no attempt to hide his affair with actress Carole Lombard.

Ria Gable arrived in Las Vegas in January 1939 for a six-week stay to establish her residency. She rented a house in downtown Las Vegas and set out to enjoy herself. At the time, Las Vegas had a population of about 8,000 and was eager to promote itself. The city took full advantage of her presence: she was feted at dozens of social events, invited to deal craps and blackjack games in the local casinos, and taken on Lake Mead boat rides. The entire time, she allowed photographers to tag along, snapping hundreds of publicity shots, which she said could be released after the divorce was final.

The actual divorce proceedings were anticlimactic, lasting less than five minutes. It was after the ex–Mrs. Gable returned to Hollywood that the Las Vegas publicity machine cranked into high gear. Stories extolling the city's hospitality to Ria Gable during her divorce ordeal appeared around the country. Almost overnight, Las Vegas supplanted Reno as the trendy place to get a quickie divorce.

### Thomas Hull and the Birth of the Las Vegas Strip

Modern Las Vegas owes a debt to Thomas Hull, a Los Angeles hotelier who had the foresight to understand the role automobiles would play in the city's future. In 1941 Hull was visiting Las Vegas and noticed the high volume of traffic on US 91, the road between Los Angeles and Las Vegas. He watched the cars for awhile and concluded that Las Vegas would make an ideal location for a resort and casino that catered to the automobile traveler.

Hull built his new resort later that year on US 91, a few miles south of downtown Las Vegas, and he named it the El Rancho Vegas. Many locals thought he was foolish to build so far from downtown. Hull, however, knew he could never build the kind of resort he wanted in a heavily developed area. He wanted an open complex of Spanish Colonial–style buildings that would be auto-friendly, meaning plenty of parking.

Hull's hunch proved to be right. The fifty-room El Rancho Hotel opened on April 3, 1941, and was an immediate success. Within a few months he was adding another sixty rooms and had spawned a few competitors, among them the Last Frontier, which opened a mile south of the El Rancho in 1942. World War II postponed further building in Las Vegas for the next five years, but immediately following the war, gangster Benjamin "Bugsy" Siegel opened the Flamingo Hotel. The Flamingo, the El Rancho, and the Last Frontier formed the nucleus of what would soon become known as the Las Vegas Strip.

As for Hull, he sold his interest in the El Rancho in 1943 and returned to his hotels in California, where he remained until his death in 1964.

### Maude Frazier

Maude Frazier was born in 1881 in Wisconsin and educated at the Wisconsin State Teachers College. In 1906 she took a job in Genoa, Nevada, as the teaching principal, and she worked in schools throughout Nevada for the next forty years. After retiring from public education, Frazier embarked on a career as a Nevada legislator. She ran for the state assembly in 1948 and lost, but when she ran again two years later, she won. Frazier served in the legislature for the next twelve years. During her tenure, she helped created Nevada Southern University, which later became the University of Nevada, Las Vegas.

In 1962 Governor Grant Sawyer appointed eighty-one-year-old Frazier to replace Lieutenant Governor Rex Bell, who had died. In accepting the appointment, Frazier became the first woman lieutenant governor in the state's history. When asked what kind of governor she would make, she said, "I've held other positions usually held by men and got by all right." She never got the chance to be governor, though—she died the following May.

### The Mysterious Mr. Hughes

One of the most bizarre characters ever to appear on the Las Vegas scene was the eccentric billionaire Howard R. Hughes. In November 1966 Hughes arrived in Las Vegas and set up his base of operations in the ninth-floor penthouse of the Desert Inn Hotel. A few months later, after the management asked him to vacate the rooms so they could use the space for high rollers on New Year's Eve, he bought the hotel.

Hughes developed an appetite for acquiring casinos, and during the next three years he purchased six more—the Sands, the Castaways, the Last Frontier, the Landmark, and the Silver Slipper in Las Vegas, and Harolds Club in Reno. He also bought a local airport, a Las Vegas TV station, several large ranches, tens of thousands of acres of land, and nearly 3,000 mining claims across the state.

Hughes's reclusive nature and intense need for secrecy—he made all his purchases without ever leaving his rooms at the Desert Inn—eventually wore thin on Nevada gaming officials. They were responsible for licensing casino operators, and the law required they personally interview all gaming-license applicants. In 1973, after one of Hughes's executives had applied for licensing to operate the billionaire's Nevada casinos, Governor Mike O'Callaghan said he was tired of Hughes's "shadowboxing"—meaning his many excuses for avoiding a personal meeting. The governor announced that he would approve the license only if Hughes met with him face-to-face to verify that the executive was his legal representative.

In the meantime, Hughes had moved to London, for unknown reasons, so Governor O'Callahan and Philip Hannifin, chairman of the Nevada Gaming Control Board, flew there to meet with him. Following the two-hour meeting, the governor said he was satisfied and the proxy's license was approved.

Hughes never returned to Nevada. He died in 1976.

### Historic Las Vegas

Las Vegas has always been the kind of place that looks forward, not back. Much of the city's history has therefore been lost to "progress." But there are some historic buildings in town worth seeking out. The oldest standing building, at 908 Las Vegas Boulevard North, is a small adobe structure that was part of the fort at the original Mormon colony, built in 1855.

A few of the city's original buildings date from its early railroad period, including several small cottages on Second Street that the San Pedro, Los Angeles & Salt Lake Railroad built for its workers in 1910. The two-story stucco Victory Hotel, at 307 North Main Street, was also built in 1910, and the first two floors of the Golden Gate Hotel and Casino, at 1 Fremont Street, were constructed in 1906.

The city's first movie house, the El Portal Theater at 310 East Fremont, opened in 1928. During the 1930s, when Hoover Dam was under construction,

*Las Vegas High School is a classic example of art-deco design.* —Courtesy Nevada Historical Society

the neoclassical post office and federal building, at 301 East Stewart, went up. At 315 South Seventh, Las Vegas High School, built in 1931, is the city's only remaining example of 1930s art-deco architecture.

One of two other historic buildings that have managed to avoid the wrecking ball is the Hitching Post Wedding Chapel, at 226 Las Vegas Boulevard South, built in 1923 as a private residence and converted to a chapel in 1934. The other, the 1941 El Cortez Hotel and Casino at 600 Fremont Street, was downtown Las Vegas's first high-rise hotel. Its exterior remains largely unchanged.

The 1950s ushered in Las Vegas's Neon Age, and one of the best examples is the giant neon cowboy known as Vegas Vic in front of the Pioneer Casino at 25 East Fremont in downtown Las Vegas. Vic, who stands sixty feet tall, has been waving his arm, smoking a cigarette, and winking at passersby since 1951.

### University of Nevada, Las Vegas

The University of Nevada at Las Vegas began in 1951 with a few extension courses taught by instructors from the campus in Reno, held in the local school district's classrooms. By 1954 the university had established a branch campus in Las Vegas, and three years after that the Las Vegas campus opened its first building on sixty acres along the Maryland Parkway. In 1968 the Las Vegas branch became independent of the University of Nevada, Reno, and by the early 1970s it was larger than the Reno campus, reflecting the more rapid growth of southern Nevada. Over the years, the school grounds have expanded into 335 acres; by the 1990s there were more than 15,000 students at UNLV.

### The Nevada State Museum and Historical Society

The Nevada State Museum and Historical Society, founded in 1982, is in Lorenzi Park. The museum's exhibits trace more than 10,000 years of southern Nevada history. Displays describe the region's people, important events, geology, and plant and animal life. The museum is also home of the Cahlan Library, which offers researchers access to hundreds of books, maps, manuscripts, indexes, and photographs related to the history of the state and the Las Vegas area.

## GOODSPRINGS

To reach Goodsprings from Las Vegas, take I-15 thirty miles south to Jean, then take NV 161 seven miles west. In the late 1860s, following the discovery of silver and lead in the region, a mining district called Yellow Pine flourished here for a short time. In the 1880s cattleman Joe Good watered his herd at some natural springs in the area—hence the name. By the 1890s a number of gold strikes in the area had attracted several hundred miners and the town of Goodsprings was established.

In 1901 the Yellow Pine Mining Company formed and consolidated ownership of most of the area's mines. The San Pedro, Los Angeles & Salt Lake Railroad reached Jean in 1905, and within a few years the mines near

Goodsprings were sufficiently profitable to support a narrow-gauge railroad between Goodsprings and Jean; it operated from 1911 to 1930.

Mining continued to thrive between 1911 and 1919. During this time, the town grew to 800 residents and had a school, a hospital, churches, businesses, and a newspaper, the *Goodsprings Gazette.* The two-story, twenty-room Fayle Hotel went up in 1917. Mining production, however, had slumped by 1920, and the mines closed. Since then, the district, which has produced more than $30 million in ore, has had a number of brief revivals.

The Pioneer Saloon, built in 1913, is one of the community's most historically interesting places. The saloon, which is still in business, is made of stamped metal in a brick pattern, and according to its owners it is America's largest stamped-metal building of the early twentieth century. In January 1942 Clark Gable spent several days in the Pioneer while waiting for rescuers to recover the body of his second wife, Carole Lombard, from an airplane that had crashed into nearby Double Deal Mountain.

# NV 169, NV 167, and NV 146
# I-15–Henderson
### 53 miles

## LOGANDALE

The farming community of Logandale on NV 169 six miles south of the Glendale intersection of I-15, was once called St. Joseph. Mormon farmers settled there in 1864 as part of a string of Mormon communities in the Moapa Valley. In 1867 fire destroyed the settlement, and the residents rebuilt it a few miles away.

The settlers deserted the new St. Joseph in 1871, when the majority of Mormons in the valley returned to Utah because of a tax dispute with Nevada. The dispute started after an 1870 boundary survey indicated that the communities along the Muddy River were not in Arizona, as most residents thought, but in Nevada. Shortly after the finding, the state of Nevada demanded that residents pay two years of back taxes, inspiring many to leave the state.

In 1881 new Mormon settlers reestablished the community. In addition to building new homes and planting crops, the residents renamed the town Logandale, in honor of Robert Logan, a prominent local rancher.

## OVERTON

Two miles south of Logandale on NV 169 is the community of Overton. The name is believed to refer to the town's situation overlooking the Muddy River. Like Logandale, Overton was one of several Mormon farming settlements established in the mid-1860s on the banks of the Muddy. But Overton's most compelling historical attraction comes from the community that preceded it—the Lost City.

### The Lost City Museum

The Lost City Museum, off NV 169, is devoted to the study of the Anasazi, or Old Ones. The Anasazi thrived in the southwestern United States 1,500 to 2,000 years ago. At the peak of their civilization, thousands of Anasazi lived along the banks of the Virgin and Muddy Rivers in southern Nevada.

The Anasazi built permanent settlements, among them the pueblo cliff villages of Arizona and Colorado. They cultivated crops and mined several minerals, such as salt. Their petroglyphs, found throughout Nevada, are among the few remaining traces of their presence. About 800 years ago, the Anasazi mysteriously departed from their northernmost villages, including those in southern Nevada.

The Lost City Museum is built on the site of an actual Anasazi village. When scientists uncovered the city in the 1920s, they were perplexed as to why it had

*The Lost City Museum in Overton.*

been abandoned and dubbed it the Lost City. But its official, more prosaic name is Pueblo Grande de Nevada, which describes the great size of the community. It is believed to have had several thousand people.

Many of the museum's artifacts were found in local excavations during the late 1930s, before Lake Mead had completely filled up behind the new Hoover Dam. The museum showcases hundreds of arrowheads, baskets, atlatl (throwing spears), skins, and pottery. On the museum grounds are several reconstructed pueblo-type shelters made of wattle and daub—woven twigs plastered with clay—on original foundations. There is also a replica of a covered underground dwelling, known as a pithouse.

### Discovering the Lost City

The men most responsible for the preservation and study of the Lost City were archaeologist Mark Harrington and Nevada governor James Scrugham, who served from 1923 to 1927. In 1924 Governor Scrugham received a package from a descendant of a pioneer Mormon family in the Moapa Valley. It contained ancient Indian artifacts found along the Muddy River. Scrugham, an engineer, historian, and amateur archaeologist, was intrigued and sent the artifacts to Harrington, a noted New York archaeologist who had come to Nevada earlier that year to excavate the Lovelock Cave in northern Nevada.

Harrington accompanied Scrugham on a trip to the site, and he later wrote, "We had not been there two minutes when my eyes rested upon a scrap of painted pottery lying on the sand beside a prickly mesquite bush. It was our first clue." He recognized the patterns on the pottery shard as an early example of Pueblo craft, previously seen in New Mexico and Arizona, but never as far west as Nevada.

Within a year, Harrington had embarked on a major excavation of the area. The governor invited the media along to publicize the excavation. He also held an elaborate public pageant at the site in 1925 that dramatically described the valley's ancient past with plays and readings. Despite its remote location, the event attracted nearly 6,000 people.

Between 1925 and 1926, Harrington and a small crew of assistants uncovered the ruins of nearly fifty prehistoric structures, including one with 100 rooms. Archaeologists later estimated that the site was settled about 300–500 B.C. and that several cultures had resided there at different times.

Harrington returned for additional digs in 1929 and 1933. The latter one involved salvaging as many items as possible as quickly as possible, since most of the Lost City sites, which were spread across nearly sixteen miles, were about to be covered by the waters of Lake Mead. After supervising the construction of the Lost City Museum in Overton, Harrington moved on to southern California, where he spent the next thirty years studying that region's prehistory. He died in 1971 at age eighty-nine.

As for Scrugham, he was defeated in a gubernatorial reelection bid in 1927 but won a seat in the U.S. House of Representatives in 1932. He served five terms there before his election to the U.S. Senate in 1942. He died in office in 1945.

## VALLEY OF FIRE STATE PARK

Valley of Fire State Park, whose entrance is thirteen miles southwest of Overton, five miles west of NV 169 on a signed road, became Nevada's first state park in 1935. The six-by-four-mile park was named for its blood red sandstone cliffs, rocks, mounds, and walls.

More than 150 million years ago, the park's unique sandstone formations started as large, shifting sand dunes. Over time the sand became stone. The wind and rain sculpted the stone into evocative shapes, a process that took centuries. Elephant Rock is one example. When viewed from a certain angle this giant arch looks like an elephant. Another amazing formation is the Seven Sisters, seven pillars rising about twenty feet from the ground. Elsewhere, several rounded sandstone domes resemble giant beehives.

There are several ancient Anasazi petroglyph sites at Valley of Fire—Atlatl Rock and Petroglyph Canyon are both excellent viewing sites and have interpretive trails. Atlatl Rock is a flat sandstone cliff covered with carvings, including one of an atlatl (an ancient spear). Petroglyph Canyon is lined with glyphs of a different sort: there are kachina figures, which archaeologists consider rare, as well as footprints, dancers holding hands, and curved lines.

*Elephant Rock at Valley of Fire State Park.*

Petroglyph Canyon's trail leads to another landmark, Mouse's Tank, a large rock catchment called a *tinaja*. This particular catch basin, which provides a regular source of water for birds and animals, was also once the domain of an outlaw Indian named Mouse, who supposedly hid in the area at the turn of the twentieth century.

Valley of Fire's ecology is also fascinating. In wet years, the park explodes with colorful desert wildflowers during April and May. There are recreation facilities and a visitor center open year-round.

## ST. THOMAS

St. Thomas, now submerged under Lake Mead, was eight miles southeast of Overton. This was another Mormon settlement established in the mid-1860s in the Moapa Valley. In its early years, St. Thomas was the largest town in the region, with more than 600 residents. Like residents of the other local settlements, St. Thomasites abandoned their community after 1871 rather than pay back taxes to the state of Nevada.

Mormons resettled St. Thomas in 1881, but it never grew as large as it had been. In the 1930s the federal government relocated the town's residents, and the rising waters of Lake Mead covered the site. In years when Lake Mead's water level is low, you can see building foundations and walls.

## CALLVILLE

Callville, founded in 1864, was Nevada's only community that could even remotely have been called a seaport. It was on the banks of the Colorado River, landlocked Nevada's only outlet to the sea. Steamboats could navigate the river from here south to the Gulf of California. The town once lay a few miles upriver from the Las Vegas Wash, but now it lies under the waters of Lake Mead.

Callville was named for Anson Call, leader of the Mormon expedition who selected the site for a port and built the settlement's first structures, including several large stone warehouses. Church leaders were interested in developing a trade route on the Colorado River because they believed it would give them access to new markets for their crops.

Callville was made the seat of Arizona Territory's Pah-Ute County in 1865. But a year later, boundary lines shifted and Callville and the other communities along the Muddy River became part of Nevada. The community prospered for a few years as a port, serving river steamers, but when the transcontinental railroad came in 1869, steamboats became obsolete and Callville faced its end. Callville was soon deserted, and today only the ruins of the great stone warehouses remain, 400 feet underwater.

## HENDERSON

Henderson, thirteen miles southeast of Las Vegas at the NV 146–US 93 interchange, was founded in 1941 as Basic, home of the Basic Magnesium plant.

The town was renamed Henderson when a post office opened in 1944. Henderson's namesake was U.S. senator Charles B. Henderson of Nevada, who was chairman of the board of directors of the Reconstruction Finance Corporation, a federal agency that funded troubled banks and industries during the Great Depression. Under Henderson's leadership, the board authorized the initial funding for construction of the Basic Magnesium plant.

By 1944, however, the plant had produced a surplus of magnesium and the government shut it down. For the next few years, the giant complex of buildings sat empty. In the late 1940s the federal government transferred ownership of the plant to the state of Nevada, which subdivided the facility and made it available to private industries. In recent years, Henderson has become a bedroom community for Las Vegas.

### Clark County Heritage Museum

The Clark County Heritage Museum, at 1830 South Boulder Highway in Henderson, is one of southern Nevada's best historical repositories. Interpretive displays, photos, and artifacts help to explain milestones such as the legalization of gambling in Nevada in 1931, the first Las Vegas casinos, the building of Hoover Dam, the arrival of Benjamin "Bugsy" Siegel, and the development of the Las Vegas Strip in the 1940s and 1950s.

Several historic Las Vegas–area buildings have been relocated to the museum grounds. Adjacent to the main museum is the restored Boulder City

*The Boulder City Depot and several Union Pacific Railroad cars have been preserved at the Clark County Heritage Museum in Henderson.*

Depot, built in 1931. A Union Pacific caboose and railcar, restored to working condition, are parked near the depot.

The museum's Heritage Street is lined by half a dozen restored historic buildings representing various eras of southern Nevada's history. The Giles-Barcus House was originally built in Goldfield in 1905, then moved to Las Vegas in the early 1950s. Will Beckley, a pioneer Las Vegas businessman, built the Beckley House in 1912. It is a California-type bungalow, a style popular in Las Vegas in the early to mid-twentieth century. The Henderson Townsite House is typical of the company-town housing built in the early 1940s for workers at the Basic Magnesium plant.

The museum also has an interpretive trail winding through displays of antique mining equipment, a replica of a Paiute camp, and a cluster of historic wooden buildings from several Nevada ghost towns, including a jail from Tuscarora.

# NV 159
# LAS VEGAS–NV 160

### 36 MILES

## RED ROCK CANYON NATIONAL CONSERVATION AREA

The 195,610-acre Red Rock Canyon National Conservation Area is fifteen miles west of Las Vegas off NV 159. Dramatic limestone and sandstone cliffs, some with vertical drops of nearly 3,000 feet, are layered in bands of red, gray, and yellow. A geological process known as thrust faulting created the layers. Sixty-five million years ago, sheets of older rock, some of it limestone, were

*Red Rock Canyon.*

pushed upward and over younger layers of sandstone. These thrust sheets are visible along a thirteen-mile scenic drive known as the Red Rock Canyon Loop.

The Red Rock Visitor Center, operated by the Bureau of Land Management, has interpretive displays of the region's natural history. There are several day-use trails, which are best hiked between October and May because of the area's extreme summer heat. With binoculars and a bit of luck, visitors can sometimes spot bighorn sheep, bobcats, and wild burros in the canyon.

### Spring Mountain Ranch State Park

Four miles south of Red Rock Canyon on NV 159 is the historic Spring Mountain Ranch State Park. It is nestled below the multicolored Wilson Cliffs in the Spring Mountain Range. The ranch was first settled in the 1830s, when the area was a campsite and rest stop for travelers on the Old Spanish Trail. The rugged terrain also made the spot a popular hideout for outlaws preying on pack trains. In 1864 an outlaw named Bill Williams is said to have built the first structures in the area for keeping his horses.

In the mid-1870s James Wilson and George Anderson filed for legal ownership of the area, which they named the Sand Stone Ranch. In the early 1880s Anderson left to start a saloon and turned his interest over to Wilson, who also adopted and raised Anderson's two sons as his own. The sons, Jim Jr. and Tweed Wilson, inherited the ranch after James Wilson died in 1906. The Wilson brothers operated the ranch until 1929, when they sold it to Willard George, a

*Spring Mountain Ranch State Park.*

longtime friend from California, who permitted them to live on the property until they died. The three Wilsons are buried in a small cemetery on the park grounds.

Since he was a furrier by trade, George began raising chinchillas as well as cattle. In 1944 George leased the ranch to a Hollywood friend, actor Chester Lauck, who had played Lum in the popular *Lum and Abner* radio program. Lauck eventually purchased the ranch and built a New England style–cut-sand-stone-and-redwood ranch house. Lauck named the property the Bar Nothing Ranch and operated it as a working cattle ranch, vacation retreat, and summer camp for boys.

In 1955 Lauck sold the property to Vera Krupp, the wife of a German munitions manufacturer. Krupp expanded the house and added a swimming pool. She renamed the place Spring Mountain Ranch and frequently entertained celebrity friends. In 1967 the Hughes Tool Company, part of the Howard Hughes empire, bought the ranch. While Hughes never visited, his company executives frequented the place. In 1972 two southern Nevada businessmen purchased the property and announced plans to construct a large housing development on the site. Public outcry ensued, however, and instead they sold the ranch to the Nevada Division of State Parks in 1974.

Today the property is still a working cattle ranch, but it is also a site for outdoor plays and concerts on summer evenings. Park rangers lead tours of the main house, the old reservoir, the Wilson family cemetery, an 1880s board-and-batten cabin, and an 1864 stone cabin and blacksmith shop.

# NV 160
## ARDEN–PAHRUMP
### 57 MILES

## POTOSI

Nevada's first mine may have been at Potosi (po-TAH-see) Mountain, twenty-five miles south of Las Vegas off NV 160. From the town of Mountain Springs, twenty-one miles west of US 93 on NV 160, an unmarked dirt road leads two miles southeast to the site of the former town of Potosi.

Several legends surround the Potosi Mine's origins. In one version, an Indian guide called Potosi showed ore samples to a Mormon batallion returning from California and the Mormons named the mine after him. Another story claims the Paiute originally worked the mine and even cast bullets from the ore prior to the arrival of the white man. That story, however, does not explain what the Indians did with the bullets, since they had no guns.

The most reliable information indicates that a local Indian led Mormons from the Las Vegas Mission to lead deposits on Potosi Mountain. Nathaniel

Jones, who had been sent by Mormon Church leader Brigham Young to develop the resource, established the mine in May 1856. Jones named it Potosi after the Wisconsin town where he grew up. Within a few months, miners were removing and smelting lead ore. However, they soon abandoned the enterprise when their crude smelting techniques produced lead of such poor quality as to be useless.

In 1861 the Colorado Mining Company began mining the region again and built a more advanced smelter at Potosi Springs. The company then platted the town of Potosi, which soon had nearly 100 residents. Although the mine and smelter closed two years later, the area was reworked periodically for the next sixty years. Today stone ruins are all that remain of the town.

## PAHRUMP

Pahrump (PAH-rump), sixty-two miles west of Las Vegason NV 160, is one of Nevada's fastest-growing communities and is home of the state's only winery. Most of the homes and businesses in Pahrump did not exist until the 1970s. NV 160, which follows the Old Spanish Trail and links Pahrump to Las Vegas, was not paved until 1954. The Pahrump Valley did not receive electrical power until 1963. But in the 1970s Pahrump began to attract retirees, snowbirds, escapees from California, and Las Vegas commuters who wanted a bit of elbow room. In the 1990s it grew to more than 25,000 residents.

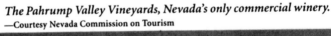

*The Pahrump Valley Vineyards, Nevada's only commercial winery.*
—Courtesy Nevada Commission on Tourism

In spite of its explosive growth, this former farming community, established in the 1870s, has retained much of its agricultural flavor. One of Pahrump's most popular attractions is the Pahrump Valley Vineyards, at 3810 Winery Road. Opened in 1990, the winery was the inspiration of Jack Sanders, a former Pahrump casino executive who has compared the climate, soil, and growing conditions of the Pahrump Valley to those of the Temecula Valley grape-growing region near San Diego, California. Sanders planted several acres of grapes around the two-story Mission-style winery building, which also has a tasting room, gift shop, and gourmet restaurant.

# US 93
# LAS VEGAS–HOOVER DAM
### 30 MILES

## BOULDER CITY

Boulder City, twenty-three miles southeast of Las Vegas on US 93, owes its existence to Hoover Dam. Work began on the dam in 1931, and shortly thereafter builders started constructing housing on the future site of Boulder City. While it is difficult to find an exact birthdate for Boulder City, several significant events occurred in 1930 and 1931, including construction of the Boulder City train station and the opening of the post office. Federal government surveyors completed a detailed map of the town site on May 26, 1931—that may be considered the town's birthday.

*Government Park, Boulder City.*

The federal Boulder Canyon Project (Hoover Dam) planners envisioned a community of 5,000 people at Boulder City; its comprehensive map designated everything from the kinds of businesses to the varieties of trees. And despite the fact that gambling and alcohol were available in Nevada, the feds enforced a ban on both in Boulder City. The plans were meticulous—government and commercial buildings fanned outward from the Reclamation Administration Building, the dam's headquarters, on a hill north of town. Residential neighborhoods were rectangular, with sidewalks constructed around the perimeter and alleys down the center of each block.

The design also featured several parks, including the large Government Park in the center of town. This greenery makes Boulder City exceptional in dry southern Nevada. To create the parks, the feds hired landscape architect Wilbur Weed to study the desert soil and determine which tree species would thrive in the harsh climate. His research showed that elms, poplars, cypresses, sycamores, and some evergreens had a good chance of survival, and his plans proved successful.

### The Boulder Dam Hotel

When it opened in 1933, the Boulder Dam Hotel, at 1305 Arizona Street in Boulder City, was southern Nevada's most elegant hotel. Its wood-paneled lobby, air-conditioned rooms, and tiled private bathrooms made the two-story Dutch Colonial hotel a favorite of America's rich and famous. Celebrity guests included movie stars Ronald Colman, Harold Lloyd, Bette Davis, and Fred MacMurray. Cornelius Vanderbilt Jr. and his new bride honeymooned in the hotel in 1935. Visitors came to see Hoover Dam and nearby Las Vegas.

*The Boulder Dam Hotel once catered to America's elite.*

The hotel's owners were real estate investor Raymond Spilsbury and builder Paul S. "Jimmy" Webb. Webb had made a small fortune building Beverly Hills mansions during the 1920s. The hotel's first few years were extremely successful. Then the federal government closed Boulder City's biggest draw, Hoover Dam, because of fears of terrorism in 1941, during World War II. In the meantime Webb had overextended himself in other business ventures and was unable to keep up on the hotel's routine maintenance.

Webb was forced to sell his share in the hotel to his partner, Spilsbury. The latter immediately began improving the property and was edging it toward profitability when, in January 1945, he mysteriously disappeared. A month later, Spilsbury's body was found in the Colorado River, his feet tied together with his own belt and his pockets stuffed with rocks. The coroner ruled it a suicide.

The hotel experienced nearly two dozen bankruptcies, closing and reopening numerous times. In the 1990s a nonprofit historical group acquired it, renovated the building, and converted it into an arts center.

## HOOVER DAM

It is no understatement to say that Hoover Dam brought prosperity to southern Nevada. When it was built in the early 1930s, thirty miles southeast of Las Vegas, the 726-foot-high, 1,244-foot-long dam, originally called Boulder Dam, was one of the largest public-works projects the federal government had ever undertaken. It remains one of the most impressive manmade structures in the world.

From 1931 to 1935, more than 5,000 men worked on the dam. It contains more than 3 million cubic yards of concrete, enough to pave a two-lane highway from San Francisco to New York. Each of its seventeen hydroelectric generators can produce enough power for a city of 65,000 people. Since its completion, the dam has been one of southern Nevada's most popular attractions, with 700,000 visitors annually.

The dam was originally proposed in the early 1920s as a means to control the Colorado River, which was prone to flooding, and to generate power for several southwestern states. In 1928 Congress approved the Boulder Canyon Project Act, authorizing the development and construction of the dam. A consortium of six construction firms, known as Six Companies, was awarded the $94-million contract.

The original plan was to build the dam in Boulder Canyon, but engineers selected Black Canyon, three miles south of Boulder Canyon, as the site. Nonetheless, the dam's name remained Boulder Dam until it was later renamed for President Hoover in 1947. Work began in 1931 with the construction of a special railroad line to transport supplies and materials. At the same time, crews blasted huge tunnels into the canyon walls to divert the river around the construction site. To produce the amount of concrete needed, the government

*An aerial view of Hoover Dam, which forms Lake Mead.*

built special plants at the construction site. Plant workers mixed and poured concrete around the clock for two straight years. The dam was completed two years ahead of schedule and within budget.

Engineers designed the dam as a giant, curved wedge, thicker at the base, where water pressure is greatest, and tapered at the top. Unlike many modern-day public-works projects, which often have a utilitarian appearance, Hoover Dam has carefully designed details. The tile floors inside the dam have a Native American motif, and the exterior intake towers are distinctively art deco. The project's planners commissioned Oskar J. W. Hansen, a noted 1930s artist, to create a pair of bronze statues to commemorate the dam. Set in a small park above the dam, the work, entitled *Winged Figures of the Republic*, is thirty feet high, one of the largest bronze monuments ever cast in the United States.

Lake Mead, the body of water behind the dam, is the largest man-made reservoir in the United States, with 822 miles of shoreline. The National Park Service oversees the Lake Mead National Recreation Area. The waters between the dam and the Arizona-California-Nevada border are now called Lake Mohave. Outside Nevada, the waters again become the Colorado River.

*Steamboats on the Colorado River*

Before Hoover Dam went in, the Colorado River traveled freely through southern Nevada. In the 1850s the U.S. Army began exploring the navigable channels of the Colorado River in the hope of establishing freight and passenger service on the river. In December 1857 Lieutenant Joseph Ives was given command of a small stern-wheeler, the *Explorer*, and departed from Robinson's Landing, sixty miles south of Yuma, Arizona, at the mouth of the Colorado River, where it emptied into the Gulf of California. The boat ascended the river for more than 400 miles before reaching the mouth of Black Canyon, adjacent to the site of present-day Hoover Dam. There, the vessel struck a submerged rock and was forced to turn back for repairs. Ives continued in a small skiff and reached the Las Vegas Wash near present-day Boulder City.

The Ives expedition proved the feasibility of steamboat travel on the river, and by the 1860s a handful of commercial steamboats were operating. While they were successful, that is not to say that the journeys were easy. Passengers suffered from intolerable heat, and submerged rocks and shifting sandbars plagued the pilots. By the 1870s the new transcontinental railroad had replaced the steamboat business.

# US 95 AND NV 163
# LAS VEGAS–LAUGHLIN
### 90 MILES

## ELDORADO CANYON AND NELSON

Miners discovered gold and silver in the Eldorado Canyon, about forty miles south of Las Vegas, in the late 1850s, making it one of the oldest mining districts in southern Nevada. A man known only as Captain Johnson, from nearby Fort Mohave, was prospecting there in 1857 and named the canyon.

There is some doubt as to who made the initial gold discovery. One particularly intriguing legend claims that a group of Spanish and Mexican miners arrived in the canyon in the 1870s with a yellowed map, said to have been about 100 years old. The miners said they had found it in a Mexican church. The treasure map showed the exact location of the Techatticup, one of the most productive mines in the region. It may have been drafted by Spanish miners who worked the area in the 1770s.

By the mid-1860s a few towns had been platted in the canyon, and people and supplies began arriving by steamboat. Soon, more than 500 people were living in the area, most working in the three main mines, the Techatticup, the Wall Street, and the Savage. Because of its remoteness—the sheriff had to come from Pioche in Lincoln County, more than 300 miles away—the area gained a deserved reputation for lawlessness. James G. Scrugham, 1920s Nevada

*An abandoned mine shaft, Eldorado Canyon.*

governor and later historian, wrote that Eldorado Canyon in its earliest days was filled with Civil War–era draft dodgers from both the Union and Confederate sides. Most had little regard for legalities, so claim jumping and murder were common, and disputes were decided by "Winchester's amendment to the Colt statute."

In 1905 miners built the town of Nelson in the canyon during an early-century mining boom. Nelson's large cyanide mills and smelter proved only marginally successful, but the town struggled along, reviving with renewed mining activity in the mid-1930s and 1940s. Today, tailing piles, stone and brick foundations, the remains of the cyanide mill, mining hoists, and abandoned shacks surround the tiny but still-inhabited town, about eleven miles east of US 95 on NV 165.

## SEARCHLIGHT

The hamlet of Searchlight is forty-six miles south of Las Vegas on US 95 at NV 164. There are plenty of stories about how Searchlight got its name. One popular myth is that it was named after a brand of matches. Another says it was named for a miner named Lloyd Searchlight. According to U.S. senator Harry Reid, native of Searchlight and local historian, there was no Lloyd Searchlight and a local wag probably made up the matches story. Searchlight's name was most likely inspired by the remark of town founder George F. Colton, who said there was gold in the area, but it would take a searchlight to find it.

Miners first prospected in the Searchlight area in about May 1897, although some believe it may have been a year earlier. By July 1898 the Searchlight Mining District had formed and a small community began to take shape. By 1907 the town had a population of several thousand. An attempt in 1908 to have the Clark County seat located in Searchlight rather than Las Vegas—which was smaller at the time—was unsuccessful.

Predictably, Searchlight's fate was largely intertwined with the mining industry's. The lode was tapped out by 1916, and by 1930 only about 137 people still called Searchlight home. Today the hills around the town remain littered

*A mining headframe still stands on the hillside above Searchlight.*

with a few aging wooden headframes and other mining equipment. About 1,000 people, mostly retirees, currently live in Searchlight.

The Searchlight Historic Museum, east of the town's center, is one of the better small museums in the state. A large wooden headframe—built in 1904 for the Ruth Elder Mine—serves as a billboard for the museum. Around the frame are other mining artifacts such as a large smelting pot, an ore cart, and an arrastra. Inside, displays include a large collection of baskets and pottery from native Southern Paiute and Mojave tribes, as well as copies of historic documents and photographs of early Searchlight.

Some sheet music on a piano makes a surprising display—it is the music for "The Searchlight Rag" by Scott Joplin. Joplin wrote the piece in 1907 as a tribute to his friends Charles and Tom Turpin, who owned a mine in the area. While the Turpin brothers did not stay long in Nevada, they evidently shared their Searchlight experience with the famed ragtime composer.

Another exhibit describes famous Nevadans who were born, raised, or lived in Searchlight, including Academy Award–winning costume designer Edith Head and pioneering Las Vegas businessman James Cashman, who opened the first car dealership in Las Vegas—which is kind of like being the first man to make cheese in Wisconsin. Movie-star couple Rex Bell and Clara Bow owned a large ranch near the town in the 1930s and 1940s.

## GRAPEVINE CANYON

The desert is an uncanny place. Despite all appearances, it manages to sustain life. A good example of a desert oasis is Grapevine Canyon, eight miles northwest of Laughlin on a dirt road off NV 163 that loops around to US 95. A turnoff from the dirt road ends at a trailhead, then it is a half-mile hike on a flat trail to the mouth of Grapevine Canyon.

There, a small stream of water trickles through the canyon and spills into a dry creek bed, where it is soon absorbed. Overhead is a series of small waterfalls. The surrounding rock walls are covered with clusters of ancient petroglyphs, some believed to be more than 1,500 years old. There are so many that in some places they seem to overlap. The images include geometric patterns, small drawings of bighorn sheep, and stick figures representing humans.

Continuing on the dirt road, past the turnoff to the Grapevine Canyon trail, you climb Christmas Tree Pass, lined with pine trees decorated with old shoes, painted cans, and other quirky ornaments. The road continues over the Newberry Mountains before dropping down and looping back to US 95.

## LAUGHLIN

In 1964 gambler Don Laughlin arrived at a spot on the west bank of the Colorado River at the Nevada-Arizona border called Mike's Camp. The place consisted of a run-down, temporarily closed eight-room motel with a bar and a few slot machines. While others might have seen the property as a money pit

*Petroglyphs carved on the rock walls near Grapevine Canyon.*

in the middle of nowhere, Laughlin saw it as an opportunity. He installed twelve slot machines and two gaming tables, added a buffet restaurant with chicken dinners for ninety-eight cents, and refurbished four of the motel rooms. He titled the new business Laughlin's Riverside.

Surprisingly, Laughlin's gamble paid off. His motel-casino-restaurant was an immediate success, catering mostly to day-trippers from Kingman, Arizona, and Barstow, California. Within a few years, other Nevada casino operators had begun to notice Laughlin's little operation on the Colorado River and opened their own places there. The growth continued through the 1960s and 1970s. In 1977 the U.S. Postal Service came in to open a post office in the little community, which at the time had no formal name. Laughlin suggested Riverside or Casino, but the postal official thought both were too common and recommended the town be called Laughlin, "a good Irish name."

*Hotel-casinos, such as the riverboat-shaped Colorado Belle (it doesn't actually float), line the banks of the Colorado River in Laughlin.*

By the 1990s Laughlin, fifteen miles east of US 95 on NV 163, had a population of several thousand and had become the third-largest gambling destination in Nevada, outranked only by Las Vegas and Reno. Today Laughlin's little motel has grown into a major hotel-casino, the Riverside Hotel, with 1,450 rooms, five restaurants, and a movie theater. Ten other hotel-casinos, offering a total of more than 10,000 rooms, have joined it on the Colorado to date.

These days, the white-maned Don Laughlin still holds court at the Riverside. A self-described night owl, the sixty-seven-year-old, who favors pastel leisure suits, can often be seen in the early morning hours wandering the casino floor or enjoying an adult beverage in one of the hotel's lounges. It's clear that no one tells him when to go to bed or what to wear. But then, it is his town.

# SELECTED BIBLIOGRAPHY

## BOOKS

Amaral, Anthony. *Will James: The Last Cowboy Legend.* Reno: University of Nevada Press, 1980.

Angel, Myron, ed. *Reproduction of Thompson and West's "History of Nevada," 1881.* Berkeley: Howell-North, 1958.

Basso, David. *Nevada Historical Marker Guidebook.* Sparks, Nev.: Falcon Hill Press, 1986.

Bergon, Frank. *Shoshone Mike.* Reno: University of Nevada Press, 1987.

Bowers, Michael W. *The Sagebrush State: Nevada's History, Government, and Politics.* Reno: University of Nevada Press, 1996.

Carlson, Helen. *Nevada Place Names.* Reno: University of Nevada Press, 1974.

Castleman, Deke. *Las Vegas.* Oakland, Calif.: Compass American Guides, 1991.

————. *The Nevada Handbook.* 5th ed. Chico, Calif.: Moon Publications, 1998.

Cerveri, Doris. *With Curry's Compliments: The Story of Abraham Curry.* Elko, Nev.: Nostalgia Press, 1990.

Cline, Gloria Griffin. *Exploring the Great Basin.* Reno: University of Nevada Press, 1988.

Curren, Harold. *Fearful Crossing: The Central Overland Trail through Nevada.* Las Vegas: Nevada Publications, 1982.

Dangberg, Grace. *Carson Valley: Historical Sketches of Nevada's First Settlement.* Minden, Nev.: Carson Valley Historical Society, 1972.

De Quille, Dan. *The Big Bonanza: The Story of the Discovery and Development of Nevada's Comstock Lode.* New York: Alfred A. Knopf, 1947.

Dunne, John Gregory. *Vegas: A Memoir of a Dark Season.* New York: Random House, 1974.

Dwyer, Richard A., and Richard E. Lingenfelter. *Dan De Quille: The Washoe Giant.* Reno: University of Nevada Press, 1990.

Earl, Phillip I. *This Was Nevada.* Reno: Nevada Historical Society, 1986.

Egan, Ferol. *Sand in a Whirlwind: The Paiute Indian War of 1860.* Reno: University of Nevada Press, 1985.

Elliott, Russell R. *History of Nevada.* Lincoln: University of Nebraska Press, 1984.

Glass, Mary Ellen, and Al Glass. *Touring Nevada: A Historic and Scenic Guide.* Reno: University of Nevada Press, 1983.

Grayson, Donald K. *The Desert's Past: A Natural Prehistory of the Great Basin.* Washington: Smithsonian Institution Press, 1993.

Green, Michael S., and Gary E. Elliott. *Nevada Readings and Perspectives.* Reno: Nevada Historical Society, 1997.

Grover, David H. *Diamondfield Jack: A Study in Frontier Justice.* Norman: University of Oklahoma Press, 1986.

Hall, Shawn. *Old Heart of Nevada: Ghost Towns and Mining Camps of Elko County.* Reno: University of Nevada Press, 1998.

———. *Preserving the Glory Days: Ghost Towns and Mining Camps of Nye County, Nevada.* Reno: University of Nevada Press, 1999.

———. *Romancing Nevada's Past: Ghost Towns and Historic Sites of Eureka, Lander, and White Pine Counties.* Reno: University of Nevada Press, 1994

Hart, John. *Hiking the Great Basin.* San Francisco: Sierra Club Books, 1991.

Hess, Alan. *Viva Las Vegas: After-hours Architecture.* San Francisco: Chronicle Books, 1993.

Hinkle, Warren, and Fredric Hobbs. *The Richest Place on Earth: The Story of Virginia City and the Heyday of the Comstock Lode.* Boston: Houghton Mifflin, 1978.

Hittman, Michael. *Wovoka and the Ghost Dance.* Carson City, Nev.: Grace Dangberg Foundation, 1990.

Hopkins, Sarah Winnemucca. *Life among the Piutes: Their Wrongs and Claims.* 1883. Reprint, Bishop, Calif.: Chalfant Press, 1969.

Houghton, Samuel G. *A Trace of Desert Waters: The Great Basin Story.* Reno: University of Nevada Press, 1994.

Howard, Anne Bail. *The Long Campaign: A Biography of Anne Martin.* Reno: University of Nevada Press, 1985.

Hulse, James. *The Nevada Adventure.* Reno: University of Nevada Press, 1969.

———. *The Silver State: Nevada's Heritage Reinterpreted.* 2nd ed. Reno: University of Nevada Press, 1998.

Inter-tribal Council of Nevada. *Numa: A Northern Paiute History.* Reno: Inter-tribal Council of Nevada, 1976.

James, Ronald M. *A Guidebook to Nevada's Historical Markers.* Carson City: Nevada State Historic Preservation Office, 1998.

———. *The Roar and the Silence: A History of Virginia City and the Comstock Lode.* Reno: University of Nevada Press, 1998.

———. *Temples of Justice: County Courthouses of Nevada.* Reno: University of Nevada Press, 1994.

Johnson, Edward C. *Walker River Paiutes: A Tribal History.* Schurz, Nev.: Walker River Paiute Tribe, 1975.

Kintop, Jeffrey M., and Guy Louis Rocha. *The Earps' Last Frontier.* Reno: Great Basin Press, 1989.

Lambert, Darwin. *Great Basin Drama.* Niwot, Colo.: Roberts Rinehart, 1991.

Land, Barbara, and Myrick Land. *A Short History of Las Vegas.* Reno: University of Nevada Press, 1999.

———. *A Short History of Reno.* Reno: University of Nevada Press, 1995.

Laxalt, Robert. *Nevada: A History.* New York: W. W. Norton & Co., 1977.

Lewis, Oscar. *Silver Kings.* Reno: University of Nevada Press, 1986.

———. *The Town That Died Laughing.* Boston: Little, Brown & Co., 1955.

Lillard, Richard G. *Desert Challenge: An Interpretation of Nevada.* Lincoln: University of Nebraska Press, 1969.

Lincoln Highway Association, Inc. *A Complete Official Road Guide of the Lincoln Highway.* 5th ed. Detroit: Lincoln Highway Association, 1924.

Lingenfelter, Richard E. *Steamboats on the Colorado River, 1852–1916.* Tucson: University of Arizona Press, 1978.

——— and Karen Rix Gash. *The Newspapers of Nevada.* Reno: University of Nevada Press, 1984.

Loomis, Leander Vaness. *A Journal of the Birmingham Emigrating Company: The Record of a Trip from Birmingham, Iowa, to Sacramento, California, in 1880.* Ed. Edgar M. Ledyard. Salt Lake City: Legal Printing Co., 1928.

Lord, Eliot. *Comstock Mining and Miners.* 1883. Reprint, Berkeley, Calif.: Howell-North Books, 1959.

McCracken, Robert D. *A History of Tonopah.* Tonopah, Nev.: Nye County Press, 1990.

———. *Tonopah: The Greatest, the Richest, and the Best Mining Camp in the World.* Tonopah, Nev.: Nye County Press, 1990.

McDonald, Douglas. *Virginia City and the Silver Region of the Comstock Lode.* Las Vegas: Nevada Publications, 1982.

McLane, Alvin R. *Silent Cordilleras.* Reno: Camp Nevada, 1978.

McPhee, John. *Basin and Range.* New York: Farrar, Straus & Giroux, 1981.

Miller, Max. *Reno.* New York: Dodd, Mead & Co., 1941.

Moreno, Richard. *The Nevada Trivia Book.* Rev. ed. Pico Baldwin Park, Calif.: Gem Guides Books, 1998.

———, ed. *The Historical Nevada Magazine: Outstanding Historical Features from the Pages of Nevada Magazine.* Carson City: Nevada Magazine, 1998.

Morgan, Dale L. *The Humboldt: Highroad of the West.* Lincoln: University of Nebraska Press, 1985.

Murbarger, Nell. *Ghosts of the Glory Trail.* Palm Desert, Calif.: Desert Magazine Press, 1956.

Myles, Myrtle Tate. *Nevada's Governors: From Territorial Days to the Present.* Sparks. Nev.: Western Publishing, 1972.

Myrick, David F. *Railroads of Nevada and Eastern California.* 2 vols. Reno: University of Nevada Press, 1992.

Nevada Secretary of State Office. *Political History of Nevada.* Carson City, 1996.

Paher, Stanley W. *Las Vegas: As It Began—As It Grew.* Las Vegas: Nevada Publications, 1971.

———. *Nevada Ghost Towns and Mining Camps.* Las Vegas: Nevada Publications, 1970.

Puzo, Mario. *Inside Las Vegas.* New York: Grosset & Dunlap, 1976.

Ratay, Myra Sauer. *Boom Times in Old Washoe City, Nevada.* Sparks, Nev.: Western Publishing, 1984.

Raymond, C. Elizabeth. *George Wingfield: Owner and Operator of Nevada.* Reno: University of Nevada Press, 1992.

Reid, Harry. *Searchlight: The Camp That Didn't Fail.* Reno: University of Nevada Press, 1998.

Rowley, William D. *Reno: Hub of Washoe County.* Woodland Hills, Calif.: Windsor Publications, 1984.

Sangwan, B., ed. *The Complete Lake Tahoe Guidebook.* Davis, Calif.: Indian Chief Publishing House, 1995.

Scott, Edward B. *The Saga of Lake Tahoe.* 2 vols. Crystal Bay, Nev.: Sierra-Tahoe Publishing Company, 1957 and 1973.

Scrugham, James Graves. *Nevada: A Narrative of the Conquest of a Frontier Land, Comprising the Story of Her People from the Dawn of History to the Present.* 3 vols. Chicago: American Historical Society, 1935.

Shamberger, Hugh A. *Goldfield.* Carson City, Nev.: author, 1982.

Shepperson, Wilbur S. *East of Eden, West of Zion: Essays on Nevada.* Reno: University of Nevada Press, 1989.

Thompson, David. *Nevada Events, 1776–1985.* Carson City, Nev.: Grace Dangberg Foundation, 1987.

Titus, A. Costandina. *Bombs in the Backyard: Atomic testing and American Politics.* Reno: University of Nevada Press, 1986.

Toll, David W. *The Complete Nevada Traveler.* Gold Hill, Nev.: Gold Hill Publishing, 1997.

Townley, John M. *Reno: Tough Little Town on the Truckee.* Sparks, Nev.: Great Basin Studies Center, 1983.

Twain, Mark. *Roughing It.* New York: New American Library, Signet Classic, 1980.

Van Tassel, Bethel. *Woodchips to Gamechips.* Lake Tahoe, Nev.: author, 1987.

Wheeler, Sessions S. *The Desert Lake: The Story of Nevada's Pyramid Lake.* Caldwell, Idaho: Caxton Printers, 1971.

———. *The Nevada Desert.* Caldwell, Idaho: Caxton Printers, 1982.

Williams, George J., III. *On the Road with Mark Twain in California and Nevada.* Dayton, Nev.: Tree by the River Publishing, 1993.

Wilson, Thomas C. *Pioneer Nevada.* 2 vols. Reno: Harolds Club, 1951 and 1956.

Works Progress Administration. *Nevada: A Guide to the Silver State.* Portland, Ore.: Binford & Mort, 1940.

Zanjani, Sally. *Goldfield: The Last Gold Rush on the Western Frontier.* Athens: Ohio University Press, 1992.

———. *A Mine of Her Own: Women Prospectors in the American West, 1850–1950.* Lincoln: University of Nebraska Press, 1997.

———, and Guy Louis Rocha. *The Ignoble Conspiracy: Radicalism on Trial in Nevada.* Reno: University of Nevada Press, 1986.


## PERIODICALS

"America the . . . " *Life,* July 1986.

Andersen, Jim. "Lost in Austin." *Nevada Magazine,* January-February 1990.

Brooks, Sheilagh, Carolyn Stark, and Richard H. Brooks. "John Reid's Redheaded 'Giants' of Central Nevada: Fact or Fiction?" *Nevada Historical Society Quarterly,* winter 1984.

Chalekian, Harry A. "Was Garden of Eden Located in Nevada?" *Nevada Magazine,* July-August 1993.

Clancy, Gwendolyn. "In Search of Will James." *Nevada Magazine,* September-October 1990.

Daley-Taylor, Andria. "Boardwalk Bon Vivants." *Nevada Magazine,* November-December 1992.

Dansie, Dorothy P. "John T. Reid's Case for the Redheaded Giants." *Nevada Historical Society Quarterly,* fall 1975.

Earl, Phillip I. "Rail Daze." *Nevada Magazine,* October 1989.

——— "A Woman of Fortune." *Nevada Magazine,* March-April 1994.

Finch, Phillip. "The First of the Bad Men." *Nevada Magazine,* March-April 1986.

——— "Twain, DeQuille, and the Comstock Classics." *Nevada Magazine,* July-August 1981.

Hayden, Carl. "Jackpot." *Nevada Magazine,* January-February 1988.

Hickson, Howard. "One Night Stands." *Nevada Magazine,* March-April 1980.

——— "Where's the Beef?" *Nevada Magazine,* January-February 1990.

Jenkins, Laird. "Exploring Hidden Cave." *Nevada Magazine,* January-February 1988.

Johnson, Ed, and Elmer R. Rusco. "The First Black Rancher." *Nevada Magazine,* January-February 1989.

MacDonald, Craig. "Nevada's First Woman Sheriff." *Nevada Magazine,* January-February 1981.

McBride, Dennis. "That Dam Hotel." *Nevada Magazine,* November-December 1989.

McMillan, Doug. "White Pine's Missing City." *Nevada Magazine,* March-April 1990.

Menzies, Richard. "The Mayor of Valmy." *Nevada Magazine,* May-June 1986.

——— "Melvin Dummar Revisited." *Nevada Magazine,* July-August 1981.

Moreno, Richard. "The Mayor of Gold Point." *Nevada Magazine,* July-August 1991.

Niderost, Eric. "Bunkerville Pioneer." *Nevada Magazine,* November-December 1982.

Powers, Rob. "In Rachel, Things Are Looking Up." *Nevada Magazine,* September-October 1993.

*Reno Evening Gazette,* Hannah E. Clapp obituary, October 9, 1908.

Roske, Ralph J., and Michael S. Green. "Gass' Station." *Nevada Magazine,* September-October 1989.

Ross, Christopher. "Dat So La Lee and the Myth Makers." *Nevada Magazine,* September-October 1989.

Smith, Roger. "Walter Van Tilburg Clark Revisited." *Nevada Magazine,* January-February 1983.

Sprenger-Farley, Terri. "The Great Train Robbery." *Nevada Magazine,* May-June 1986.

Toll, David W. "Butch Cassidy and the Great Winnemucca Bank Robbery." *Nevada Magazine,* May-June 1983.

————— "Edna and Charlie." *Nevada Magazine,* November-December 1994.

————— "E. E. Roberts and the Politics of Personal Liberty." *Nevada Magazine,* November-December 1982.

————— "The Last Stagecoach Robbery." *Nevada Magazine,* March-April 1983.

# INDEX

275

## ABOUT THE AUTHOR

**Richard Moreno** is the publisher of *Nevada Magazine* and author of four books, *The Backyard Traveler: Fifty-four Outings in Northern Nevada*; *The Backyard Traveler Returns: Sixty-two Outings in Southern, Eastern, and Historic Nevada*; *Desert Lows and Mountain Highs*; and *The Nevada Trivia Book*. He also co-edited *The Historical Nevada Magazine: Outstanding Historical Features from the Pages of Nevada Magazine* and has written a syndicated newspaper column about Nevada history and travel since 1987, as well as numerous articles about the Silver State.

Mr. Moreno received his master's degree in journalism from Columbia University in 1980 and moved to Nevada in 1982. He worked as a newspaper reporter for the *Reno Gazette-Journal* and other papers for several years and was named Outstanding Young Journalist of the Year by the Nevada Press Association in 1983. Prior to joining *Nevada Magazine*, he worked for more than seven years as director of advertising and public relations and public information officer for the Nevada Commission on Tourism. In 1987, he won a Travel Industry Association of America public relations award for his "Highway 50: The Loneliest Road in America" promotion.

In addition to writing and publishing, Mr. Moreno has taught a Nevada history course at Western Nevada Community College since 1996, and he has served on the boards of the Children's Museum of Northern Nevada and the Carson City Library. He was also Nevada advisor to the National Trust for Historic Preservation from 1991 to 1994. He resides in Reno with his wife, Pamela, and their two children.

We encourage you to patronize your local bookstore. Most stores will order any title they do not stock. You may also order directly from Mountain Press, using the order form provided below or by calling our toll-free, 24-hour number and using your VISA, MasterCard, Discover or American Express.

Some other Roadside History titles of interest:

_____Roadside History of Arizona, Second Edition    paper/$20.00

_____Roadside History of Arkansas    paper/$18.00    cloth/$30.00

_____Roadside History of Colorado    paper/$20.00

_____Roadside History of Louisiana    paper/$20.00

_____Roadside History of Montana    paper/$20.00

_____Roadside History of Nebraska    paper/$18.00    cloth/$30.00

_____Roadside History of Nevada    paper/$22.00

_____Roadside History of New Mexico    paper/$18.00

_____Roadside History of Oklahoma    paper/$20.00

_____Roadside History of Oregon    paper/$18.00

_____Roadside History of South Dakota    paper/$18.00

_____Roadside History of Texas    paper/$18.00

_____Roadside History of Utah    paper/$18.00

_____Roadside History of Vermont    paper/$15.00

_____Roadside History of Wyoming    paper/$18.00

_____Roadside History of Yellowstone Park    paper/$10.00

Please include $3.50 per order to cover shipping and handling.

Send the books marked above. I enclose $ _____

Name _____

Address _____

City/State/Zip _____

☐ Payment enclosed (check or money order in U.S. funds)

Bill my: ☐ VISA   ☐ MasterCard   ☐ Discover   ☐ American Express

Card No._____

Expiration Date_____ Security Code #_____

Signature _____

**MOUNTAIN PRESS PUBLISHING COMPANY**
P.O. Box 2399 • Missoula, MT 59806 • Order Toll-Free 800-234-5308
E-mail: info@mtnpress.com • Web: www.mountain-press.com

Printed in the United States
150189LV00004B/2/P

9 780878 424108